THE LAVONNE HOULTON
COMPENDIUM
PONIES, POETRY AND PROSE

Historic Horse Articles
with an emphasis on the Morgan Horse
Cowboy Poetry and A Heritage in Prose

LAVONNE HOULTON

Edited and Compiled by
Janet Gingold
Tucson, Arizona

Cover photo: LaVonne and Minnie at Cold Creek Ranch, 1943, courtesy of LaVonne Houlton.

Back cover photos: LaVonne 1999 (©Olan Mills), courtesy of LaVonne Houlton; Redman with Warren Halliday and Sonfield with Jean Hill, courtesy of the National Museum of the Morgan Horse; Janet Gingold and Roy El's Harmony, courtesy of Janet Gingold.

Cover design: Janet Gingold

Text design and layout: Janet Gingold

First printing, May 2015.

Designed and printed in the United States by AlphaGraphics Commercial Printing Services, Tucson, Arizona.

This book is dedicated to

LaVonne Houlton
July 24, 1925 - June 11, 2009

Morgan Horse Breeder
Historian and Poet
American Treasure

LaVonne's beloved daughters
Robin and Leslie

Figure aka Justin Morgan
Progenitor of the Morgan Breed
"America's Breed"

Acknowledgments

This compilation would not have been possible without the support of many people. I would like to thank Kathy Furr, Kathy Raymond, Amber Broderick and Helen Herold of the National Museum of the Morgan Horse in Shelburne, Vermont for providing such excellent historic photographs to use in the book. Their long hours of research finding the exact photos used in LaVonne's previously published articles to include here were well worth the effort and much appreciated.

Many thanks to Chris Koliander, former editor of *The Morgan Horse*, and to Stephen Kinney, current editor, for their terrific support. Chris provided the computer file for the article "California Mares of the Twentieth Century," and was so supportive of both LaVonne and me through the years, always ready to print our articles! A big thanks also to Joanne Hoefer (Northern California Morgan Horse Association, now defunct), Melodie Lawson (Siskiyou County Historical Society), Loretta Veiga (California Thoroughbred Breeders Association) and Christine Hamilton (*Western Horseman*) for giving full release for reprints of articles. I have found no information that *The Piggin String* and *Horseman's Courier* are still in existence.

Margo Metegrano, editor of CowboyPoetry.com, was invaluable for providing access to LaVonne's poetry and prose published on the CowboyPoetry.com website. The website features poems, prose and songs of contemporary and classic poets and songwriters, and tugs at the heartstrings of those of us who grew up with Roy Rogers and Dale Evans, Hopalong Cassidy, Gene Autry, The Lone Ranger, Zorro and other cowboy heroes of the small and large screen.

LaVonne's poem, "Ern Pedler (1914-1989)", was of great interest to me, as my first Morgan mare was a double granddaughter of Ern's well-known stallion, Flying Jubilee (aka "Little Fly"). It was such a treat to meet Ern years ago at an AMHA convention. His daughter, Lynne Pedler Boren, writes, "I would be honored, and so would he I believe, to have a picture of him on Flying Jubilee in your book. The picture of Dad and Little Fly on the cover of the June, 1966, issue of *The Morgan Horse* in memoriam to Little Fly following his death, was one of his favorites, because it represented what they loved to do together in the mountains and on the desert. You know, I used to ride Little Fly bareback in the hills above our home in the canyon. Dad was proud of me as a good rider, but he was more proud of his horse, that as a stallion and hard working mountain horse, he was gentleman enough to allow me to ride bareback and be responsive to me as the rider. I was eight years out of my parents' home and living in Idaho when Little Fly died. I couldn't believe it, and Dad's sorrow was palpable."

Fellow Morgan historian and author Gail Perlee shared her enthusiasm, support and encouragement throughout this long endeavor and was eager to help in any way she could. As a former librarian, Gail has a well-indexed research library of her own, containing hundreds of magazines and books covering the entire history of the Morgan breed. Gail was always ready to dig through her magazines, find a needed article and copy it, then pop it in the mail for me. Gail's own articles include: "The Western Working Family of Morgans," *TMH* November 1995, p. 97; "Working Western Sires of Utah," *TMH* April 1996, p. 80; "The La Osa Horses: a Morgan Mystery Solved," *TMH* July 2006, p. 118; "The Morgan/Quarter Horse Connection," *TMH* September 1997, p. 179; "Morgans on Hawaii's Parker Ranch," *Writing For the Brand*, 2WF Club Newsletter 2003; "Mountain Air: the Story of the Ayr Morgans of Colorado," *Writing for the Brand*, Vol. 2, 2WF Club Newsletter 2007; "Drumming Hoof Beats: the Story of the Indian Reservation Morgans," a five part series in *Rainbow Morgan News*, Spring 2009 - Spring 2010; "Stuart Hazard and his Funquest Morgans," *Rainbow Morgan News*, Fall 2010 and "The Morgans of Wyoming's LU Sheep Company," a three part series in *Rainbow Morgan News*, Fall 2011 - Spring 2012.

Little did I know when I started this project with LaVonne that I would finish without her. Although she had been in ill health for over a year, I was unprepared for her passing on June 11, 2009. It was an incredible honor and pleasure working with LaVonne for seven years on this special project. She was an inspiration and mentor to me, and I shall be forever grateful for her friendship, total support and trust. LaVonne was truly a treasure not just for Morgan lovers, but for historians who value her unique perspective of the development of the West and the Morgan breed's influence on the westward expansion of our great country. LaVonne's poetry brings to mind cowboys of old sitting around the campfire sharing their life stories, and her prose speaks of her devotion to family.

During my editing, I corrected typos and grammar as needed, but also embraced LaVonne's unique manner of story-telling. Much of her research focused on the Sellman/Hill/Hearst breeding programs, and the reader will find that there is redundancy in some of the articles. This is for two reasons: firstly, these historic articles cover a period of 35 years, and several of them were reprinted in different magazines; secondly, LaVonne had an absolute LOVE of the "western working Morgans" from these bloodlines, and her own breeding program was based upon them. These Morgans exemplify some of the best in the breed, and it's encouraging to know that dedicated breeders across the country continue the legacy of Figure/Justin Morgan.

LaVonne's longtime friend, Twana Williford, had this to say: "LaVonne and I met when I was riding a neighbor's horse that was not shod and went lame. I saw a horse trailer across the way, knocked on the door and asked to pay for its use. LaVonne immediately came to the rescue. This was around forty years ago. We were great friends ever since and ironically, LaVonne and I had lives that were so close we couldn't believe it. Our younger years were almost identical and in the same area. We loved Morgan horses, poetry, music, family, and much more, and went through sad and glad times together. A very gracious, talented lady. I feel lucky to have been included in her life and she told me the same." I was so sad to read online that Twana passed away February 23, 2012.

My heart belongs to the Morgan breed and I am blessed to have shared my life with incredible horses, my beloved mares: M. M. Jubilee Pride, Aladdin's Sweet Pea, Mary Mels Dolley and Roy El's Harmony. I bought Sweet Pea for my daughter in 1982; Pea was a light in our lives - showing, trail riding or just "hanging out." These mares embodied all that is Morgan: a generous, kind spirit, can-do attitude, beauty, courage, strength and stamina, intelligence, a sense of adventure, and a bottomless warm soul. My children, Missy and Matt, have enjoyed our horses and have had much patience with me, as I headed out the door saying, "Going to the stable; be back in a couple hours." They knew better, the hours did stretch a bit….I dedicate this work of love to my children and horses as they have enriched my life beyond words.

I would be remiss in not acknowledging other special people who provided encouragement during this long project: Joyce Quigley, Judi Anderson, Kathleen Kahrl, Jim Vasquez, Sonya Woehlecke, Nancy King, Joan McCarthy, Marjorie Hazelwood, David Ladd, Anne Britt, Cary Newman, Jean Bagley Tremethick, Bea Wiltse, Marge Pracht-Gehrmann, Charlie Burton, Kevin Jones, Nancy and Tom Lurie, Marilyn Silver and Don Coates, Terri Caminker, John McFadden, Phyllis Shopbell, Jeff Albright, Marianne Muller, Linda and Dick Sampliner, Susie Adams, and to those I may have missed, I do apologize. Many have long awaited this publication. My life has been full of twists and turns, and I was unable until now to devote the time and energy to finishing this important project that is a fitting tribute to LaVonne Houlton, my dear friend. Her love of the Morgan horse shines through every word she wrote. I know she is peering down from heavenly clouds grateful that her words are being shared and honored.

Janet Gingold

A Tribute to Ern Pedler

May 31, 2014 was the 100th anniversary of my father's birth. Ernest (Ern) Joseph Pedler was born in Prospect, South Australia, the third child of William Joseph Pedler and Lily Violetta Cook. When he was between 2 and 3 years of age, the family emigrated from Australia to Salt Lake City, Utah, after his parents were baptized into the Church of Jesus Christ of Latter-day Saints. He loved horses and owned one to several all of his adult life. He rode them in the Wasatch and Uintah Mountains and on the west desert of Utah, where he chased and caught wild horses, until that became illegal. Later in his life, he was able to live on a ranch in the Vernon area and lived the life of a cowboy, his long-time dream. He died in his home there on 17 November 1989. *Lynne Pedler Boren.*

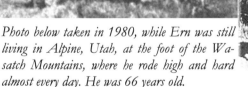

Photos: left, Flying Jubilee (aka Little Fly) 1963; center, Flying Jubilee and Ern; right, Mary Mels Dingo (aka Adios) and Ern, courtesy of the National Museum of the Morgan Horse.

Photo below taken in 1980, while Ern was still living in Alpine, Utah, at the foot of the Wasatch Mountains, where he rode high and hard almost every day. He was 66 years old.

Photo below rt., Sept. 1985, in the west desert mountains above Rush Valley, where Ern had moved to live his life-long dream of being a working cowboy. The ranch where he lived was large, raising alfalfa for winter cattle feed and grazing rights in the mountains for summer range. His mount is Mary Mels Dingo, whom he fondly called Adios. He would have been 71 years old.

Photo lower left, taken in October, 1988, while Ern was working the fall roundup. This picture gives one the real idea of the ruggedness of the country where the cattle grazed from late spring to early fall, and what a challenge finding and

moving them to their wintering grounds in the valley would be. Ern was 74 and the horse is Adios. This was his last roundup. Photos courtesy of Ern's daughter, Lynne Pedler Boren.

Table of Contents

Poetry: Cowboy Poetry

Prose: A Heritage in Prose

Bibliography

Index

Introduction

I was born in Eau Claire, Wisconsin in 1925. We moved to South Dakota in 1926. I was lucky to have had an uncle and aunt who ranched in the Dakota Badlands in the early days. Their cattle and horses grazed on land that's now a part of the National Grasslands of North Dakota -- near Bullion Butte, and along the Little Missouri River. From my uncle, I heard many tales of colorful characters - like Bill Follis, one-time boss of the 777 outfit and a veteran of many cattle drives on the old Chisholm Trail. And like Pete Pelissier, the "Buffalo Bill of the Missouri Slopes," who rounded up wild horses every year, and once ran a Wild West show of some renown. I heard of the old Hashknife outfit, of Teddy Roosevelt and the Custer Trail Ranch, of round-ups and disasters, of long gone but well remembered horses named Van Zandt and Bon Dieu.

We moved to Modesto, California, in June 1930. In 1931 my folks purchased a ranch near Modesto, where we had a small Jersey dairy and raised turkeys, milk goats, chickens and Emperor grapes. My father was a grocer, so much of the care of the stock fell to my mother, with help from me.

Knowing how I loved horses, my uncle, Ed Titus, would take me along to watch night harness races in Stockton. One of his Belgian mares had twin foals the year I was nine. The twins were a colt and a filly, and both survived. This was a rare enough event that the trio was photographed for the *Modesto Bee*, and rated a special exhibit at the California State Fair. I got to go along to help with the exhibit. A year or so earlier, my cousin Olive and I, in long dresses and sun bonnets, had participated in Modesto's Fourth of July Parade, with Olive driving a matched pair of Belgians pulling a covered wagon.

My first "mount" as a five-year-old in California was a burro named Cecil. He taught me agility, as his main goal in life was to scrape me off on the side of a building, or to knock me out of the saddle with a fig tree branch. He was fun, nonetheless, as you could both ride and drive him. At my uncle's farm I would ride Major, a big Belgian gelding, home from the fields at the end of the summer workdays. Next came a red and white pinto pony named Ginger, who proved to be more cooperative than Cecil. There was at one time a Shetland Welsh cross mare, and I even rode the fat and congenial Hereford bull, Prince Domino, a few times.

Uncle Ed taught me important things about horsemanship and horse care, and was a stickler about riding properly: Have the stirrups under the balls of your feet, don't turn those toes out or you'll get caught in the underbrush, and keep those heels well down, elbows close to your sides, hands light on the reins. One thing he couldn't change was that I always rode what he called "left-handed." I should have held the reins in my left hand, so I could swing a rope with my right, he said, but that always felt awkward to me. I never got very good at swinging a rope anyway!

Morgans first entered my life in 1939. My aunt and uncle (Titus) had acquired the 1,280-acre Cold Creek Ranch in Siskiyou County, near the Oregon border. I spent all my teenage summers at Cold Creek Ranch. One horse had come with the ranch – Bessie, a well-built bay mare with an excellent disposition and great talent at working cattle. She was part Morgan. So was Minnie, the small bay mare my uncle bought for me. I wrote about her in my poem "Cold Creek Remembered." We were both fourteen, and from the start we went together like ham and eggs! Minnie was sweet-tempered and pretty, always willing, extremely sure-footed, even in the roughest terrain, and she had endless bottom. Minnie and I covered many miles of tough, lava-strewn terrain in Northern California's Siskiyou Mountains. She worked well with cattle, too. The interesting thing about these two bay mares is that the only Morgan horses in that area when they were born were Sellman-bred Morgans owned by Reginald Parsons, of Mountcrest Ranch in nearby Hilt, California.

There were Herefords and horses, dreams to dream, and many trails to follow. And in the evenings there were the stacks of *Western Livestock Journals*, with poems by Bruce Kiskaddon and Cowpoke Cartoons by Ace Reid with which to while away a few hours.

Up the Copco Road from us was the Silva Ranch, and Joe Silva owned the Morgan mare Balkitty 04437, foaled in 1923, bred by Parsons. Balkitty was a pretty, good-bodied mare, light tannish chestnut. Joe also had her unregistered daughter, who looked just like her. Balkitty was by Baldie's Boy 7117, out of Kitty E. 03308, who was also the dam of Mountcrest Sellman 7289, one of the best California stallions of his generation. Byron White, who lived a few miles south of us, registered two of Balkitty's colts, one by King Shenandoah, the other by North Fork.

One summer we gathered up a large group of Herefords to be sold in Los Angeles. They were trailed the ten miles down the road to the rail-head at Ager. Uncle Ed rode the stallion North Fork 8082 (Don Juan x Roverta), borrowed from "Jiggs" Kuck of Montague for use on the drive. North Fork enchanted me. He would stand stock-still, relaxed and gazing at some far-off scene, but you'd better be alert when you put foot to stirrup – he was already in motion while you were still swinging into the saddle. He was an "all business" cow horse, such fun to watch!

Another grand Morgan I admired back then was the Mountcrest Sellman son, Redman. This fine stallion was well-known in Southern California by the time Warren Halliday moved his Morgans to a property he called Blue Heaven Ranch near Etna, in Siskiyou County south of Yreka. Two notable mares Halliday bred there were the Redman daughters, Redlass and Etna. Redlass was the dam of Keystone, a premier sire in the Pacific Northwest, who in turn was the sire of Keystone's Rome Beauty, a marvelously versatile mare out of Etna. Redman and his get were the epitome of what we now call the Western Working Morgan - the kind I fell in love with as a teenager.

Was it mere coincidence that the first yearling colt I bought in 1959 traced twice to North Fork through his sire, or that the red chestnut yearling filly I bought the next year had Redman in her pedigree?

Disposition, conformation, and that willingness to do were characteristics of the Sellman/Hill/Hearst Morgans that so many of us Western owners prized highly. Those Morgans had pretty well blanketed the West from the mid-1920s until after World War II. Many were found on the big ranches of the era, working cattle and earning their keep during the week, then polished up and shown to blue ribbons on the weekends. By the 1960s it seemed that our splendid Morgans had been nearly forgotten beyond our borders, as the emphasis switched to Eastern bloodlines, and shows where park saddle and fine harness horses were the stars.

I was surprised when I visited throughout New England in 1966 to discover that folks there thought of our Western Morgans as somehow inferior to their Eastern counterparts. I remember so well one fellow who brought out his stallion, stood him up for us, and then said proudly, "There – you don't have anything like that out West, do you?" Politeness stilled my tongue!

When I returned home, I continued to chronicle the history and the current achievements of the Morgan breed in the West. Their history began with California's Gold Rush, when men of great wealth and social prominence chose Morgans imported from New England, and prized them highly. Late in that century, Morgan blood was crossed on Standardbred stock, to add stamina to the speed of trotters and pacers. The first two decades of the 20th century contain no ongoing California Morgan history. Then, in the early 1920s, Roland Hill, Reginald Parsons and F. A. Fickert brought fine Sellman Morgans from Texas to California. They were the men who sold Morgans to Dr. C. C. Reed, Sheldon Potter, William Randolph Hearst and others. Today, breeders of Western Working Morgans cherish any portion of those old bloodlines that can be found.

With two exceptions, all the Morgans I had over the years were descendants of stock that had originated with Richard Sellman, through what I called the Sellman/Hill/Hearst family. I loved the conformation and disposition that seemed so consistent among our California Morgans of that line. They were horses that could take you over the mountain, and look very handsome doing so. My foundation mare, Gimma 010133 (Dannie Lu x Linn's Black Beauty) was a granddaughter of Dapper Dan (Trilson x Bess Gates). Three of my broodmares were by Muscle Man (Trilson x Flika). These two sires were full-brothers in blood, descended from W.R. Hearst's government-bred stallion Uhlan, and out of full sisters of the old Sellman breeding.

Because I'm Norwegian, I called my place Viking Morgan Ranch, and "Viking" was my registered prefix. The operation was small, as I was a working mom (social services supervisor with the county welfare department) with two daughters to raise. The largest foal crop I had was six, but most consisted of one or two foals a year. One interesting fact was that in 1976 I had five generations on the ranch, beginning with Linn's Black Beauty 09779 (1952-1980). In 1979 "Beauty" (Monte L. x Luccia) baby-sat a colt of her 6th generation when he was weaned.

When my daughters were in grammar school they participated in 4-H, with projects in Guide Dogs, Beef Cattle and Light Horse. I was leader of the horse project, and also of the cooking class. In high school, the girls were members of a youth parade group, the Rimrock Riders. Our registered half-Morgan gelding, Viking Fury, was the only horse in the group that would consent to carry the flag. This Fury was one of those who could "go" all day, and still come home prancing. He was the North Fork descendant I bought first in 1959. His dam, Ginger, was one of those unfortunate Morgans who was sold and re-sold until no one knew if she'd ever had papers. Years later, I registered a purebred Morgan colt with the name Viking Fury in honor of the first one.

Here are just a few of my Morgans and their descendants: Blossom's Lass 013320 (Muscle Man x Anita Blossom) was 1965 Golden West National Junior Champion Mare. Her son, Viking Coronado 20154 (owned by my daughter Leslie), was successfully shown both in-hand and in park saddle stallions, and won his last in-hand championship at age 18 (the judge later told me he thought "Cory" was about 9). "Blossom" was never out of the ribbons at halter for me, never below 3rd, and often first and champion. She was also shown in English pleasure, pleasure driving, and lead line. She produced beautiful, sweet-tempered offspring like herself.

LaVonne and Viking Captor 30033 (Cap's Nugget x Viking Vanity). Photo courtesy of LaVonne Houlton.

Viking Cavalier 15808 (Dapper Dan x Satina) was a consistent winner in family classes and hunt-seat for the Needham family of Walnut Creek. Viking Show Time 029892 (Windcrest Showboy x Gimma) was the dam of O.L. Show Stopper, owned and successfully shown by Martin and Glenda Drake, and an excellent sire in Southern California as well. Viking Vanity 012963 (King Bob x Gimma) produced two foals for the Point Reyes National Seashore Morgan Horse project, and while there she became the superintendent's choice to ride. They also put the less-experienced rangers on her, because she wouldn't get anyone into trouble on the trails. Viking Caprice 016535 (Muscle Man x Gimma) gave me several fine foals, among them Viking Capri 91353 by Valiant Turk, now owned by Susanne Coe of Mokulumne Hill, California, who uses him on cattle drives, etc., as well as at stud. Capri has the most fabulous disposition!

I sold my last Morgan, the 12-year-old stallion Viking Capri, in June 1995. He was so easy to get along with that I kept him for several years after retiring from the business. The stalls and pastures seemed awfully empty after he left! Now I'm delighted when owners send me letters and photos of descendants of Morgans that I raised.

I've written articles for *The Morgan Horse, Western Horseman, Thoroughbred of California, Horse Lovers, Horseman's Courier,* and *California Horse Review.* In the 1960s I wrote a monthly column, "LaVonne's Line," that ran in the old *Piggin' String* magazine for a decade or so, and sometimes I included a poem or one of my "Peanuts Horse" cartoons. My column covered various equine events and horse people, primarily in the central California area. When my daughters and I took a 99-day trip by car across Canada, from Vancouver to Quebec, and then back across 17 states, I took the column "on the road," reporting on people, places, horse farms and special events along the way.

One year at the Northern California Morgan Horse Show in Monterey, California, I was introduced to the wife of a prominent Arizona breeder. "Oh," she said, "I'm so pleased to meet you. They say you are the Mabel Owen of the West!" To me, that was a wonderful compliment. Some twenty years later, another Morgan owner wrote me, saying, "You and Mabel Owen are my all-time favorite writers. Both of you rise above the mere 'cataloging' phase…and write with analysis and purpose – and tell a good yarn in the process."

In 1985 the San Simeon Press published *The Horses of San Simeon,* by Austine Hearst (Mrs. William Randolph Hearst, Jr.). This is a large, richly illustrated and interesting "coffee table" book, with many drawings and sketches by the well-known equine artist, Sam Savitt. I was delighted to be contacted by Mrs. Hearst for assistance with the book's chapter on Morgan horses. It seems her trainer had suggested she contact me because I "probably knew more about the Hearst Morgans than anyone else."

Chapter 8 covers "The Morgans and Morabs." Five of the pictures in this chapter are of my horses. One is a full-page colored picture of Blossom's Lass, another shows her as a 2-year-old. Another is Blossom's son, Viking Coronado, ridden by my daughter Leslie Young. Another shows Jaye P. Collins in a walk-trot class, ridden by my 7-year-old grandson, Nathan Young. The fifth is of Viking Mystic, wearing the blue ribbon for halter geldings at an Elk Grove Morgan show.

Mrs. Hearst, in mentioning the stallion Uhlan, said, "The Uhlan line has also been continued by Mrs. LaVonne Houlton at the Viking Morgan Ranch in Modesto, California…" She also said, "I am deeply indebted to her for much of my information on the Hearst Morgans…(She is) a fount of Morgan History."

One outcome of all my writing that really pleased me was being named an AMHA Master's Certificate winner for 1999. The Western Working Family Morgan Horse Club (2WF) nominated me for this award, and that made me appreciate the certificate all the more!

I have written poems since I was 12 years old, quite a few of them being narrative cowboy tales. Cowboy poetry isn't about kings, tycoons or posh surroundings. It is about the extraordinary lives of ordinary people, whether set in the past or in the present. It covers an important time and aspect of American life that many people cherish, and children still dream of (when I was 7 or 8 my playmates and I would argue over whether we would be Bob Steele or Tom Mix in the fantasy of the day). I believe that poetry portrays the cowboy and the West better even than prose can do. I have a number of my poems posted on the Cowboy Poetry website (www.cowboypoetry.com). In 2002, "Ace" was a runner-up in the Lariat Laureate competition, and in 2003 my poem "Ern Pedler" won the same distinction. In March 2004, I was honored as the winner of the prestigious Lariat Laureate competition for my poem "Town and Country." I was also very pleased to receive awards from the World of Poetry: 1989 Golden Poet Award; 1990 Who's Who In Poetry (for "The Beauty of Words"); and the 1990 Silver Poet Award.

LaVonne Houlton

About CowboyPoetry.com

CowboyPoetry.com, also known as the BAR-D Ranch, was established January 1, 2000. Over the years, it has grown to be a central resource for Western and Cowboy Poetry and associated arts. Always commercial-free, the BAR-D has been mostly a volunteer effort by an energetic and devoted group of people who have worked to create a vibrant community.

In 2001, New West Library published *The Big Roundup*, a collection of contemporary and classic poetry from CowboyPoetry.com. Some proceeds from the book's sales help maintain Cowboy-Poetry.com. The Big Roundup was awarded the Will Rogers Medallion Award and the Buck Ramsey Best Poetry Book Award.

CowboyPoetry.com inaugurated Cowboy Poetry Week in 2002 with the "Favorite Cowboy and Western Poems Project," which invites people to share comments about their favorite poems. The project was inspired in part by former American Poet Laureate Robert Pinsky's "Favorite Poem Project." In 2003, Cowboy Poetry Week was recognized with unanimous resolution by the U. S. Senate. We celebrate the week each year during Poetry Month, the third full week in April.

CowboyPoetry.com offers thousands of poems by contemporary and classic poets, classic cowboy songs, and lyrics by current Western songwriters. Its Lariat Laureate competition recognizes excellence in writing.

The Cowboy Poetry website has organized a non-profit organization, the Center for Western and Cowboy Poetry, Inc. to sustain our current work, broaden existing programs, and take on new projects. With additional funding, CowboyPoetry.com can work with its supporters to expand programs such as Cowboy Poetry Week, create print publications, compile another anthology, encourage youth and library programs, and do more educational outreach.

Center for Western and Cowboy Poetry, Inc.

The specific purposes for which the Center for Western and Cowboy Poetry, Inc. is organized are to maintain a central resource to publish and archive educational material relating to Western and Cowboy Poetry for poets and for the public; to promote the work of poets and related organizations; and to research and preserve Western heritage as practiced in Western and Cowboy poetry and associated arts, through but not limited to electronic and print publication, broadcasting, and electronic and physical library repositories.

The Center for Western and Cowboy Poetry, Inc. was formed to serve a mostly rural and underserved community of rural Western writers, musicians, and artists; to help preserve Western and Cowboy Poetry and its associated arts; to offer a central resource for poets, libraries, schools, and the public; and to educate the public about the history and value of Western and Cowboy Poetry and its associated arts.

PONIES
Historic Horse Articles
with an emphasis on the Morgan Horse

Figure, also known as Justin Morgan
Progenitor of the Morgan Breed.
From a woodcut, courtesy of the
National Museum of the Morgan Horse.

California Morgans of Yesterday - 19th Century
1966

From Gold Rush days on, the Morgan Horse has been known and appreciated in California. Ardent Eastern breeders imported quality stock to the West Coast between 1850-1880, and found a ready market. The history of many of these animals has been lost to us, but we do know about a number of the fine Morgan stallions that came to the West in that period. Some crossed the plains; some came by ship, via Panama; others came later by rail. Some served as pleasure mounts, others as carriage horses; not a few were entered in trotting races, or shown to 1st Prize at state and county fairs. And, almost without exception, they were used as breeding stallions, to upgrade the native stock. As sires, they were much in demand – especially since over 2/3 of this early group were direct descendants of the fabulous Black Hawk 20. At least 10 of his sons and 16 grandsons, plus many of the 3rd and 4th generation, are among those listed below.

These early Morgans often commanded premium prices – fabulous prices when the value of the dollar then is considered against the inflated dollar of today. For example, Nicholas Ehle, of Kenosha, Wisconsin, brought several black Morgans West in 1860. One was Benecia Boy 1184, a grandson of Black Hawk. This horse was later owned by C. L. Hutchinson, Mayor of Sacramento and President of the California State Agricultural Society. He won 1st at the State Fair, 1860, and 2nd in 1863. Mr. Ehle sold three Black Hawk sons – all "jet black and beautiful" - for a total of $14,200.00, the highest bringing $7,000.00.

Young Stockbridge Chief 1205, by Stockbridge Chief 102, son of Black Hawk, sold for $4,000.00 to Charles Hosmer, San Jose, and won several good races here. David Hill 2nd 1092 left much good stock, both in Wisconsin and California. His owner, J. G. McCracken, refused an offer of $10,000.00 in gold for him when gold was worth $2.50 in paper. This bay grandson of Black Hawk won 1st premiums at the State Fair in 1864, 1866 and 1868, the latter two when shown with ten of his get – one of them his California-bred son David Hill Jr. 1093, also a 1st prize winner. Ansel Easton paid $2,800.00 for Dave Hill 1267, son of Black Hawk. The horse was shipped to San Francisco via Panama, and stood at $100.00, a very popular sire. San Francisco banking tycoon, William C. Ralston had a fast four-in-hand team, all sired by this Morgan. Wine Creek Black Hawk 1323, by Black Hawk, sold for $1,000.00 at 1 1/2 years old. Brought to California in 1861, he stood at the Union Ranch near Folsom. Comet 201 was delivered to Benjamin Fish in San Francisco in 1856, purchase price $1,750.00. Foaled in New York, 1853, by Young Black Hawk by Black Hawk 20, and out of a mare by Morgan Tally Ho 35, son of Woodbury Morgan 7, Comet was a handsome, fast horse whose colts were fine, spirited roadsters. Comet won a 5 mile race in Oregon in 15:21, against Mohawk. He lived to be twenty-four years old. L. J. Rose paid "an extravagant price" - $3,000.00 - for Flying Morrill 226, and brought him to California in 1858. Indians killed the horse in 1859, before Rose could get any colts from him. Conrad's St. Clair 598, foaled in California about 1863, sold to W. Todhunter for $1,500.00. The horse was still living in Yolo County in 1889. Easton's Wizard, by Black Hawk, out of *Fairy Queen (Thoroughbred), sold in 1861 (age three) to Thomas Lett, Novato, for $6,000.00. Bred by J. B. Redmond, San Francisco, Wizard was called "one of the finest young horses that walks this state."

Rollin J. Jones and Sylvester B. Rockwell frequently brought good Black Hawk Morgans to California. In 1860 William P. Morrison, San Mateo, purchased a 3 year old son of Ethan Allen 50 from them for $2,500.00. Spring of 1861 found three more "Black Hawks" arriving on the ship Cortez. One 3 year old harness horse sold promptly to Dr. E. S. Holden of Stockton. Another was a bay son of Black Hawk, out of "one of the finest Henry mares in the Atlantic States." The third was Challenge 1002, black, foaled 1859, by Sherman Black Hawk 51 out of a Henry mare by Black Lion 1080; 2nd dam, a gray mare of Morgan type. Challenge, highly admired on both coasts, won many prizes at fairs. He produced racing offspring, and died in 1874, property of William Doty, Meriden, California. The partners brought three others in 1861 – two Black Hawk sons and a young black son of Prince 1415. The older two were full brothers – Black Eagle 198 and Black Warrior 2038. Black Eagle, a highly regarded, stylish horse, left much fine stock here. He won 1st in 1861 at the State Fair. He was owned first by Charles Reade, Knight's Landing, and later by William Clark, Yolo, California. Rollin Jones paid $2,000.00 for Redfield's Vermont 121 (by Independence 1025, son of Peck Horse 120, by Black Hawk 20) a black stallion brought West by Tulett and Muzzy. Vermont stood one season in the Rogue River Valley, Oregon, then sold for $7,200.00 to a company. His offspring were very fast. Jesse Carr of Salinas purchased him in 1871.

Another Jones purchase was Keokuk 107, brought west by Daniel Blodgett in 1855. Jones made a $2,000.00 profit on the sale of this son of Black Hawk. Keokuk stood near Sacramento in 1857. One of his good sons was Index 1121, foaled 1865, bred by E. J. Winegar, Scott River, California. Index's dam was by Morrill 55. His colts were speedy. Two other sons of Ethan Allen 50 came West – Vick's Ethan Allen 1564, and Rollin Jones' gray Rappahannock 1444, who went to George Butler, Los Angeles. J. G. McCracken was a prominent California Morgan breeder. In 1860 he brought McCracken's Black Hawk 131 (by guess who?) to California, where he was a noted sire in the Stockton-Sacramento area. His son, Billy McCracken 1050, sold to D. E. Knights, Marysville, in 1861. "Billy" trotted five miles in 14:10, and his owner challenged any stallion for a 5 or 10 mile race: no takers. Others of the same line were Lancet 1054, Paul Jones 1055, McCracken's Golddust 1056 and Black Boy 1057.

The second earliest recorded arrival was Burgess' Sherman Morgan 843, dark gray grandson of Sherman Morgan 5, a stylish, good-dispositioned show winner, sold in 1850 to T. K. Burgess, Sacramento. Worth mention as sires are Uncle Shube 930, Black Ralph 1095, Killarney Pacer 1096, and Iowa Chief 1368. Primus 1714, by Marshall Chief 112, a phenomenal trotter, sired Magdallah, one of the fastest horses on the West Coast. Black Prince 179, a beautiful, gentle animal, could pull a buggy 8 miles in half an hour. He sired 15-20 excellent colts. Magna Charta 58 came to California in 1870. Green Mountain Morgan Jr. 447 had arrived in 1858. Flaxtail 628, grandson of Pilot 104, was still alive in 1886 (32 years old), and John Bull 653, a double grandson of Pilot, produced race-winning offspring here. Bertrand Black Hawk 1161, a double Black Hawk grandson – a fine trotter – sold to Californian Major Rathburn in 1866.

In 1849, a soon-to-be-famous sire crossed the plains and arrived at Hangtown (Placerville), California, in the lead of an ox team. This horse with a clouded history got between 600-700 hundred foals, mostly bay or brown, fast and typey. Advertised as a Morgan Horse – which his description bears out – he was possibly by Barden Morgan 47, who stood in Illinois where the dam was bred. His pedigree was destroyed by fire – symbolic, since he too burned to death in an 1864 stable fire. His name? St. Clair 48. Among his sons were Medoc 597 (sire of Occident, 2:16 ¾), Fred Low 605 (winner of three State Fair firsts), Shootz's St. Clair 601, and Dietz's St. Clair 602. Two of St. Clair's fast grandsons were Child's St. Clair 599 and Yolo Chief 4039.

There were many more – but let these few stand as a memorial to the worth of the Morgan horse, from Justin Morgan I down to his living descendants of today.

LaVonne's Line-The Piggin String
1966

August

This month's "Line" comes to you from Banff, Alberta, Canada. The Stoney Indians of the Banff area are holding their annual Indian Days Celebration. There are parades daily…gaily decked Indians and horses come single file down Banff Avenue, braves in front, squaws next and children last.

Other daily events are an Indian-style rodeo, ceremonial dances and chants by campfire, and a variety of games and contests. Large white teepees dot the Indian Grounds, many of them decorated in bright colors, with designs of bear, buffalo and wolf.

The setting is beautiful, and somehow just right, with stands of pine and aspen throughout the grounds, and the great peaks of Cascade and Rundle Mountains in the background.

This annual celebration dates back to 1889, when the Bow River washed out the railway line, stranding several trainloads of summer tourists. To keep the visitors entertained, the people of Banff asked the Indians to put on a show, and the tradition has been carried down to today.

The first stop on our trip was at Montague, California, where we met Morgan owners, Mr. and Mrs. Silvio Regnani, whose stock consists of Hildegarde, her weanling bay colt by Siskiyou Lad, Lad's Silvana, and Little Fella. Silvana is a three-year-old chestnut mare by Lad, out of Easter Bunny. Hildegarde, a bay, is eighteen years old, rather short and chunky. Silvio says she has great stamina, and doesn't know what it means to quit. She has won a number of blues at the Siskiyou County Fair. Her sire was the great old Morgan stallion, Gay Mac; her dam was Hannabelle.

Little Fella, the Regnani's two-year-old bay stallion, is a son of Hildegarde, and was sired by Phil Morrison's Aranafield. He has a nice head, small pert ears, and shows promise of being a good horse.

We loved Oregon; the state is beautiful from border to border. Our next "horsey" stop was a most enjoyable stay with Jeanne Mehl at Glendale, Oregon. Mr. Mehl was in Costa Rica, so we didn't get to meet him, but we did see his remarkable trophy room. Mounted heads of water buffalo, caribou, sable, lesser kudu, and many more, attest to Mr. Mehl's skill as a big game hunter.

Mrs. Mehl has a lovely band of twelve Morgans, not an inferior one in the bunch. I ended up with half a dozen "favorites." Her stallion, Merry Warlock, carries some of the best blood in the breed, being by Merry Knox, out of Conniedale. Warlock has an exceptional head, is well conformed, and has one of the nicest dispositions I've seen in a stallion.

His foals are a lot like him, so he should have a bright future in Oregon. He's only four years old now. I just loved the sweet-faced mare, Mary Todd, and her '66 filly is a DOLL. The thirteen-year-old mare, Our Girl Friday, is a full sister to Muscleman, and her filly was another typey charmer.

The other mare in the band is Jesto's Merryminx, a daughter of Broadwall St. Pat, out of Mary Todd. Toddy's offspring are all good, even her grandchildren are pretty. Minx's yearling daughter, Mehlwood Zoosa, was SO nice we wanted to take her home. Unfortunately our suitcases were already full.

Ballerina June (Muscleman x Roseta Mae) showed off for us by racing around in her pasture, and Mehlwood Squire, a chestnut yearling by Warlock and Toddy, came up for inspection.

After dinner Jeanne showed us a number of slides of Eastern mares and stallions, which were very interesting to us, since we will be seeing those horses ourselves in a few weeks. Next day we said a reluctant goodbye to Mehlwood, and pressed on for Washington. Had planned a couple more stops in Oregon, but time would not permit.

There was a huge pumpkin moon riding over Seattle's sparkling skyline the night we stayed there. Next day we toured the interesting Woodland Park Zoo, and then went to Bothell, where we visited briefly with Gladys Koehne and Yvonne McDonald. These ladies are also Morgan breeders. They showed us Keystone's Missfire and Keystone's Starfire, both by Keystone, out of Lady K. Gates. These two young horses are whip broke, and were worked in a small round arena for us.

Here we saw another daughter of Gay Mac, the fine old black mare, Laurinda, owned by Elizabeth Equals. Mrs. Koehne then drove us out to see her stallion, Chowtime, who is in training. I had seen pictures of this horse, but none of them did him justice. He is a very upstanding, flashy moving fellow, dark brown and showy.

Our next stop was supposed to be Mount Vernon, but an international conference going on in Vancouver, B. C. had taken up all accommodations for many miles around, so we kept driving, and driving, and driving. Finally reached Abbotsford, B. C. at 2:30 a.m., so tired by then that we slept the clock around.

Next afternoon we ran into fellow Californians, Dr. and Mrs. H. P. Boyd and Gloria Jones, who were in Abbotsford with the Fahrnis. Small world!

Mr. and Mrs. Gerald Fahrni own Skyfield Farm, out the old Clayburn Road from Abbotsford. Their home perches among the pines, overlooking the beautiful Fraser Valley. Their stables are old and enormous, and contain many fine Morgans. Their two stallions are Skyfield and UVM Colfield.

Skyfield resembles his sire, Sonfield, quite a bit. He was High Aggregate Performance Horse at the 1965 All Morgan Show up here. Colfield was brought out from Quebec last February, and is a fine addition to the roster of sires in Western Canada. He is black-chestnut, over 15 hands, and very flashy. He had numerous wins to his credit in Eastern Canada, including blues in Get of Sire (against all breeds), high point awards, and Grand Champion Stallion six years. His '67 foals are anxiously awaited at Skyfield Farm.

The Fahrnis' mares are Lady Margaret, Oradust (who was once paralyzed by a bolt of lightning), Ranchita Queen, Easterglo, and Skyfield Patricia. Miss Merilee Fahrni has a two-year-old colt, Skyfield Golden Glen, that she thought might be a hunter prospect. Cutest of the foals, to me, was a little bay fireball named Skyfield Rebellion. He is a real clown, and I couldn't resist taking several pictures of him.

We spent two VERY enjoyable evenings with Mr. and Mrs. Ab Thiessen, at Sardis, B. C. Here again we saw good Morgans, and the hospitality shown us "furriners" by this fine couple was one of the high points of our trip so far. (Come to think of it, they remind me a lot of Lu and Dick Kibler!)

At this small ranch we saw the cutest little red and white barn, which Ab designed himself. I liked it so much that he gave me pictures of it, as well as some colored snapshots of their horses.

The Thiessens own the aged mare, Sharen Vermont, by Kenelm Morgan, out of Ro Boss. This breeding goes straight back to the fine Sellman stock, which has been responsible for much that is good in Western Morgans today.

Three of Sharen's offspring are owned by the Thiessens – two-year-old Shari Rockwood, King Rockwood, a yearling colt with light mane and tail, and a nice chestnut foal called Stormy. The horses we liked best were My Gay Pixie (Sonfield x Laurinda) and her weanling filly, Pixie's Gay Diamond, by Orland Royal Don. This liver chestnut filly was impossible to fault, and should certainly be a winner.

Ab and Eleanor Thiessen took us to Chilliwack, where we met some more nice folks, Ted and Peggy Williams, who have three Morgans. Their black mare, Zelpha, reminded us of Satina, a black mare we sold recently, and it turned out that both mares have Chief Bugler as a grandsire. It is interesting to pick out these family characteristics within a breed, and such family similarities certainly do exist.

The other two Morgans here were both bay, a full brother and sister by Sundust out of Zelpha. Bay Baron is a three-year-old stud, with the mildest eye, and the kind of temperament Morgan owners boast about. Zelpha Zee is a roly-poly two-year-old filly. It was obvious in looking at these horses that Ted does not stint on the feed.

Incidentally, Ted makes beautiful trophies for the local Morgan shows. His collection of ceramic horses makes quite a conversation piece.

After leaving the Fraser Valley, we concentrated on the scenery, and on getting to Banff Springs Hotel on time. British Columbia presents a continuous vista of beauty. The barns in the Fraser Valley are very large, and quaint by California standards. This is wonderful farming country, and everyone was busy putting up hay. Most of it seemed to be alfalfa.

Deep into the mountains we passed a number of historic-looking old shanties made of rough-hewn logs, topped by thatched roofs. The highway here follows the route of the old Cariboo Trail.

Many of the towns along the way were early settlements created by the Northwest Company or the Hudson's Bay Company. Most towns of any size still have a Hudson's Bay Company store. Beyond Savona the road paralleled the long Kamloops Lake, which stayed beside us for nearly twenty-eight miles.

Farther on we noticed a beautiful ranch, with large green meadows, trees and shrubs, a windbreak row of poplars beside a white ranch house, white board fences, and herds of fat Herefords. Such a pretty place! This was the Cherry Creek Ranch, where registered Polled Herefords and Quarter Horses were raised. Wish we could have stopped, but it was getting late.

Between Kamloops and Golden we again drove through some fine-appearing farm country, and every ranch seemed to have several horses. The scenery all the way was exceptional. Again our road ran beside a long lake, the Shuswap, and we passed through Revelstoke and Glacier national parks. Glacier is in the heart of the Selkirk Mountains, a range far older than the Rockies. Scenery was all around us…it was hard to know WHERE to look! The next day found us in Banff National Park, in the Canadian Rockies, and across the Great Divide.

If you ever wonder what to do with your vacation, come to Vancouver, B. C. and follow the Trans-Canada Highway to Banff. You couldn't possibly regret the choice. This is a land that can only be described in superlatives!

At Banff Springs Hotel we were met by kilted doormen, and awoke next morning to the skirl of bagpipes in the courtyard below. The view from our window was completely out of this world, and we could hear Bow River Falls roaring somewhere below us.

There are many excellent riding trails both at Banff and at Lake Louise, and you can bet that the Houltons took a "busman's holiday" ride at both places. From Chateau Lake Louise, the ride around the lake is especially lovely, with the picturesque chateau at one end, Victoria Glacier at the other. Lake Louise laps the shore on one side, while pines whisper to you on the other. It snowed our last night at the lake, and we poor Californians nearly froze!

The Sundance Arabian Ranch is located in Banff, headed up by the champion Arabian stallion, Saracan AHCR 23879. Saracan was champion at the 1966 Fifth Annual Canadian Partbred Arab Show, and also champion at the 1966 Calgary Horse Show. The ranch owners also operate the Sundance Riding Stables, and the name of both is derived from a local mountain range.

September

Quebec – September 16th. The "Line" has stretched a long way, since I wrote to you from Banff! Before leaving that city, we drove through the "Buffalo Paddocks," where one of Canada's three herds is maintained. This herd roams naturally over acres of wooded terrain, and their coats are rich and glossy…not like the typical moth-eaten zoo buffalo. They're magnificent animals, and the old bull is enormous!

At Calgary, we went through the Horsemen's Hall of Fame, located at the Brewery Grounds. The hall pays homage to early West Canadians, with life-size wax figures and dioramas. It includes a fine collection of Charles Russell's paintings, sketches, and sculpture.

We spent an afternoon at Calgary's Heritage Park. This is a sixty-acre re-creation of a nine-teenth century Canadian community, complete with railway line, steamer, fur trading post, village, Indian encampment, working farm, etc. One side of the farm's field is fenced with the wicked buckthorn barbwire of the '70s. At Hull Carriage House, built in 1905, we saw some fine old car-riages, which are pulled by the park's two Hackney Horses, Animation and Seal's Sensation, a pair of matched bays.

At nearby Okotoks, there are a number of fine horse ranches. I heard that Johnny Longden is part owner of a Thoroughbred farm here. One of the outstanding horse farms is 2-C Ranches, owned by an American, J. F. D'Arcy. It features Quarter Horses - training and boarding. D'Arcy's stallion is Sugar Bud, a grandson of Three Bars. The barns here are large and modern. Morris Ericcson is trainer and general manager.

We were houseguests of Mr. and Mrs. A. J. Mills, who have an outstanding band of Morgans. All are remarkable for their muscular development…wonderful chests and hindquarters. Their sen-ior stallion, Mills Pride, is one of the nicest I've seen anywhere. He has many championships to his credit. The display of ribbons and trophies at the Mills' attest to the quality of their stock. Did you know that in Canada the first prize ribbon is red?

My girls had a ball riding Mills Pride. They worked him both English and western, and pro-nounced him a powerful horse, all stallion, but very well-controlled. The Mills own two stallions, a gelding, three mares and a colt, all registered Morgans, and a larger hunter type mare, plus having a few boarders. Our favorite Morgan was the typey dark brown mare, Mills Gay Lady, a real cat-footed dynamo under saddle!

Mrs. Mills came by her interest in horses quite naturally. She is from Dartmoor, England, fa-mous for its ponies. Her grandfather once owned all the horses used on the mail carts in southern England. He kept special four-in-hand teams to be used for weddings, funeral corteges, etc. and also bought and sold jumpers and hunters for use by the British gentry.

At Regina we toured the Royal Canadian Mounted Police Barracks, and watched a group of recruits go through their morning equitation drill. Twenty-nine young men, all mounted on dark bays, browns or blacks, worked in a huge brick indoor arena, under direction of a mounted instructor. All exercises are performed at the trot, and include a variety of close-order maneuvers, and a session on how to "present swords."

An interesting museum at the barracks covers early history of the R.C.M.P. Regina has been known as the "Home of the Mounties" since 1905, when their headquarters were moved here from Walsh. The city has an outstanding Museum of Natural History, which no one visiting Saskatchewan should miss.

On our way to Winnipeg, on August 18th, we were treated to a display of the Northern Lights! I was still fascinated by Canadian barns. On the prairies, people add color to the flat land through their buildings. We saw barns of white, with roofs of bright blue or green; brilliant red barns trimmed in white, even pale green barns with bright red roofs. We passed one darling little New England style church of gray stone, with white woodwork and a delft blue roof.

We toured beautiful old Lower Fort Garry, an 1831 fortress and trading post on the banks of the Red River. Next day we attended the opening day of harness racing at Assiniboia Downs Raceway. Only one of the Standardbreds that day was a trotter, the others were all pacers. Nearly all were Canadian owned, only four being entries from the States.

Smoky Seven Up, a nice black gelding, won the 6 ½ furlong first race, and later won the one-mile pace. We especially liked another black gelding, Mac Counsel (Glenwood Counsellor x Allie Guy), owned and driven by G. S. MacDonald, and Mac was nice enough to win two races for us!

The third race was most exciting. Buddy Bree, a four-year-old gelding by Champ Adios, stayed way back until he was deep into the far turn. Then he just SURGED forward, to lead them all under the wire!

Another son of Champ Adios won the fourth race, Adios Richard, a five-year-old bay stallion. Emery Learfield of Canby, Oregon, came in second in that race with his mare, Etta Richard, the only U. S. horse in the money.

A Saskatchewan entry, Donna L. Worthy, took "show" position in one race, then came back later to win a mile at the pace. She is by Mack Harvester, out of Sue Elworthy. A stallion, Pistol Pointer, won the eighth race, and another Champ Adios offspring, Nancy Adios C., came in second.

I love harness racing…think I could sit and watch forever! I tend to pick my "winners" primarily by pedigree, topped by the look of the horse when he makes his warm-up trip down the track. Standardbreds are notable for their great racing families, and I kind of like to watch how these families do. Mac Counsel, by the way, was oldest on the track that day…age thirteen…and he showed all the "youngsters" his heels…twice.

Canadians are great racing fans, and every major city has its racing calendar, for harness and flat racing, even in the winter. Windsor, Ontario has one of the finest raceways in North America, where harness races are conducted from early October through mid-March.

Racing is conducted on a special "Tartan" track, a synthetic plastic material that guarantees uniform racing conditions through the fall and winter meets. Fans enjoy air conditioned, shirt-sleeve temperature in the glass-enclosed clubhouse and grandstand. The raceway is equipped with special closed circuit television that transmits pictures and data on the race in progress. TV sets are located wherever the raceway doesn't overlook the track.

At St. Catherine's Garden City Raceway, Kinnel Lodge, an outstanding two-year-old trotter, whipped older horses to tie a track record of 2:09 3/5 for the mile. He is owned by veterinarian John Findley, and this race gave Dr. Findley his 58th win of the season. The young doctor annually ranks among the leading money winners on the Ontario circuit. His horses earned over $100,000 in 1964 and in 1965.

The offspring of Sheila Lee, dam of Kinnel Lodge, have won more than $175,000. All were trained by Dr. Findley, who owns Madawask Farms in Arnprior. He is director of the Canadian Standardbred Horse Society, and third vice president of the Ontario Harness Horsemen's Association.

The Thoroughbreds were running at Toronto when we were there. Pine Point, a dark bay colt owned by Saul Wagman, Willow Down Farm, won the $10,000 Yearling Sales Stake on September 6th. Pine Point is considered by many here to be the top two-year-old prospect. Purchased for $4,000 at last year's Canadian Thoroughbred Horse Society's yearling sale, he has already earned more than $37,000. He was sired by All Hands, whose offspring have been very impressive on the track this season. All Hands is by Turn-To, a Royal Charger offspring, and out of Best Risk, by Blenheim II.

Here's a cute trick. A racehorse named Jolly Jet was found to run better just after he comes out of a shipping van. So, now he is driven around in a van for a couple of hours on the morning of the race…and it works!

The Canadian Thoroughbred Horse Society's annual yearling sale was held at Woodbine on September 6th and 7th. One hundred thirty yearlings brought $345,000, with five offspring of Nearctic (sire of Northern Dancer) bringing $86,000. Top selling yearling, a chestnut colt by Nearctic, out of Questage, went to M. J. Boylen for $25,500. Next, at $25,000 was a bay colt by Victoria Park out of Salix. Both colts are half brothers of stakes winners, and their prospects are bright, as Nearctic and Victoria Park are noted for their speedy offspring.

A Reuter's dispatch from London told about Greg Lougher's heart-breaking problem. Thirty of Greg's best horses were stranded aboard a freighter in London. Greg had asked Queen Elizabeth, Prince Phillip and Prime Minister Wilson to help untangle the quarantine deadlock.

Seems there was a one-night stop-over at LeHavre and, because there was an outbreak of swamp fever in France, the horses were forbidden to disembark in England even though they did not leave the ship in France. They could not remain on the ship either, since it was scheduled to go into dry dock. Greg had paid nearly $20,000 to transport the stock to England, where they were to spend a six-month quarantine period before proceeding to Australia.

There was a hard decision to be made…find another $20,000 to return the band to America, or destroy it. Lougher said he couldn't destroy what had taken a lifetime to build, and raising the money to do it all over again was tantamount to bankruptcy. What a choice! I hope the Queen, horsewoman that she is, was able to help.

Lady Escar is a great-hearted three-year-old filly who wins her races, but nobody wants her. The most remarkable horse running in Canada today, she has won more races than any horse this season, finishing in the money fourteen times in fourteen starts. She is royally bred, by Canadian Champ, out of Bull Tan, and wins despite tremendous handicaps…but no one will buy her.

You see, Lady Escar is a horse with problems, and her owner, Ernie Lieberman, holds his breath every time he enters her in a race. Her list of ailments is fantastic. She has chips in her front ankles and knees that need continual treatment. She has injured a stifle bone in her hind leg, and has pulled a shoulder muscle. She is pigeon-toed, and needs a special shoe. She gets cortisone shots in her legs and ankles up to forty-eight hours before a race.

Afterward, a painkiller is put into her feed, poultice bandages are put on her ankles to draw out the heat, and her legs are placed in tubs of hot and cold water containing salts. She seems like a cripple, requiring constant care from her trainer, groom and vet.

But when the starting gate opens, she runs like the wind, and leaves all the sound horses behind…a great lady, with a heart bigger than most!

From Toronto we traveled to Oshawa, to visit the National Stud Farm, third largest stud farm in North America, and internationally famous for the championship horses it has produced. We were VERY fortunate in being able to go through this fine establishment, and take all the pictures we wished, as it was not open to visitors when we were there.

The tour of the stallion barn was really a treat. Here were many of Canada's greatest stallions, including the fabulous Northern Dancer, 1964 winner of the Kentucky Derby. He is a handsome bay, very muscular, and quite short. There's a special platform for him in the breeding arena.

In the next stall was the Dancer's sire, Nearctic, who is a brown-black, taller and longer than his son. These two have fine heads and nice mild eyes. Among the stallions we saw were other fine sires, like Gray Monarch, Victoria Park, Canadian Champ, New Providence and Startus.

The farm is owned by Canada's foremost Thoroughbred breeder, E. P. Taylor, and consists of nearly 2,000 beautiful wooded acres. There were ten stallions and about 266 mares and foals, a number of them outside mares, there for breeding. Mr. Taylor was to hold a sale of sixty-four yearlings in late September.

Northern Dancer won over a half million dollars during his track career, and now stands at stud for $10,000, live foal, to approved mares. Many top American mares are being brought to him now. Nearctic's fee of $7,500 may go up next year.

If you're planning a trip to Canada next year for Expo '67, be sure to include stops at Old Fort Henry in Kingston, and Upper Canada Village near Morrisburg; both are an absolute must for the Ontario tourist!

Two things will always stand out in our minds when we remember the time we spent in the Province of Quebec. One was the caleche ride we took through the historic city of Quebec.

Our other good memory will be of Hillhead Farm at LaChute, and its very nice owners, Mr. and Mrs. Atlee Clarke. The Clarkes are Arabian breeders, and their 250-acre farm is situated in beautiful hill country, north of Montreal, and near the Laurentian Mountains.

The Clarkes currently have seventeen Arabians, and their breeding program is similar to that being carried out at Al-Marah. Their stallion is the International Champion Ikhtiyarin, by Indraff x Imagida. He is a small horse, well-developed, with a true Arab croup, with a perfect Arabian head, which he is passing on to his offspring. Two of his daughters were especially attractive, and one of them should be familiar to Arabian admirers…Gay Minx, out of Gay Semiha. She is a beautiful young gray mare, quite small, with the daintiest head imaginable.

Her half-sister, Micky, out of Maraga, is just about as nice, and is actually a more colorful gray, since she has black mane, tail, and points.

Another beauty with an exquisite head was the rose gray yearling filly, Khara Mia. The young stock is all classic in appearance, showing proof of an excellent breeding program.

It is a pity that the Clarkes are the only Arabian breeders in this part of the world, as their stallion would surely be in great demand wherever Arabian owners were found. All the stock here is very gentle and well-mannered. We walked out into the field to see the mares, who came up to get acquainted, and caused no trouble whatever. One was a Crabbet mare, another was Polish, several were gray, and a few chestnut. There were four nice weanlings, two rose gray, one dark gray, and one tiny fellow who is a dark, rich chestnut like his sire.

Hillhead is a most attractive place, quite new, and efficiently planned. Near the home are an outdoor riding ring, a stable with foaling stalls, and quarters for the weanlings. An intercom connects this barn to the house, and there is a sleeping room and a trophy room at one end. The weanlings' pasture is in sight from the barn. Farther away are the trainer's house, the main stable and pasture area. Here are the large indoor arena, many stalls, more living quarters for help, and a tack room and lounge. A picturesque brick ruin stands between the two homes, near the road… remnant of the first farmhouse on this land.

Sufficient stabling is a necessity in this deep-winter country. You don't dare let your horses run outside in the winter. The cold air would burn their lungs and kill them. They are only let out for a few minutes of mild exercise. Mrs. Clarke said the horses get so used to walking on snow that, when spring comes, they avoid the patches of exposed ground and step in the snow!

To top the day, we had dinner at the famous LaChute Golf and Country Club, where Mrs. Clarke guided us through a delicious selection of French foods, including specialties unique to this club. It had been weeks since we'd had a real chance to talk "horse," and it was a pleasure to spend an evening with these very nice people.

October

The "Line" this time is being written in Greenville, Pennsylvania, where we have been visiting with Dot and Dayton Lockard. The Lockards are a very interesting couple, with a variety of talents.

For several years, Dot wrote a homespun type article for *The Morgan Horse* magazine, titled "Just Hossin' Around." She has a lot of fun trading in antiques, and probably has forgotten more about Early Americana than I'll ever learn. She also breeds dogs…Cocker Spaniels and Miniature Schnauzers.

Dayton trains horses, and occasionally judges. Their horse is the Morgan stallion, Archie O's Archie. I really enjoyed watching this horse, because he has a kind of freedom denied to many stallions. Archie runs free in a large pasture, with a river at one edge, and a hilltop from which to survey the world. He has a gelding for companionship, and the two run and play together. One evening we called Archie, but he was too far away to hear. The gelding heard us though, and he galloped down the hill to where the stallion grazed. He must have "told" Archie we were calling, because in a minute both horses came flying up to the gate!

The official state animal of Vermont is the Morgan, and in that state we visited ten Morgan farms, seeing many fine examples of the breed.

At Towne-Ayr Farm we saw the venerable Lippitt Rob Roy, now twenty-five years old. He's still a very handsome stallion, fat and shiny.

The Townes have been raising Morgans for years. We saw four generations of mares from one family. First was the black mare Dream Star, who produced Towne-Ayr Belle, first foal born on the farm. Belle's beautiful daughter, Towne-Ayr Carillon, won the Justin Morgan class at the 1966 National Morgan Horse Show. This class is a test of versatility, and to compete, a horse must trot a half-mile under saddle, and a half-mile in harness, and also pull a weighted stone boat. Carillon's yearling filly, Diane Jacobs, was the fourth generation of this family, and she was a very flashy dark chestnut with flaxen mane and tail.

At Richmond, Vermont, we visited Paramount Stables, owned by Dr. E. F. Paquette. Here we saw the handsome Paramount Ambassador, fifteen-year-old son of the noted Upwey Ben Don. He was Vermont Champion Open Morgan in '62 and '63, and several of his offspring have also won state championships. He is a good-sized horse, with a tremendous chest, shoulder and neck.

Everyone who owns a Morgan, or admires the breed, should visit the University of Vermont Morgan Horse Farm at Weybridge! Go in late September, to see the fall foliage at its flamboyant best. The Vermont hillsides are covered with maple trees, turned to bright shades of gold, crimson or maroon, all mixed with dark evergreens. The road to the farm takes you over a picturesque covered bridge spanning Otter Creek. Soon you see fields with mares out grazing, and then the white barns and houses of the farm come into view. On a rise of ground before the main barn, stands the fine bronze statue of Justin Morgan, foundation sire of the breed.

There are 54 Morgans at the farm. They have three outstanding stallions: UVM Flash (Upwey Ben Don x Norma), coal black, very short backed, lots of depth, and a marvelous head; UVM Highlight (Orcland Vigildon x Symphonee), a fine-boned bay; and UVM Cantor (Tutor x Sugar), the senior stallion. Cantor is a bright chestnut, with a long, long forelock, wonderful disposition, and lots of personality, plus the most fantastic action.

We spent three hours at the farm, seeing all the horses, watching some of them work out, and chatting with Leonard Wales, the manager, and his assistants. Later, we met Dr. Leonard Balch, who is in charge of the UVM Farm.

Another of the impressive Vermont Morgan establishments is the Green Mountain Stock Farm at Randolph, owned by Californian Robert Morgan. This farm is set in lovely, wooded country. The Horseman's Book Stall, a well-stocked book and novelty shop, is in one of the barns, and overhead is quite a collection of old horse-drawn sleighs. Another barn contains a number of antique buggies and carriages. Trainer Raymond Rooks was very hospitable, and brought out several of the Morgans for our inspection. We were quite taken with Green Trim's Top Miss, a three-year-old filly who can really move. Their chestnut stallion, Great Hills Atlantic, is a double grandson of Orcland Leader. He moves well, and looks great in harness.

We came upon another ancient covered bridge at Tunbridge, Vermont, when we went to visit Mr. and Mrs. Harold Childs at their historic farm, Harolyn Hill. As we drove up through the vibrantly colored hills we came upon the Justin Morgan Memorial, which identifies this farm as the place where the original Morgan horse died. This memorial is in a lovely, grassy plot in the woods, bounded on three sides by white board fence. As we stood there, the years whizzed away, and we could almost feel that this was 1825 and the plucky little bay stallion was coming up the hill, pulling a load of logs behind him! Then we went on up the road, past Justin's descendants grazing where he too must have once nibbled grass.

Two horses will stand out in our memories of Harolyn Hill. One was quite young, the other very old. Lippitt Mandate, at twenty-seven, is one of the few remaining sons of the great Government stallion, Mansfield. This enchanting old codger shows his age…grizzled face, and hollow back, but he has all the pride and fire of a young stud. He challenges every stallion led past his stall, and he keeps one eye on the band of mares, too! The young stallion is High Pastures Ivanhoe, owned by Mrs. Harriet Hilts, and he was our favorite of all the stallions we have seen on our trip. He's light chestnut with a great, thick mane shot with gray. His conformation was excellent, his disposition superb. Mr. Childs has trained him to be very versatile…English, Western and harness. All last winter he was driven to a sleigh!

Mrs. Frances Bryant has one of the loveliest farms imaginable, near Woodstock, and her band of Morgans was exceptionally uniform and handsome. Her senior stallion is Lippitt Ashmore, whose get were all very typey and pretty headed. Here at Serenity Farm we got to go for a drive. Pulling our cart was the very handsome David Ashmore, three-year-old son of Lippitt Ashmore.

Mrs. Bryant has been raising Morgans for many years, and her breeding program has produced a fine group of horses. She does not show, but horses raised at Serenity Farm are sold trained and gentle, ready to go on for their new owners.

Harriet Hilts and her trainer, Mary Turgeon, showed us ten nice Morgans at High Pastures Farm. One was Royalton Bobbin, who at age fifteen and heavy in foal, placed third in the lightweight division on the Vermont 100-mile trail ride. Mrs. Hilts' horses have lots of substance, and true Morgan disposition.

In southern Vermont we visited Bald Mountain Farm, where Mr. and Mrs. Keynith Knapp have been raising Morgans for over twenty years. A car killed their well-known stallion, Easter Twilight, this spring.

At Tamarled Morgan Farm, Brattleboro, we saw a new 74 x 150 foot barn and arena, where a "barn warming" and clinic was to be held in mid-October. This place, like many we saw in New England, has a well-stocked tack shop, in conjunction with the breeding farm.

We spent a week with Wally and Evie Dennis, in Durham, New Hampshire, and these nice people took us somewhere every day to meet all the Morgan owners in the area. We even watched the final day of the Deerfield Fair Horse Show. In the Dennis barn we saw Foxy Wallect, UVM Keepsake, and Lynda, whose colt was by Donlyn of Windcrest. Wally Dennis is highly regarded as a horse show judge in this area.

Donlyn of Windcrest was another of the exceptionally good stallions we saw in New England. He is by Upwey Ben Don, out of Ingrid, and is owned by Dr. and Mrs. Charles Thompson, Highover Farm. The Thompsons own eight Morgans. Their Bar-T Coronet won the mare and foal class at the '66 National Show, with her fine bay filly, Highover Crown Jewel. They have a very pretty young mare, Highover Yankee Lass, which my girls both enjoyed riding.

Kay and Tommy Thompson took us on a drive through the woods up to Blueberry Hill, where a short climb brought us to a breathtaking "top of the world" view of the country, for miles in all directions. The blueberry fields had turned to red and were all about us. The rocks and boulders we stood on were filled with mica, glittering in the sunshine. It was a balmy afternoon, and a marvelous place to be.

At the University of New Hampshire, we saw another "ancient" of the Morgan world, the thirty-two-year-old stud Melysses (Ulysses x Melba). We were disappointed with the UNH stock, which seems to have downgraded over the years. We also visited with Ruth and Lyman Orcutt, where Orland Dondarling and many other well-known show horses make their home.

Mary and Freddy Crafts have the most beautiful barn…three levels, lots of windows; shutters on the front make it look just like a house from the road. They have two very nice stallions, Ethan Twilight and Tinderbox, who is what we call the "old type" Morgan. He is outstanding under saddle and in harness.

Mr. and Mrs. Clayton Conn have one of the snuggest and neatest stables, room for lots of horses, but right now they have just three. Their mare, Syndicate's Anastasia, did very well at shows this year.

At Le Chat Noir Stables we saw a variety of horses, including Green Dream Figure, a nice black son of Orland Dondarling. One interesting horse was eighteen-year-old Salvador, an Arab-Welsh Cob cross from England.

The Gardner Stones have several Thoroughbreds, and part-breds, by their stallion Mr. Covell (Boswell x Anna Covell). Their mare named Catnip is a tremendous bay heavy hunter, seventeen hands high, out of a registered Percheron mare, U. C. Kon Konilda. Catnip looks like her Thoroughbred sire.

Mr. and Mrs. Dennis also treated us to a drive along the Atlantic coast through Hampton Beach and Rye Harbour, to Wentworth by the Sea, Portsmouth Harbour, and up to Kittery, Maine.

Next day we said reluctant farewells, and drove to Richmond, Massachusetts, where we attended the 9th Annual Greed Meads Weanling Sale.

Green Meads Farm, owned by Mr. and Mrs. Darwin Morse, is another lovely and well-planned breeding farm. We were greatly impressed by their young stallion Green Meads Marauder (Upwey Ben Don x Abbington of Shady Lawn), and his full brother and sister. They all had beautiful heads, and the most gorgeous, big, gentle eyes. Marauder's little daughter, Green Meads Desire, was a chip off the old block.

At the sale, nineteen good colts and fillies brought $19,375.00. The top price was $2,100. Only two weanlings sold for under $700. Kay Thompson's pretty filly, Highover Sugar Candy, by Donlyn of Windcrest, brought $1,550.

In New York we spend an afternoon at Voorhis Farm, with Jeanne Mellin Herrick, noted artist, author, and horsewoman. Her studio is a big house trailer, an ideal setup for an artist's workshop. She showed us two marvelous paintings she was working on, one of which was commissioned by Robert Morgan.

We saw the Voorhis Morgans, including the famous Pecos, now about twenty-three, one of those small but mighty horses who look bigger somehow than they really are. This is a very picturesque farm, because the green paddocks border a hillside apple orchard.

Kingston was friendly and inquisitive, and came up to the fence to visit with us. Pretty mares and foals also came up when they saw us, and Sealect of Windcrest watched us from his paddock. The trophy room at Voorhis Farm is very impressive. Many winners have been produced here, under the capable hands of Jeanne and Fred Herrick.

After a close look at Niagara Falls from the Canadian side (WOW!), we drove to Pennsylvania. Our first night there, the Lockards took us to visit some of the Morgan owners nearby. It was a cold and drizzly night, but the horses looked good just the same! Now we're taking off for Lexington, Kentucky, which I'll tell you about next month.

November

The "wanderers" are home again. We were gone over three months, and put some 13,000 miles on the speedometer. We saw so many places that were beautiful, and met so many wonderful people all across Canada and the United States, and learned a lot about horses all along the way. It was a wonderful, never-to-be-forgotten experience. We got so used to traveling that now it seems strange not to be packing up and moving on!

The most interesting place we visited on our trip through the South was, of course, Lexington, Kentucky. More than three hundred horse farms make this truly the horse center of America, and a lovelier place would be hard to imagine.

The country is a succession of gently rolling hills, dotted with trees turned soft yellow in the fall sunlight. I never saw so much white board fencing…miles and miles of it, stretching in all directions for as far as the eye could see. Some of the farms had fine gray limestone fences, and I noticed a few had switched to the new idea of painting their pole or board fences black…very effective.

Thoroughbreds, Standardbreds and American Saddle Horses are raised here in Big Business fashion. The historic and beautiful Keeneland Race Track is here, and the famous "Red Mile" Trotting Track for Standardbreds. Most of the farms are open daily to the public between 9 a.m. and 4 p.m., and you can go by Blue Grass bus tour, or make the circuit in your car, whichever you prefer.

The Fayette County Chamber of Commerce prints a nice little map which identifies all the big farms…a very handy piece of paper.

One of the lovely estates is Walnut Hall, at the intersection of the Newton and Ironworks pikes. It covers hundreds of acres of pasture and woodland, and is the oldest Standardbred horse farm in the world. Out the other direction from town is Almahurst Farm, where the world champion Greyhound was foaled.

The Helena Rubenstein horse farm, Main Chance, is very impressive, and houses some notable racing stock. The names of farms are intriguing…Providence, Dixiana, Winganeek, Spendthrift, Darby Dan and Calumet.

Many of them have fine statues erected to a favorite or famous horse of their breeding. The Man O' War statue is fabulous. One-fifth larger than life, it stands on raised ground, surrounded by a cement dry moat, and circled by trees. "Big Red" himself lies buried in front of the statue, with two of his sons, and under the trees nearby are markers for two other sons, and his dam. When Man O' War died, his body was embalmed and placed in a fine casket lined with his stable colors, and he lay in state at Faraway Farm for three days. Giant horseshoe floral pieces were sent to the farm from all over the world, and then the great Man O' War was laid to rest, with mourners present at the graveside ceremony.

Roxie Highland was considered one of the greatest three-gaited mares of all time. She won 257 firsts out of 260 times shown. When she died in 1939 she also was buried with full honors, at Spindletop, and a fine statue of her marks the site, done in bronze by sculptor George F. Yostel.

We spent some time at the American Saddle Horse Museum, where the executive director, Mrs. Esteray Goggin, was very informative and friendly. The collection of horse portraits comprising the Saddle Horse Hall of Fame is very fine, and included many George Ford Morris originals.

Wing Commander's portrait hangs over the mantel with his trophies, ribbons and shoes displayed below. This is the wonderful Saddle Horse who won the Grand Championship Five Gaited Stake at the Kentucky State Fair every year from 1948 through 1953, and who was World's Grand Champion Saddle Horse from 1948 through 1955. Now almost twenty-four years old, this great king of the show horses may be seen at Castleton Farm, on the old Ironworks Pike, across from Walnut Hall.

Some of the other great horses to whom statues have been raised are Bull Lea at Calumet Farm, and Fair Play, sire of Man O' War. There is an excellent statue of General John Hunt Morgan, astride a powerful, lovely horse, in the center of downtown Lexington. Funny thing though, General Morgan's mount was a fine black mare, but in the statue she's turned into a stallion!

Stallion Station, out the Russell Cave Pike, is an unusual farm in that it is not a breeding farm. About fifteen top stallions stand here, and mares are brought to them from all over the area.

The gates at many of the Blue Grass farms are very interesting. They are so constructed that they can be opened by a person driving a horse, without leaving the cart. Two long wooden arms and a pulley arrangement make this a very handy way to get in and out.

One thing that interested me at Elmendorf was the fact that Ben Ali Haggin built a house there. Ben Ali was a colorful figure from California during the Comstock era. He was an enthusiastic horseman, and extremely wealthy. He is best know for his eastern breeding and racing stock, but he also was a Morgan horse enthusiast, and once ran large numbers of them on his huge central California ranches.

The grounds and lovely old southern mansions at many of these Blue Grass farms are so picturesque, and really give you a sense of the past melded to the present. We stayed right across from the University of Kentucky Experimental Farm, a beautiful old place with white board fences, rolling green pastures, many trees, fine old buildings, and fat, black Angus cattle. We went one day to see Ashland, Henry Clay's fine, old red brick, white pillared home.

The gateways to so many farms are works of art…at Keeneland, Winganeek, Spindletop, and so many more. In addition to the horses, you see many fine herds of cattle and sheep near Lexington. The area is a treasury of Civil War lore, with many monuments erected as Confederate memorials. The homes out Lexington's Main Street are mostly colonial architecture, with fine lawns and a gracious air. It's fun to just drive around slowly, for hours on end, and look, and look…

From Kentucky we cut through the Ozarks, across Oklahoma, down Route 66. When we reached Arizona we stopped at Holbrook, and there one of my girls said, "Hey, there goes the Jack Tone horse van!" We really felt we were getting close to home!

Like all good tourists we toured the Painted Desert, Petrified Forest, Meteor Crater, and Grand Canyon. That Arizona country looks more like it belongs on the moon than on earth…strange but beautiful.

We drove into our yard on Halloween, and my dad thought we were trick-or-treaters!

Roy Bush and Jon Scholten have sold their J-R Ranch property in Sonora, and have purchased a 240-acre ranch near Prospect, Oregon. The new place boasts a lovely view of the mountains along the Rogue River, and will one day be stocked with cattle and Morgan horses.

The two partners are busy mending fence and building a stable to house their two Morgans, Satina and Dee, and the two mares leased from Viking Morgan Ranch, Gimma and Viking Vanity. All three mares are due to foal the same week in March, which should make for an interesting spring at the new J-R Ranch.

We drove over with the Willifords recently to visit Mr. and Mrs. Henry Trantham, to see their young stallion Kellfield. The Tranthams also have an old Morgan mare, Sunday Gold D, and her two bay fillies by Dapper Dan, and out of the good Fleetfield mare, Falene, and we found him to be an unusual horse.

You frequently hear about stallions with good dispositions, but this young fellow is pretty amazing. He is actually mild and gentle as a kitten, yet he has enough zip to be fun to ride. In spite of coldness of the day, my daughter, Leslie, had a great time riding him. He has a good head carriage and is nice and light on his feet. He is still kind of green, but with more work should make a fine mount, because he is eager to go and anxious to please.

As an example of his unruffled disposition, the Trantham's little boy often swings from a rope tied to a big tree branch down onto Kellfield's back, and it doesn't faze this nice young stud a bit!

15

The National Stud Farm
1967

Oshawa, in the Canadian province of Ontario, is a pleasant community some thirty miles east of Toronto. Several large industrial plants are situated there, including General Motors of Canada.

The city has many points of interest for the tourist. The fine, lighted monument in Memorial Park was built of stones from the countries of all the World War I Allies, and from most of the battlefields where Canadian servicemen have fought. One stone came from Westminster Abbey. Nearby is the Canadian Automotive Museum, containing a complete chronology of the automobile, from a 1769 French Cugnot to the latest in modern developments. Not far away is the Henry House Historical Museum, where relics from the early settlement of the area are on display.

During World War II Sir William Stephenson, a Canadian millionaire, represented British Intelligence in the United States. He purchased a farmhouse at Oshawa and set up a training school for instruction in the fine arts of sabotage and subversion. His staff included two former members of the Shanghai police, and experts in the fields of safecracking, lockpicking and housebreaking. Among the students at the center for a short time was Ian Fleming, author of the James Bond stories.

One of the most interesting establishments at Oshawa is E. P. Taylor's National Stud Farm, located at the north end of town. This, the third largest stud farm in North America, is world famous for the championship horses it has produced. Taylor, who is often called "Mr. Thoroughbred," also owns Windfields Farm, a fine racing stable at Willowdale, near Toronto. He has bred thirteen Queen's Plate winners, over seventy stakes winners and seven holders of the title, "Canadian Horse of the Year." His annual yearling sales are an important event in the Thoroughbred horseman's schedule.

The National Stud Farm is a beautiful 1,700-acre showplace, situated in lush, rolling farmland, framed by trees and edged by black board fences. It is also a scientific plant, devoted to the production and care of top quality Thoroughbred horses. The farm maintains a staff of some fifty employees, under the direction of manager Gil Darlington.

A self-contained operation, National Stud Farm has its own laboratory and treatment center, complete with portable X-ray unit. If a foal is noticed lying too still in a field, a call goes out over the intercom from the administration office to the nearest barn for someone to check whether it is just asleep or ill. There is a large lay-up barn for injured horses from the track, and foaling barns for expectant mares. Pastures are routinely checked for calcium content, and rigid parasite control is practiced.

The laboratory and veterinary center are housed in the administration building, and a more complete and efficient facility would be hard to imagine. Blood tests and cultures are run in the lab, pregnancy tests are made, and a special virus-abortion flu vaccine is produced. Stallions and racing stock have blood-count checks each month, and mares are blood-tested quarterly. On the supply room shelves are antibiotics, tetanus vaccine and other medications vital to the well-being of the farm's valuable stock.

Each foal has a "case file," which includes periodic X-ray pictures that indicate the growth and development of its all-important leg bones. After all, Taylor's foals are intended for the track. Also, a small band of nurse mares is kept at the farm for easy availability when a substitute mother is needed.

The farm's proven speed sires, among them Northern Dancer, Nearctic, *Grey Monarch, Victoria Park, Canadian Champ and New Providence, are housed in fine box stalls at one end of the large breeding barn. A new stallion barn is under construction. A raised platform stands in the center of the sand-floored breeding arena, for use by the 15.3-hand Northern Dancer, who is nicknamed "Shorty."

Last fall there were 266 mares and foals at the farm, and Mr. Taylor was readying sixty-four yearlings for a late September sale. Many Thoroughbred mares are brought here from Canadian and United States racing farms to be bred. Some arrive while carrying foals, and these are carefully tended until they have foaled and are bred, checked and pronounced safe in foal again.

To give some idea of the quality of the stock produced by the stallions named above, the results of the annual summer yearling sale at Woodbine Sales Pavilion in Toronto are of interest. The 1966 sale, conducted by the Canadian Thoroughbred Horse Society, was held on September 6 and 7, and when it was over total sales had reached $345,300 – an average of $4,194.60 for the 130 head. From this group twenty yearlings by Victoria Park, Nearctic, *Grey Monarch and Canadian Champ brought a total of $182,700, or over one-half of the entire sales proceeds (an average of $9,135 each). A Nearctic foal topped the sale with a price of $25,500.

Taylor's stallions are considered "proven" when their offspring begin to do well on the track. Their ability to breed speed is more important to him than their individual records. For example, Victoria Park, a grandson of Gallant Fox, was a Queen's Plate winner and placed second in the Preakness and third in the Kentucky Derby during his turf career. In 1966 his son, Victoria Era, won nine stakes races, including the Durham Cup at Woodbine, where he carried 133 pounds – the highest impost assigned in Canada in twenty-two years.

The Dancer's sire, Nearctic, has a number of offspring which have competed successfully on northern tracks, and his foals generally command premium prices at the sales. He has pedigree as well as performance, being of the great Nearco-Hyperion cross. His stablemate, *Grey Monarch, a stakes winning grandson of Nearco, sired offspring that ran third in the Queen's Plate. Several of Canadian Champ's offspring have also done very well on the turf, especially the extraordinary Lady Escar, who finished in the money in all fourteen of her 1966 races despite a combination of leg problems that would have shelved most horses.

Northern Dancer is by far Canada's greatest racehorse, and the spotlight shines brightly on him this year. He won over half a million dollars in his brief racing career. His first crop of foals will be eligible to run in the 1968 Queen's Plate race, and he now commands the highest stud fee in Canada. His immense popularity in the United States stems from his winning the 1964 Kentucky Derby and the Preakness. He also won the Queen's Plate that year. There were over a dozen American foals dropped at the National Stud Farm in 1966, out of U.S. mares sent up to be bred to the Dancer.

The fact that mares from the United States are coming to the court of Northern Dancer is causing concern among Canadians, because of its possible influence on future Queen's Plate races. The Queen's Plate is Canada's prestige race – the equivalent of our Kentucky Derby, and it may well become a $100,000 race from this year on. The Plate is open to Canadian-breds only. This is a somewhat confusing term, which means that eligibility depends solely on *where* the colt is born. Now it is possible that horses that are not technically Canadian will be able to take the Queen's Plate by 1968. To use a far-out example, a California Thoroughbred mare, in foal to an Argentine stallion, could be brought to Oshawa prior to dropping her foal, to be later bred to Northern Dancer. That foal, though it was not conceived in Canada, and neither its sire nor dam were Canadian, would be an eligible Canadian colt, since it was born in that country. If its owner made the required payments, that colt could run in the Queen's Plate and just might win the cherished race.

Richard Sellman's Morgans
1967

PART I

In the history of any light horse breed, the names of a few breeders stand out in bold type. Occasionally, fortune smiles on a particular horseman just by chance. But more often than not a man's program succeeds because he has spent years of careful study, not only on bloodlines, but also on results. He selects the best of stallions for his mares, and concentrates always on breeding up. If he has been as wise as he had hoped to be, breeders generations later will proudly say their horses trace to his stock.

Such a man was Richard Sellman, who planned so wisely, and succeeded so well, that descendants of his Morgans pretty well blanket the West today.

Sellman, a Marylander, moved to Rochelle, Texas, in the late 1800s, and founded the beautiful 40,000-acre Mountain Vale Ranch. At one time the

Headlight Morgan, a noted early Morgan sire owned by Sellman for almost 12 years. This horse lived to be nearly 33 years old and sired nearly 200 registered Morgans. The photo was taken in his later years. Photo courtesy of the National Museum of the Morgan Horse.

ranch was said to have carried four thousand head of Angus cattle, eight thousand sheep, and over four hundred registered Morgans.

The number of Morgans identified as Sellman's in Volumes III, IV and V of *The Morgan Horse Register* is an astounding one - 689. He also had over twenty broodmares designated by color only, sired by Major Gordon, and apparently foaled between 1886 and 1899. One of his first mares was sired by an English Coach Horse.

From 1905 through 1925, Sellman-bred foals were produced by 273 mares. The peak year was 1921, when 54 colts and fillies were born. The average over the first eighteen years was 35 foals. Then, in 1924, only four colts were registered. Richard Sellman had fallen ill, and a vivid chapter in Morgan history was about to end.

When Sellman began his breeding program, there was much cross-breeding going on – a practice which he deplored. In a limited sense, the infusion of blood from other stocks was necessary, but in some areas this was carried to such a degree that the true Morgan pattern was being lost. Sellman wanted to save the old-time, distinctively-typey Morgan for posterity. For this purpose he selected six of the most representative stallions to be found, trying to stay within eight generations from the foundation sire, Justin Morgan. This breed is unique, in that it is the only one that ever sprang from a single stallion. If Justin Morgan had not been a mutant, of tremendous prepotency, there would be no Morgan horse today.

The stallions chosen by Sellman descended in tail-male lines from two of Justin Morgan's best sons, Sherman Morgan 5 and Woodbury Morgan 7. Major Antoine, Gold Medal, The Admiral, and

Red Oak traced, through two sons of Black Hawk 20, to Sherman Morgan. Major Gordon and Headlight Morgan sprang from descendants of two of Woodbury Morgan's sons.

Many mares used in the early stages of the breeding program at Mountain Vale Ranch were daughters of Major Gordon, a stylish black stallion with a star on his forehead. He was foaled about 1880, and lived to be nineteen years old. Sellman purchased him about 1886. Major Gordon stood sixteen hands, weighed 1,260 pounds, and had very fine action. His sire, Young Octoroon, paced, trotted and ran, and won races at each gait.

Headlight Morgan was one of the breed's outstanding sires. He was a deep red-chestnut, with a wide stripe and one white foot. He was beautifully bred, and through him has come the only remaining trace, in male line, of the blood of Bulrush 6, son of Justin Morgan. Bulrush was renowned for his soundness, powers of endurance, muscular development and longevity - traits which he passed on to his progeny. Twenty-seven-year-old Red Flash, owned by Jerald Rhine, Oakdale, California, is the closest living descendant of Headlight Morgan, and even in his latest foals the characteristics of this line are retained.

Headlight Morgan was the kind of horse that inspires legends. Foaled in June 1893, he was already twenty-one years old when Richard Sellman bought him, and he lived almost twelve more years. He was bred in Illinois, foaled in Kansas, and orphaned when just a few weeks old. He ran with the range horses all summer, and was brought in with the weanlings that fall. From this bad start, he was a runt as a yearling, and had a thick, shaggy coat that stayed with him until he was two. He was broke to saddle and harness, and was used as a cow horse for several years. His owner even roped coyotes off him.

Headlight Morgan's first registered foal arrived in 1899. The following year he was selected by the Morgan Horse Club of America as the best living representative of the original Morgan type, and awarded a silver trophy. Richard Sellman must have purchased him late in 1913, since his first crop of Texas foals didn't arrive until 1915. From then through 1921 he produced 112 foals for Sellman.

This was a fast and agile horse, with a reputed 22-foot stride from a flat-footed start. He had a wonderful disposition, and a very handsome appearance. The stunted orphan colt, who weighed only 850 pounds as a young horse, developed into a powerful, heavily-muscled, 1,200 pound stallion, beautiful enough to capture the silver medal as the best of his breed. He was a sure sire, and had 174 registered sons and daughters of fine quality. He fully deserved the name he was often given, "King of the Morgans."

Another Sellman horse was Major Antoine. Through the second dam of his grandsire, Meteor, Major Antoine carried the blood of Revenge, another son of Justin Morgan. Major Antoine was foaled in 1901 in Amboy, Illinois. His sire, Meteor Jr., won six firsts at state and county fairs from 1897-1899. Richard Sellman purchased the black colt from his breeder, Mrs. C. Antoine, and had 47 fillies and 16 colts sired by him. Probably his best son was The Jew, who also sired fillies almost exclusively. Major Antoine disappeared from the pages of the *Register* after his 1908 foals were recorded.

Major Antoine and Gold Medal had almost identical breeding, both being by Meteor Jr., out of daughters of

Gimma 010133, owned by Viking Morgan Ranch, Modesto, California. In this mare's extended pedigree, the six Sellman stallions appear 64 times; she has 18 crosses to Headlight Morgan alone. In all, 57 Sellman mares and stallions are named 125 times in her extended pedigree. Photo courtesy of LaVonne Houlton.

General Lee 936, sire of six race-winning Morgan trotters. Gold Medal's career at stud was short, too – he had twenty-eight foals between 1906-1910, then was sold, and evidently not used at stud again.

The only stallion in the Sellman group to produce more purebred foals than Headlight Morgan was The Admiral, with 187. Foaled in 1903, this chestnut son of Jubilee de Jarnette would have stood out in any group of stallions. He came from a line famous for its beauty and accomplishments. Reading backward up the tail-male line we find Justin Morgan, Sherman Morgan, Black Hawk, Ethan Allen, Daniel Lambert, Jubilee Lambert, and Jubilee de Jarnette – all outstanding in appearance and trotting speed. Daniel Lambert sired over 100 race winners, nine of which won fifty races or more. He was the source of fine trotting stock for generations. His son, Jubilee Lambert, also won on the trotting track, and was good enough to be chosen as the mate for the incomparable Lady de Jarnette, probably the greatest show mare of all time. Their colt, Jubilee de Jarnette, was exceptionally attractive, and a show-ring star in his own right.

The Admiral 4871 (Jubilee de Jarnette x Morrill Queen).
Photo courtesy of the National Museum of the Morgan Horse.

On his dam's side, The Admiral traced to Morrill 55, descendant of Bulrush. This combined the very best in Morgan bloodlines, giving The Admiral a full measure of beauty and speed from Sherman Morgan, plus the extra soundness and development from the Bulrush strain. It is no wonder, then, that he sired many of the best quality Morgans of his era. His band of daughters was outstanding; they were uniform in appearance and disposition, and they in turn produced foals of excellence.

The last of the stallions purchased by Sellman was Red Oak, a powerful, handsome bay horse, who stood fifteen hands, and weighed nearly 1,100 pounds. Foaled in 1906, in Middlebury, Vermont, Red Oak was also deep in old-time Morgan blood. His sire was General Gates 666, great-grandson of Ethan Allen 50. His dam was Marguerite, whose pedigree contained the names of Sherman Morgan, Black Hawk, and Hale's Green Mountain 42. The latter had also won the silver cup for being nearly a replica of old Justin Morgan.

General Gates was the senior stallion at the U.S. Government Morgan Horse Farm in Middlebury. This black stallion was said to closely resemble the great Black Hawk. The colts of General Gates were – as he was – exceedingly beautiful, sound, and strong. He was named the outstanding sire in rigid cavalry tests, which his progeny passed with flying colors.

As a yearling, Red Oak was first in a class of twenty colts. He was then purchased by the U.S. Government Morgan Horse Farm. Red Oak was one of the most popular stallions bred at Middlebury. He stood at stud for several years at the State Agricultural College in Amherst, Massachusetts. Sellman probably purchased him in 1918. Between 1919-1925, Red Oak sired eighty-four foals for Sellman and four for Texas A & M College.

According to many authorities, it is of little value to breeders to check beyond the third generation in a horse's pedigree. They feel that the blood of any one ancestor beyond that point can have little bearing on the product of the present mating. There are sixteen horses in the immediate pedigree of a registered animal. Behind that sixteen stand hundreds of horses within the extended pedigree. The possibilities for gene combinations are staggering. The chance of one animal seven generations back having great influence over the make-up of a new foal is very slight.

Yet, in the long view, these early progenitors do have great value to the breed as it is today — especially in the case of volume breeders like Richard Sellman. The progeny of the six Sellman stallions were responsible for whole families of Morgans, in many areas of the West. Because their owners liked the original stock, they stuck pretty close to the family system, frequently keeping within the same strain, rather than infusing the blood of outside stallions to any great degree. Often, when outside blood was desired, these breeders turned to another distinctive family group — the sons and grandsons of General Gates.

PART II

Richard Sellman used many sons of his six major stallions later in his breeding program, and did purchase a few other studs. He grouped his mares into family units, and bred them accordingly. In the first half of the program, daughters of Major Gordon were bred to Major Antoine, The Admiral and Gold Medal. The Admiral was used on the Major Antoine mares.

Sellman crossed some of The Admiral's daughters back to their own sire, or to one of his sons, but most of them were bred to Headlight Morgan. Still later, he bred mares by Headlight Morgan to Red Oak and his sons, and so on. Sellman didn't want his breeding program to end at his front gate. He often sold mares by the carload, with a carefully selected stallion to accompany them. In this manner, many units of Sellman-bred stock moved to other areas.

In May 1920, Reginald Parsons of Medford, Oregon, purchased Baldie's Boy, a three-year-old son of Headlight Morgan, out of Baldie Antoine. That year, Parsons moved to the Hilt, California area, and in December a carload of Sellman mares arrived at his beautiful Mountcrest Ranch. Five of the mares were in foal to Joe Bailey (by Headlight Morgan), and two carried foals by Dot, a son of Morgan Chief. Three colts and four fillies were foaled in the spring. One of the colts was Mountcrest Sellman, who grew up to produce a family history of his own.

Baldie's Boy sired one colt in 1922, and four fillies in 1923, out of the Sellman mares. In 1926, the mare Berta produced Mountcrest Wonder, by Mountcrest Sellman, and this about ended the Parsons' breeding program. Between 1924 and 1927 he sold most of his Morgans to northern California and southern Oregon people. In 1932, Mountcrest Sellman was purchased by the Piedmont Land and Cattle Company, San Simeon, California. No transfers are recorded on the last eight horses.

Richard Sellman's interest in the Morgan horse was not a selfish one. He not only wanted to save the old-type Morgan for posterity, he wanted to promote the breed, and acquaint horsemen with the worth of the Morgan. He liked to see someone new get started, and was interested in helping when he could. He was also interested in Texas A & M, a college of agriculture in Brazos County, Texas.

Sellman proposed that the college place a few Morgan horses in its stables on the basis of a gift and loan from him. He place three mares — Blondie, Rofanny and Black Rose — there, with a stallion, Bobbie Burns (by Headlight Morgan), and said these could be kept, or returned to him, at the pleasure of the college. He further agreed to keep the college in suitable breeding stallions without cost, on an exchange basis. Bobbie Burns was transferred to the college as a gift, and later, with Sellman's permission, was sold to one of the students, Raphael d'Avila Oliveira, of Rio de Janeiro, Brazil. Black Rose produced four foals for Texas A & M, and then was sold. Blondie and Rofanny remained at the college.

Rofanny was a daughter of Red Oak, out of a mare by Headlight Morgan. From her, the college had five foals – all but one by her own sire. Red Oak himself had by this time been "loaned" to the college. This was really a generous gesture by Sellman. Red Oak was a prized stallion, beautiful, well-bred, and an excellent sire. He was shown extensively throughout Texas, and won many championships. When Sellman died, Red Oak's papers were transferred to the college by his estate.

Red Oak was highly regarded by everyone, and when he was finally put down because of old age, his head was mounted as a museum piece, and hung in the large lecture room of the Animal Industries Building at Texas A & M.

The third mare, Blondie, produced twelve foals for the college between 1918 and 1930. Her daughter, Blonella, was the dam of Headlight Alamo, also foaled at the college. In all, Texas A & M raised twenty-one registered Morgans from the three mares, and had the use of three excellent Morgan sires: Red Oak, Bobbie Burns and Alamo. The latter was transferred back to Mrs. Sellman in October 1925, after her husband's death.

John C. Burns was head of the Department of Animal Husbandry in 1918, and it was he who received the original Morgans from Sellman. He resigned in 1920, and was succeeded by W. L. Stangel. Later department heads included F. I. Dahlberg and D. W. Williams, who has been associated with Texas A & M University since 1919.

O. D. Butler, present head of the department, states that the program with Morgan horses was successful in terms of the purposes in mind. They were used to familiarize students with the breed, and were ridden, used in buggy work, in teams, and big hitch farm work. They were also used in cross-breeding experiments. The Morgans were shown extensively at the State Fair of Texas in Dallas, and the Southwestern Exposition and Fat Stock Show, in Fort Worth, where they won most of the first places and championships.

Morgans were not the only breed at Texas A & M, but they were eventually discontinued because of lack of demand. The last Morgan mares were traded to Tom Hogg, for a five-gaited stallion named Liberty Loan.

In 1922, Roland Hill made a decision that had far-reaching effects. He sent an employee to Texas to buy a Morgan stallion from Richard Sellman. Redwood Morgan (Headlight Morgan out of Bonnie A., by Major Antoine), a four-year-old brown stallion, soon arrived in a boxcar.

Hill had been breeding a variety of horses for use on his sprawling cattle ranch. His operations, under the name of the Horseshoe Cattle Company, ranged over the years from Tehachapi to Tres Pinos, Gustine, Keene, Bakersfield, and Chowchilla, California, and to the forty-square mile Blue Horse Ranch in Nevada. Hill needed good stock horses, with stamina, cow sense, and disposition. As a breeder and horse show judge, he was also interested in type and conformation.

Hill liked his new Morgan stallion. In May he went to Texas and selected thirteen mares, some sired by Headlight Morgan and his sons, the rest being daughters of The Admiral. Three more mares were sent to him later in the year. In 1923 he sold Redwood Morgan, replacing him the following year with Querido, a Government-bred grandson of General Gates. This was a happy choice. Querido's foals had disposition to burn, as well as substance and innate cow-savvy. He was a great broodmare sire, and his daughters, when bred to Sonfield, produced some of the best breeding stock on the West Coast. Sonfield was the son of Querido's full brother, Mansfield, a highly-regarded sire.

Roland Hill returned to Mountain Vale Ranch in February 1924, and purchased ten Red Oak mares, two Headlight Morgan daughters, and two mares by Sooner, a son of Headlight Morgan.

Richard Sellman had wanted, as was his practice, to select a suitable stallion to accompany the mares. At the time, Hill felt this would represent too much inbreeding, and he did not take the stallion, which he later regretted. In 1925, he purchased two more mares from the Sellman estate.

Over the years he bought, used, and sold a number of stallions, but apparently was most pleased with Querido and Sonfield. He purchased one more Sellman-bred mare, Headstar, in 1930, from F. A. Fickert, who had owned her since 1912.

From 1992 on, Roland Hill was knee-deep in Morgans. Through 1954 he registered 558 of them, and their names are scattered throughout California pedigrees today. A whole book could be written about this one breeding program.

Roland Hill and his brother, Russell, ran mustangs off the Blue Horse Ranch. They found that the Morgan horses could out-do and out-last the other breeds formerly used at the ranch. Both could relate many instances of Morgan endurance and hardiness, well-proven in their rough, ranch country.

Following Sellman's death, his family sold most of the stock, and the ranch was broken up. The stallions Rojeneiro and Woodcliff and twenty mares went to D. D. Kellogg of Wauneta, Nebraska. Horses were sold singly, in small units, and in large groups. In April 1926, Robert Dean of Rochelle, Texas, purchased five stallions and nineteen mares from the Sellman estate. Unfortunately, Dean died within a year. Most of his horses then went to W. S. Jacobs of Houston, Texas.

John Williams, then head of horse work for the U.S. Department of Agriculture, accompanied his brother, D. W. Williams of Texas A & M, to Rochelle in 1925. There, he selected seventeen mares from the Sellman estate. These mares, several in foal or with foal, were shipped in two carloads to the U.S. Range Livestock Experiment Station at Miles City, Montana, to be used in the station's horse breeding program.

Among those purchased was the fine old broodmare, Baby Lu 099, sired by The Admiral, out of a daughter of Major Antoine. Part of her family went with her – an eight-year-old daughter, Travis K., by Headlight Morgan; Travis K.'s filly Jobaria, by Joe Bailey; and Baby Lu's last foal, Emalu, by Rojeneiro, by Red Oak. Five other mature mares in this group were by Headlight Morgan. All but one had 1925 foals by Red Oak. The fifth was bred to Rojeneiro.

Half of the mares sent to Miles City were two-year-olds. Most were by sons of Red Oak, out of Headlight Morgan daughters, the others being by sons of Headlight Morgan out of mares by The Admiral. All were Sellman-bred, and the influx of this Morgan stock into Montana had impact enough to reach down to today.

From 1926 through 1929 these mares were bred to Revere, a Government-bred stallion by Mansfield. Revere sired sixteen foals for the station through 1930. Monterey, also by Mansfield, sired thirty-one foals for the station from 1931 to 1935. Many Morgans from the Experiment Station were sold to individuals throughout the Pacific Northwest.

Revere and Monterey were both qualified as Remount stallions. The War Department began its Remount Program soon after World War I, selecting breeding sires on the basis of rigid tests for soundness, conformation and size. The General Gates line continued to retain these qualifications.

As an example of the U.S.R.I.E.S. breeding program, let's take one colt: Delbert, a light chestnut, with a short strip and snip, foaled May 5, 1930. His sire was Revere, his dam Alibirdie, a granddaughter of Red Oak and Headlight Morgan. Delbert was sold as a yearling, then sold again in 1940 to J. C. Jackson, of Harrison, Montana. Delbert sired more studs than fillies, over sixty foals in all. One of his sons was Julio, an excellent stock horse, out of Katelina. Delbert also sired Chocolate Katy, dam of the Jackson's fine stallion, Fleetson. The Jackson ranch has always been noted for good working stock and strong performance Morgans. It has been under continuous family ownership since 1869, and was one of the first in the West to use Morgan horses on the range.

Although Richard Sellman passed away over forty years ago, the luster has not dimmed from his early dream. Other men continued to breed along the lines he had established, and an excellent family of typey, versatile Morgans continued to grow, and to spread across the West. One of these men was William Randolph Hearst.

As a boy, "Willie" Hearst spent much of his time in the saddle. At San Simeon and Piedra Blanca ranches he rode for hours on end, and it was here that he developed skill as a horseman, and a life-long love of animals. His father raised race horses, and young Hearst no doubt took an interest in the functioning of the stables. As an adult, politics, antiquities, and journalism engaged his fancy and his fortune. Still later, he turned again to horses, and his preference was for Arabians and Morgans. For his Morgan stock he went to Roland Hill, purchasing one mare in 1928, thirteen in 1929, and eight more in 1931. These were daughters of Querido and Pongee Morgan, out of Hill's Sellman-bred foundation mares.

In 1930, Hearst purchased the stallion Uhlan, from the U.S. Government Morgan Horse Farm in Vermont, to use on his mares. Bennington, by General Gates, was the sire of Mansfield, Querido and Uhlan.

In 1932, Hearst obtained Mountcrest Sellman from Reginald Parsons, and thereby intensified the old-time bloodlines in his breeding program. He must have liked the Headlight Morgan strain, since he purchased another grandson, Hacienda Chief, in 1940, from Russell Hill. Each of these stallions produced good families of their own.

From Mountcrest Sellman came the greatest of these families. His most outstanding son was Redman, a great horse in his own right, and a very productive sire. Other fine sons of Mountcrest Sellman included Antman, Montabell Gift and Kenelm Morgan.

Redman, a top Morgan sire of "doing" horses some 20 years ago, and a great horse in his own right. Warren J. Halliday is up, with Long Lake and Bishop Pass in the background. Photo courtesy of NMMH.

Sharen Vermont, a 23-year-old broodmare by Kenelm Morgan, is owned by A. B. Thiessen, Sardis, British Columbia. Her dam was Roboss, bred by Richard Sellman, foaled in 1920, by Red Oak, out of Bossie A., by Major Antoine. In West Linn, Oregon, there is a horse named General Ken, by Kenelm Morgan, owned by Nathan Wright. General Ken's dam was Lulu Mae; his second dam, Lulu Belle, by Mountcrest Sellman, was bred by W.R. Hearst. Lulu Belle's dam was bred by Roland Hill, out of a Sellman mare.

If Redman had sired only one colt, and that one had been Blackman, he would still deserve his fame. Blackman died in 1965, but he had sired over 120 purebred foals. Blackman mares have always been in demand, and many of his sons proved to be fine sires, too.

Uhlan was also responsible for a sire line of exceptional quality. His son, Katrilan, sired Katrilan Prince, whose best son was Trilson. Trilson, in his turn, had two outstanding sons, Dapper Dan and Muscleman. These two stallions are very popular in central California, and their daughters are especially good. Muscleman has sired such fine mares as Honey Bun, Toy Ann, Jodie Collins, and Blossom's Lass, to name a few. These are a rich, almost black-chestnut color, with excellent conformation, and the presence and beauty that catches a judge's eye. The offspring of Dapper Dan

24

are also of show-ring caliber, and have excellent dispositions as well. Dapper Dinah has twice been grand champion mare at the Northern California Morgan Horse Show. Dapper Dolly is one of the best young stock horses in Southern California. "Dapper" himself has won grand championships, and get-of-sire classes, and has an excellent head.

Hacienda Chief produced a good line of broodmares, and his son, War Chief, stood at stud in Ripon, California for several years. His horses seem to be long-lived. Major Louise D. Bates, Arlington, Washington, has a 24-year-old mare, Hacienda Dot, by Hacienda Chief, out of Red Dot – one of Roland Hill's mares. Another daughter, Hacienda Kitty, produced twin foals when she was twenty-three.

William Randolph Hearst was interested in a Morgan-Arab cross, and he purchased desert-bred Arabian stallions to mate with his purebred Morgan mares. Hearst's "Morab" foals were very good – Antman, mentioned earlier, was one of them. However, Hearst couldn't get others as enthused about the Morab as he was, and he gave up the idea. In all, Hearst registered about 120 foals, many under the Piedmont prefix – for his Piedmont Land and Cattle Company. This company was succeeded by Hearst's Sunical Packing Company, and the prefix changed to Sunical. In the mid-and late 1940s, foals were registered by an organization with the impressive title, Sunical Land and Livestock Department, Hearst Magazines, Inc., San Simeon Stables, Hearst Ranch, Cambria, California.

Blossom's Lass 013320 (Muscle Man x Anita Blossom).
Photo courtesy of LaVonne Houlton.

Morgans descended from the Sellman band have gone just about everywhere. A good idea of the scope of Richard Sellman's legacy comes from the following:

Two pages of Volume IX of the *Morgan Horse Register* (foals of 1958-1963) were chosen at random. Of the twenty-five Morgans listed, fourteen traced at least once to one of the six Sellman stallions. They are not all Western horses – some are in Michigan, Minnesota, Pennsylvania and Massachusetts.

Mary E. Smith of Camarillo, California, had remarkable success in breeding pure-black Morgans by Hedlite – a grandson of Redwood Morgan – out of some of the Piedmont mares. The Hedlites carried Sellman breeding on both sides of their pedigrees, and descended partly from horses raised by Sellman, Hill and Hearst. Waer's Play Boy, owned by Frank and Frieda Waer, Orange, California, has won at least seven grand championships. His sire is Hedlite's Micky Waer, owned by Howard and Pat Splane, of Applegate, Oregon.

Oregon's 1965 reserve high point champion harness horse was Sonoma's Gabriel, owned by Phil Morrison of Grants Pass. Gabriel's sire was Sonoma (Piedmont Apache out of Rose B.). Here again, in both sire and dam, we find Sellman mares and stallions in the pedigree. Sonoma's Gabriel is out of an own daughter of Sonoma. Morrison owns the 28-year-old Sonoma and four of his get.

E. W. Roberts was a prominent Morgan breeder in the San Diego area, favoring the Redman bloodlines. After Roberts' death, E. Glen Francis continued along the same pattern, and has raised many good Morgans from Blackman and his sons. Warren J. Halliday of Etna, California, also preferred Redman as a sire.

Halliday sold two daughters of Redman to breeders in Washington. One, Redlass, was bred to Pomulus, and produced the fine stallion, Keystone. The other mare, Etna, was later bred to Keystone, and in 1958 produced Keystone's Rome Beauty, one of the finest trail horses on the West Coast. Owned and ridden by Marjorie Hambly of San Bernardino, this great mare has won many awards on the trail and in the show ring during the past four years.

Red Cal, a 15-year-old Morgan gelding, owned by Dick King, Vista, California, is another top western trail horse. Red Cal's sire is Red Gates (Redman – Bettina Allen), and his dam was Baja Cal (Blackman – Sunical-Dot), both bred by E. W. Roberts. Bettina Allen was by Tehachapi Allen (bred by Roland Hill), whose dam was a Sellman mare. Sunical-Dot was raised by W.R. Hearst. Her sire was Red Dot (bred by Hill), whose dam was also a Sellman mare. Red Gates still had a youthful appearance and zest enough for trail ride competition when past twenty years of age.

Another good southern California trail and show horse is Mijito, owned by Sam Siciliano. Mijito's sire is a great-grandson of the Sellman-bred Romanesque, and his dam is Cruz (Blackman – Bettina Allen). Rayito F., a full brother to Mijito, owned by Joy Cummins of San Diego won about twenty awards at six shows in his first few months in the ring.

Bob Roth's Ramona Warrior has been high-point horse at the Morgan Horse Breeders' and Exhibitors' Association Show two years' running. Warrior's specialties are trail, reining, and pleasure classes – both English and Western. He and his young rider, Robin Roth, have won a great many ribbons in the past two years. Ramona Warrior also follows the bloodlines mentioned above, being by Otto McClure, son of Blackman, out of Jipsey Allen, by Tehachapi Allen. All of which proves that the Redman family is very hard to beat in the show ring and on the trail.

Domino Vermont with his owner, Gene Davis, up. Domino was prominent on the California show circuit a few years ago. He traces to Jubilee de Jarnette three times through his sire, Red Vermont. Photo courtesy of NMMH.

The offspring of Redman, Red Gates, Blackman, and Blackman Allen are found in large numbers in western Canada, in Oregon and in Washington. Florence Hindmarch, Noti, Oregon, owns Blackman Allen and his full sister, Jeanne Allen (Blackman – Bettina Allen), and the daughter of both, Lady of Allen.

H. M. Hughes, Creswell, Oregon, has several deeply inbred horses from this line, including the very handsome young stallion, Red-Jo Allen. This seems to be one family that can stand up well even when intensely inbred. Barclay Brauns, of Entiat, Washington, owns 21 Morgans, including Red Bess, by Redman, a good producing mare, and several others from daughters of Redman and Pomulus. Clarence Shaw of Walla Walla has over 60 registered Morgans at Shawalla Ranch. Four are Sonfield daughters out of mares from the Sellman background. He owns Bettina Allen, now 21 years of age.

One could go on almost without end, following down the many paths taken by all the Sellman mares and stallions. The more pedigrees that are searched, the more clear it becomes that Richard Sellman's Morgans did help preserve and pass on the versatility and appearance of their progenitors. He succeeded far better than he ever knew.

The Spanish Jennet: Its Origin and Influence
1968

PART I

Spain once had a breed of horses so highly regarded that the word for "horseman" became synonymous with the name of the breed – "jinete," or Jennet.

The Jennet developed in Spain's southern regions, from stock that reached back into antiquity, and during the Middle Ages it was counted among the best of breeds. Physically, the Jennets were rather small and finely made, and very handsome. Their heads were attractive and well-formed, topped by very small ears. Their bodies were compact and close-coupled, with well-sprung ribs, good quarters and broad chests. The legs of the Jennet were slender, clean-boned and strong.

The Spanish Jennet, conceptual artwork by Leslie Houlton 1967. Artwork courtesy of LaVonne Houlton.

During the sixteenth century, Spain was the greatest nation on earth, and Jennets were the favorite mounts of the nobility. Stables and equipment of the wealthy were often worth a king's ransom. Horses wore carmine velvet horse cloths, and black, purple or yellow velvet saddles trimmed with gold nails. Pillions were fashioned of cordovan leather, and breast straps and silver headpieces were strung with tiny, tinkling bells.

Four qualities for which the Jennets were especially prized were swiftness, docility, courage and easy gaits. It was said that for speed these horses exceeded all others "so far as the eagle exceeds all birds of the air, or the dolphin passeth all the fishes in the sea." Because of their gentleness and easy gaits they were very popular as ladies' mounts.

English soldiers of the Middle Ages at first looked down upon the Spanish cavalry mounts. It seemed to them that a horse of such small stature must also be of small courage. Instead, they found the Jennet was not only cool and fearless in battle, but was also an expert at the pesade, courbette and capriole. Soon the English joined the Spaniards in high praise of the Jennet's courage. They had seen these stout-hearted animals carry their riders miles away from the battlefield, after the horses had been "shot clear through the bodies with harquebuses." The harquebus was a form of portable gun used before the development of the musket. It was carried in a sole-leather case attached to the war horse's harness.

The gait of the Spanish Jennet was an easy amble, or pace. This way of going had been most prized from the middle of the fifth century, and remained the favorite for well over a thousand years. The Jennet was the horse of his times. Mention of this breed continued down to the close of the eighteenth century; then they seemed to vanish, which makes one wonder: where did they come from in the first place, and where did they go?

The Libyan Horse

To find the answer to the first question, we must go back many centuries, to the continent of Africa. As far back as the fourteenth century B.C. the Libyan tribes, living between the Nile River and the Atlantic Ocean, were great horsemen. It is said that they possessed the best breed of horses that the world has ever known. Just how early the Libyans had domesticated the horse is not known, but they drove horses long before they rode. Their horses were driven in pairs hitched to very light chariots, and at a later time were yoked in teams of four.

By the seventh century B.C. even the Libyan women were expert and frequent riders. The mobility of these early desert tribes was responsible for the introduction of Libyan horses into neighboring lands, from which they spread to faraway places.

The Libyan horse was dark bay, with a star on its forehead. He was small, spirited and extremely gentle. He was lightly built, yet strongly made, a beautiful animal with a finely chiseled head, arched neck, and high set tail. For swiftness, he was unsurpassed.

The breeding of these horses was carefully attended to by the tribal kings and the strain was kept pure for over 1,500 years. The ancient historian, Strabo, reported that by 20 B.C. the annual foal crop of Libyphoenician horses was estimated at 100,000. Strabo noted that these horses were so docile they followed their masters like dogs, without being led. In battle, they wore bridles made of rushes, and could be guided by the touch of a switch.

Libyan horses were introduced into Egypt, Numidia, Greece and Arabia at a very early time. Just when they first reached Spain is not known. Iberians first settled the Spanish peninsula about 3000 B.C. The northern regions were inhabited by Celts about 1000 B.C., and within a hundred years the Phoenicians had founded trading posts along the Spanish coast. Greek traders arrived in the seventh century B.C., followed by the Carthaginians. Probably the Libyan horse came to Spain with one of these early merchant groups. Roman dominance, beginning with the Second Punic War (218-201 B.C.), brought what was probably the largest influx of Libyan horses into Spain.

When Hannibal began his campaign against the Romans in 219 B.C., his cavalry consisted of 12,000 men, mainly Numidians, who rode with neither bridle nor saddle, and Spaniards, who did use bridles. His brother, Hasdrubal, was left in charge of troops and cavalry brought for permanent station in Spain. The cavalry consisted of 300 Libyphoenicians and 1,800 Numidians and Mauritanians – meaning that over 2,000 Libyan horses arrived at one time. Most of these horses were stallions, since they did not use geldings, and mares were kept for breeding. The influence of this fine-bred stock upon the native horses of Spain must have been astounding.

The horses of the Andalusian, or southern, regions of Spain largely retained their dark color. Farther north, where the Libyan was crossed on the old striped dun of the Spanish sierras, elements of gray and black appeared. The Libyan blood was further diluted in the north about 409 A.D. when Visigoths and Vandals invaded, bringing with them their heavy German horses. Here, in northwest Spain, two breeds developed, the Galician and Asturian, both of which were pacers.

Saracen invasions to the south of Spain, meanwhile, brought about a further infusion of the old Libyan desert strain, through the arrival of 300,000 head of fine Arabian and Berber horses. The Moorish invaders bred their animals to the best of the Iberian stock in Spain. The result was a beautiful breed of classic appearance, compact build, fine temperament, great speed and easy gaits.

These were dark-colored horses, mainly bay, with some black, gray and chestnut, resulting from infusions of the northern stock, which also brought with it the pacing gait. The breed that evolved from these matings became known as the Spanish Jennet. The Lipizzan is a direct descendant of stallions and mares taken to Austria from Spain in 1580, when the Jennet was at the height of its popularity. The present day Andalusian horse carries Jennet and Libyan blood as its foundation.

And, although the Jennet as such has vanished, he lives on today, both in Europe and the Americas, where he had a part in the formation of several breeds.

The Peruvian Paso

The Conquistadores brought two types of horses to the New World. One was the aristocratic beauty of southern Spain; the other, the plain, stout breed from the north.

Hernan Cortes began his 1519 expedition into Mexico with sixteen horses, at least two of which were Jennets. Though most of these were killed in battle, hundreds like them soon followed.

In 1535, Spanish colonists at Buenos Aires fled from attacking Indians into Paraguay, leaving behind five Andalusian mares and seven stallions. When the city was resettled in 1580, a large band of horses, descended from these twelve, roamed the plains. Some were captured and tamed. The rest continued to multiply, forming the huge herds that ranged for miles south of the La Plata River.

Meanwhile, north of the La Plata, huge bands of wild horses had sprung from stock abandoned at San Juan Bautista about 1554. It is interesting to note that ninety percent of these horses, called Baquales, were bay – the inherent color of the Libyan horse, retained through centuries of breeding.

Two breeds of horses, now extinct, the Costena and the Chola, were once found in large numbers in Peru. The description of the Costena matches that of the Andalusian-Jennet, while that of the Chola parallels the Galician-Asturian horse of northwest Spain. Again, we find that the Costena was the choice of the upper class. He was the peacock of the horse world, swift, beautiful, and proud. His way of going consisted of variations of the pacing gait. His stamina at high speeds for long distances was outstanding.

The Chola was a plainer, less animated animal, but he had more strength and agility that the Costena. He too had pacing gaits, though he did not lift his feet so high, nor have quite the variety of gaits.

The best individuals of these two vanishing breeds were mated, forming a new species that carried the desirable qualities of both parent stocks. The new horse had beauty and animation, great endurance, a gentle nature, and five natural, easy-riding, stylish gaits. He was called the Peruvian Paso.

The Mustang

Spanish Conquistadores brought to Mexico and Texas both the fine-bred southern horse of Libyan extraction, and the more inferior breeds of the northern region. These carried a wide variety of colors, from the dark bay with a star, down through the duns, grays and piebalds.

Juan de Oñate established a Spanish colony near present day Santa Fe, New Mexico, in 1598, bringing with him twenty-five stallions, one hundred fifty mares and one hundred fifty colts. The Spaniards remained in the area until 1680, when Indians attacked and killed most of them. During that 82-year interval, the band of 325 horses must have increased many-fold.

To be purely hypothetical, say that seventy-five new foals were born each year, and that every year ten horses died. At that ratio, the original band of 325 would have grown to 5,525 head in eighty years. To this would be added all stock brought to the settlement by later arrivals. It is from this large band that the wild Mustangs of the West descended, as well as the horses captured and ridden by the Plains Indians. Interested horsemen have been searching for the best remnants of the old Spanish Mustang type, and have recently established a breed registry for them.

PART II

The influence of the intrepid Jennet was felt not only in the Spanish colonies of Central and South America, but also in the North American West. Even while Oñate's band was increasing on the Western plains, the Spanish Jennet found its way into the upper reaches of Puritan New England.

The Narragansett Pacer

Roger Williams established his Rhode Island colony on Narragansett Bay in 1636, eleven years after the Pilgrims had imported the first horses from England. The Rhode Island founders soon profited from horses, for Massasoit, Great Chief of all the tribes from Cape Cod to Narragansett Bay, would trade tracts of his kingdom for guns, horses, rum and cash. In 1656, the governor gave Massasoit's son, Philip, a young black stallion – which Philip, as king, rode in raids against the colonists twenty years later. By then, Rhode Island had a well-established horse breed of its own, the Narragansett Pacer.

*The Spanish Jennet, conceptual artwork by Leslie Houlton 1968.
Artwork courtesy of LaVonne Houlton.*

The original imports had been big "Dutch" mares, English stallions, and mixed stock from the British Isles. The New Englanders were sea traders, and the West Indies were on their trade route from the beginning. Newport, Rhode Island, was a principal port of entry on the old triangular trade route from New England, to Africa, to the West Indies. Up from the Indies came the ambling, pacing Spanish Jennets, stallions of beauty to improve the captains' inferior stock.

The nature of the Narragansett area made containment of the horse band, and establishment of a type, quite simple. At Point Judith Neck, the bay, ocean, and a chain of lakes, surrounded three sides. It was only necessary to erect a short length of stone wall to the north. Since the soil was rich, and crops abundant, the contained band of horses was strong and healthy, and multiplied well. Stallions imported from Andalusia and Tripoli, and West Indian imports, improved the quality of the stock and fixed the pacing characteristic. Captain John Hull and Governor Robinson were among the early Narragansett breeders.

By the late 1600s Spain had toppled from her position as Queen of the Seas. Her far-flung outposts could no longer count on regular supply ships from the mother country. French and Spanish planters in the West Indies needed more and more easy-gaited horses to ride over their vast sugar plantations. And the Bristol merchants were ready now to meet their needs. Captain Simeon Potter carried pacers hobbled on deck, and ropes of onions stored below, to the sugar islands around 1670. Later, he expanded his cargo to include African slaves. By 1686, Colonel Nathaniel Byfield was also shipping pacers and onions to the Dutch Guianas on his sloop, the "Bristol Merchant." Many ships carried these horses to Jamaica and Havana over the years as the demand for them steadily increased, both in America and the sugar isles. One Rhode Island farmer exported one hundred pacers annually to Cuba. Cuban agents visited Narragansett Bay, buying full-blooded pacing mares at high prices.

Virginia planters also found the pacing gait desirable, and bought up many of the Narragansett horses. Stallions found a ready market from Boston down to Charlestown.

Again, a pacing horse was the choice of the gentry. New England's few roads were rough tracks through a wooded and rocky country. A horse that was sure-footed, easy to sit, and hardy, was much in demand. Narragansett Pacers filled the bill. They could travel long distances at a swift pacing gait without tiring either the rider or themselves. Stories of Narragansetts having covered 100 miles in a day were quite common. They could pace a mile in just over two minutes. These pacers were fine-boned, rather small horses, generally chestnut in color, though some were bay or black. Stamina and easy movement accounted for their great popularity as saddlers in the Colonial period.

Pacing races were held each year on the hard sand beaches of Newport and Narragansett before 1700, where the winner always received a silver tankard.

The Narragansetts were never broke to harness, being considered too valuable to have their joints stiffened by heavy pulling work. As roads were improved throughout the country, people rode less on horses and more in carriages. A different type of horse was needed, and the American trotter was evolved. Consequently, the market for pacers dwindled, fewer were raised, and by 1800 it was said that only one full-blooded Narragansett Pacer was left in Rhode Island.

Still, experts have said that the bloodlines of every racing American pacer of today traces back to the old Narragansett Pacer. How did this come to be?

The Canadian Pacer

While interest in pacing horses was dying elsewhere, the French-Canadians of southern Quebec had acquired a real penchant for them. It didn't take the canny New England horse trader long to discover this new market for his dwindling stock. As the 18th century waned, any number of Narragansett pacing mares were taken north of the border. From about 1795 a Vermonter named King made numerous trips to southern Quebec each year, taking six or seven pacing mares at a time, and disposing of them on a swing through Fairfield, St. Caesaire and St. Hyacinthe, P.Q. A Mr. Bernard took Narragansett Pacers in droves from Rhode Island to the French country around Quebec City, where he readily sold them, or traded for stout, white French horses, often with cash to boot.

So avidly did the French-Canadians seek pacing stock that even the most weak and rickety mares — anything that could make the long trip — sold with ease and profit. Some of these old pacing mares, coming from Northern Vermont, were traded in foal, either to Justin Morgan, founder of the Morgan breed, or to his son Brutus, or one of his other very early offspring.

One Frenchman who eagerly snapped up pacing mares was Louis Dansereau, of Contre Coeur, P.Q. He developed a pure black strain of pacers, known as the Dansereau Family, that became renowned throughout the province.

Dansereau's foundation mare was a black pacer, obtained from a Yankee trader. He bred the mare to Voyageur, whose pacing dam was also got from a Yankee trader. Their offspring was the remarkable black pacing mare, Jeanne d'Arc, dam of a fine line of black pacing stallions. The Dansereau strain was largely inbred, and from it came old pacing Pilot (son of Jeanne d'Arc), Pilot, Jr., Columbus, Petit Coq (Beppo), and others, all bred at Vecheres, or nearby. The original Pilot was bred by Louis Dansereau, and foaled in 1823. After several sales and much travel Pilot arrived at Louisville, Kentucky in 1831. He lived to be thirty years of age. During his twenty-two years in Kentucky he sired some of the finest pacing and trotting stock ever to be developed in that state.

The first Canadian Pacer to go to Kentucky was Copperbottom, a sorrel stallion foaled in 1809. His description sounds quite familiar – "very strongly built – broad chest – round barrel – short back; good neck and head, and a handsome appearance." He was the fastest pacer of his day. Next came Tom Hal, similar in appearance, also having extraordinary speed. Another was Davy Crockett, and he too had very similar characteristics to the others.

All came from southern Quebec, where the Narragansett mares had gone. They had uniformity of type, pacing characteristics, and flashing speed – a heritage without doubt from their distant Jennet ancestors.

Montpelier Men and Their Morgans
1968

The first Morgan horse to arrive in Montpelier, Vermont, was the progenitor of the breed himself, Justin Morgan I. Jonathan Shepard paid William Rice $200.00 for the stallion in the summer of 1796, and bred some mares to him late that season.

For the stallion, 1796 was an eventful year. In the spring he won two races at Brookfield, Vermont, against Sweepstakes and Silverheels. His actual ownership is a bit clouded at that point. While he was raced by the singing master, Justin Morgan, Rovert Evans had had the horse during the winter and William Rice of Woodstock took him late in the spring to clear a debt that Evans could not pay. At any rate, within weeks of his arrival in Woodstock, "Figure," as he was then called, traveled north with still another master, Jonathan Shepard, who had paid a high price for him considering that a good horse cost $50.00 at the time.

Shepard was one of Montpelier's early settlers, having arrived in 1793. For the first couple of years he worked for Col. Jacob Davis, clearing the colonel's land, and the village site. His salary at that time was probably about $9.00 a month. Shepard was an enterprising young man though, and soon built and equipped a blacksmith shop, the first in the village.

In February 1797, Shepard traded this shop and the Morgan stallion to James Hawkins, for a farm at the mouth of Dog River. Shepard remained in Montpelier, an active and respected citizen. He operated a popular tavern on Main Street for nearly 30 years, served in the War of 1812, and was one of the organizers of the Congregational Church. He raised other Morgans over the years, and died at the ripe old age of ninety-one.

James Hawkins kept Justin Morgan I for over a year, undoubtedly making good use of him. Hawkins, one of the original Montpelier settlers, was the town's first blacksmith, and a fine carpenter. He was one of the voters who took part in the organization of the town, and served as selectman at the first town meeting in 1791. Hawkins settled on land about a mile east of Montpelier, that he purchased from its original owner, Ziba Woodworth. He built the town's first frame house, and, in 1791, its first store – which stood until 1873. He built many more in rapid succession, fine homes, stores and hotels. Undoubtedly Justin Morgan had his share in this construction, bringing in logs and lumber, and carrying Hawkins about on business.

During his stay in Montpelier, the gentle bay stallion was sometimes borrowed by David Wing, Jr., for saddle and carriage use. Young Wing was one of Montpelier's most illustrious citizens. He began as schoolmaster in 1790, was Proprietors' Meeting clerk in '92, and served as town clerk, town agent, town representative, selectman, chief judge of the county court, and finally secretary of state. He was a charter member of the Winooski Turnpike Company in 1805. David was a charming, brilliant and handsome man. His wife, Hannah, quite a style-setter, created a sensation at a meeting in 1803 by wearing the first silk dress to be seen in the town. Wing's untimely death from typhus in 1806 stunned the entire state. Justin Morgan no doubt carried Wing about on important town business now and then during 1796-1798, and Hannah Wing apparently made quite a pet of him. In 1798, the stallion went back to Sheriff Rice in Woodstock, and was owned in Montpelier no more. What horses he had sired there we do not know.

In 1822, Sherman Morgan 5 stood at stud in Montpelier and Waterbury, and to his service Jonathan Shepard brought a mare. The following spring she dropped a fine dark bay colt that grew up to greatly resemble his grandsire, Justin Morgan. This horse, named Wicked Will 774, because of a cross disposition, stood 14.2 hands high, and was described as very handsome, well-built, and a "splendid" traveler. Young Brilliant, a dappled bay stallion that Shepard advertised in 1829 may possibly have been a brother or half-brother of this horse. Shepard did raise and keep a son of the old crosspatch, called Wicked Will II, which in turn sired a number of good Vermont Morgans, including Kate, the dam of Fremont 1028.

About 1835 Lucius B. Peck purchased a black mare, supposedly Thoroughbred, from the governor of Vermont. In 1845, she produced a typey black colt by Black Hawk 20. The Peck Horse, named Cottrill Morgan 120, grew up to be a sixteen hand, 1050 pound, stylish stallion. He had a fine head, beautiful neck, good legs, and a lovely, wavy tail that he carried proudly. What he looked like between these extremities we are not told. Presumably his conformation matched the "fine points," since he sired some excellent stock in Vermont, and in West Virginia, where he was taken when he was about twenty-four years old.

Lucius Peck was an important member of early Vermont society. A native of the Green Mountain State, and a resident of Montpelier for forty years, Peck was admitted to the bar at the age of twenty-three, and soon after was sent to the state legislature. Over the years he served as town representative, as congressman from Vermont (he delivered a stirring speech to Congress on "Slavery in the Territories" in 1850), and as U.S. District Attorney. He was twice nominated for governor. He served as general counsel for the Vermont Central Railroad, and was president of the Vermont and Canada Railroad. The Morgan horses that Peck owned were surely active participants in this busy lawyer's life and travels.

Sons of Cottrill Morgan 120 in the Montpelier area were Daniel Webster 1024, Fremont 1028, Sterling's Black Hawk 1033, Farwell Horse 2410, Henry Clay 2635, and Page Horse 3103. The fine stallion Independence 1025 was sired by Cottrill Morgan, as was the dam of Black Hawk Morrill 3961. The black Farwell Horse, foaled at Barre, Vermont, was owned by a Mr. Sibley of Montpelier, who took him to Alabama about 1855.

The Page Horse was a very showy stallion, chestnut, with one white hind foot; he was 15.2 hands high and weighed about 950 pounds. He only lived five or six years, which was unfortunate, since he was noted for his fine action. His owner, Addison L. Page (or Paige), was in the livery business in Montpelier for many years, and also served at one time as sheriff. Page also owned Young Black Hawk 996, a black stallion with a star on his forehead, by Sherman Black Hawk 51. This stallion fared better than Page's other one. He lived to be twenty, and sired many fine carriage horses.

Fremont 1028, by Cottrill Morgan, was out of Kate, a daughter of Wicked Will II; 2nd dam a black mare, said to be a Morgan. Fremont was bred by Daniel Baldwin, and foaled at Montpelier in 1852. Of a kind disposition and great energy, this stallion was sold to Wisconsin as a two-year-old, and left excellent stock there. His breeder, Daniel Baldwin, was another of Montpelier's favorite sons.

Born in Norwich, Vermont, in 1792, Baldwin was orphaned at two years, and came to Montpelier to live with his brother in 1806. Starting out in the carpenter's trade, Baldwin's talents were such that he soon became prominent in civic affairs. He was active in almost every activity and enterprise of the village's early days.

One of Cottrill Morgan's sons, Sterling's Black Hawk 1033, was bred by the man for whom Peck's horse had been named, Mahlon Cottrill. This Black Hawk was out of a brown mare, said to be by Royal Morgan II. Foaled between 1851-54, he was sold to J. M. Sterling of Ohio about 1860.

Mahlon Cottrill owned the Pavilion, one of New England's best hotels. Constructed in 1807, this brick building was noted for its ornate moldings, carved woodwork and fresco paintings. Cottrill was in the stage and mail contracting business for thirty-five years. His great, central stage route through the state was the main thoroughfare between Montreal and Boston. As host of the

Pavilion, he was widely known as the "Prince of Landlords." Cottrill sold Black Hawk 1033 shortly before he contracted to carry the U. S. mail between Kansas City and Santa Fe.

The full brothers, Daniel Webster 1024 and Henry Clay 2635, and their half brother Andrew Jackson 154, were bred by Barnabas and Lawson Hammett at East Montpelier. Andrew Jackson, foaled 1850, was black, sixteen hands, and 1150 pounds, sired by Black Hawk 20. Daniel Webster, foaled 1851, was also black, stood 15½ hands, and weighed 1,050 pounds. He was sired by Cottrill Morgan 120, as was Henry Clay, foaled 1852, a 15½ hand bay with star, weight 1,000 pounds. The dam of all three was the Robinson Mare, by Andrew Jackson, son of Young Bashaw. She was a trotting mare of record, but was unpredictable in races due to a very high temper. Barnabas Hammett purchased her in Philadelphia, and sent her home to his brother, Lawson. Andrew Jackson received 2nd premium at the 1853 Vermont State Fair, and 1st premium at the Pennsylvania State Fair in 1855. All three stallions had been taken to Philadelphia; however, Andrew Jackson was returned about 1860 to East Montpelier, where he died at the age of sixteen. Barnabas Hammett bought property in the village in 1792 or '93, and he and Lawson helped prove the area's claim to fostering longevity.

Daniel Webster sired Bonny Doon, a high-headed, brown trotter from New Jersey that won nineteen of twenty-two races, with a record of 2:35 for the mile.

In 1853, Dr. Beriah Shortt of North Montpelier bred a dark brown daughter of Hale's Green Mountain Morgan 42 to Andrew Jackson 154. The following year she produced a dark chestnut colt, Paul Jones 156, from this mating. He was a very showy, fast, harness horse, and he sired foals of high quality. Shortt had sold Paul Jones as a foal to his brother, Dr. Azro A. Shortt, who in turn sold him some years later to a doctor in Ohio. At the Ohio State Fair in Columbus in September 1865, Paul Jones collided in a race with his son, the Kurtz Horse, and died of the injuries sustained. In 1858, Dr. A. A. Shortt's mare by the Hollister Horse, a grandson of Sherman Morgan 5, produced an outstanding colt by Morrill 55, called Hagler's Morrill. The colt's second dam was Beriah Shortt's mare, mentioned above. Hagler's Morrill sold as a five-year-old for $1,000.00. He was considered to be an excellent sire in Ohio, where he died in 1885.

Among the stallions standing at Montpelier in the early days were Napoleon and Silver Gray. Napoleon was dark bay, a nicely proportioned horse, and a very fast trotter. Lorenzo Willard advertised him to stand the 1831 season at Montpelier, Middlesex and Plainfield. Silver Gray (Newell's Gray?) was bought in about 1830, and described as a very beautiful horse, and a nice traveler. He sired the dam of Paris' Hambletonian and was quite probably also the sire of Pink, the second dam of McMonagle's Warren Horse. No pedigree data is given for these two, but they were assumed by Colonel Battell to be of Morgan extraction.

Another early stallion was Vermont Champion (Town Horse) 785, a small but powerful black horse. He had a fine disposition, smooth action, and lots of "go," and he sired many fine, fast horses that sold for high prices. He was by Vermont Morgan Champion 13, out of a "Dutch" mare. He stood at stud in the Montpelier area from 1840 to 1865, where he was variously owned by Joseph Bradish, Dr. George M. Town and Benjamin Town. He lived to be about thirty-two years old.

On Election Day, October 12, 1848, the store owned by Erastus Hubbard was crowded with men. Hubbard was a manufacturer of tinware, and he sold stoves, hardware and agricultural implements. Some of the men puffed at cigars while Hubbard weighed out a parcel of gunpowder for a customer. Suddenly, there was a tremendous explosion, which lifted the second floor of the building about six inches, and set the store ablaze. Two men died, and a few others were badly maimed. One of them was Erastus Hubbard, who was terribly burned. For months he wavered on the brink of death, and though he finally recovered, he was scarred for life.

In 1855 Hubbard purchased the good road horse, General Putnam 304, son of Putnam Morgan 303, out of a daughter of General Hubbard. Mr. Hubbard sold the stallion in 1856, and purchased Green Mountain Morgan Jr. 447 the following year. This was a very stylish, showy horse, a fast walker and a good trotter. He was by Green Mountain Morgan 42, out of a daughter of Gifford Morgan 30. He went to California in 1858. Hubbard was again harassed by fire in 1875, when his new three-story brick block was among the buildings badly damaged by flames.

Fire was a constant hazard in those days, and many fine horses were lost in burning barns. One of them was the ill-fated Vermont Reindeer 267, by Morrill 55, only five when he died in a Montpelier blaze. He was in the care of E. H. Gilman at the time. Gilman owned a half-interest in his dam, a black full sister of Blood's Black Hawk 59 (Black Hawk 20 x Old Polly). Gilman had luckily one fine son of the lost black stallion, Reindeer 268, foaled in 1862. He was also black, with a small star and snip, a small horse of 900 pounds, standing just 14.2. The little horse could move, though. His stride when speeding measured twenty-

Hale's Green Mountain Morgan 42, woodcut.
Artwork courtesy of the National Museum of the Morgan Horse.

two feet. Reindeer was kept at Montpelier until 1883, when he stood in New Hampshire. He was sold in 1885.

One of Reindeer's offspring was the chestnut mare, Sparkle 02366, bred by Theron O. Bailey of Montpelier, and foaled about 1870. Her dam was a fast running mare that Bailey had purchased in Boston. Theron gained early fame in constructing and furnishing the famous Pavilion Hotel, one of the most perfect hotels of its time in New England. He was just one of George W. Bailey's six interesting and successful sons. George, Jr. served as secretary of state for four years; James was a New York doctor; Warren a grain merchant and town official; Edward had business interests in Vermont and the western states, and Charles engaged mainly in furnishing horses, cattle and sheep to the Boston markets.

The evening edition of *Walton's Daily Journal*, Montpelier, February 24, 1862, carried this item: "Two hundred and twenty horses, purchased for the 8th Regiment (Col. Thomas) by the Bailey Brothers, left Montpelier this noon for Boston, where they are to be shipped for the South. They filled thirteen cars, and are an excellent lot of horses - probably as good as any that have left the State." Thus, Warren and Charles Bailey gave the Union Army a gift deemed worthy of million-aires, as their patriotic contribution to The Cause. It is interesting to note, however, that Charles Bailey was among the town's ten drafted men who paid commutation to release them from service.

The 8th Vermont Regiment was mustered in on February 18, 1862, and included eleven men from Montpelier. The original 220 had dwindled to 156 by the time the regiment was engaged in the battle of Cedar Creek, in October 1864 (when Sheridan and Rienzi turned the tide of battle). Of the 156 engaged, seventeen were killed, sixty-six wounded and twenty-three missing - 67.9 per-cent of the total regiment. It is doubtful that many - if any - of the 220 Morgans and other horses shipped by the Bailey Brothers ever set hoof again in the Green Mountain State.

One soldier who did come safely through the Civil War was Perley P. Pitkin, of East Montpelier. He enlisted June 6, 1861, at the age of thirty-five, and was commissioned Quartermaster, 2nd Regiment, Vermont Volunteers. He was soon promoted to captain, then to colonel, and made head of the Depot Department of the Army of the Potomac. After the war, he resigned his colonelcy and was elected Quarter Master General of Vermont, and had charge of the state arsenal. By selling surplus military supplies to foreign governments he helped the state treasury reduce tax rates. General Pitkin held a number of civic and business offices, both before and after the war.

Just before the war, General Pitkin purchased the Morgan stallion Woodstock (John Morrill) 249, son of Young Morrill and a gray mare of Quicksilver blood. Woodstock was a large horse, sixteen hands, and 1100 pounds, foaled in Topsham, Vermont in 1857. He was sold to the old singing master, Moses Cheney, and then to others, prior to 1864. The general bred a mare believed to be by Cottrill Morgan 120, and out of a daughter of Gifford Morgan 30, to Young Morrill about 1885, and the resulting foal was Black Hawk Morrill 3961. This black stallion matured at fifteen hands, and weighted about 960 pounds. Pitkin sold him to Samuel Wheat, of Putney, Vermont.

Redfield's Vermont 121, foaled at Montpelier about 1855, had a very colorful career. Bred by Judge Redfield, he was sired by Independence 1025, out of a mare believed to be by Royal Morgan 11. The dam of Independence had been used as a family mount by the Redfields for many years. She was stated to be by Gifford Morgan 30. Twice sold, Vermont was taken across the plains to California about 1859. He was again sold twice, first for $2,000.00 to Oregon, then for $7,000.00. Next he was purchased by well-known horseman Jesse D. Carr of Salinas, California. Redfield's Vermont sired a number of race winners on the West Coast. He sired the dam of Saladin, who for a long time held the fastest record for a mile to harness in a winning race.

The Redfields were an illustrious Vermont family. Isaac F. Redfield was Judge of the State Supreme Court for twenty-five years. He authored several law books and was considered one of the foremost jurists of the age. His younger brother, Timothy, was Phi Beta Kappa at Dartmouth, and graduated with high honors. Admitted to the bar in 1838, he became senator from Orleans County in 1848. Like his brother before him, Timothy Redfield was elected Judge of the State Supreme Court, a post that he held for many years.

Young Myrick 202, a black son of Sherman Black Hawk 51, foaled 1848 at Panton, Vermont, was owned for several years by Cyren Joslyn of Montpelier. At the 1857 Vermont State Fair, Young Myrick trotted the mile in 2:50, and was purchased by Mitchell and Huston, Bedford, Indiana, for $1,600.00. In 1858 J. A. Mitchell took a mare said to be by Black Hawk 20 to Bedford from Montpelier. She was the dam of black Patsy, who produced Braxton's Morgan Emperor 811. Young Myrick was kept at Bedford for twenty years and he sired many foals. His son Rocket 203 was the sire of Bellfounder 878, bred by F. W. Randall, Montpelier, foaled in 1871. Bellfounder was chestnut, with a strip and white hind ankles, and a heavy mane and tail. He weighed 1,100 pounds, and stood 15.3 hands high. Colonel Randall served in the 13th Vermont Regiment during the Civil War. This was one of the units that participated in Brigadier General G. J. Stannard's famous flank movement at Gettysburg, on July 3, 1863. Randall returned to Montpelier after the war, and became a charter member of the local chapter of the G. A. R. His son, Frank, Jr., also enlisted in the Union Army, as a musician, Co. F., 13th Regiment, when he was just eleven years old. In 1864 the boy re-enlisted as a musician with his father's new outfit, Co. E., 17th Regiment, and served to the end of the war. The family moved to Brookfield in 1877, taking Bellfounder with them. He was later sold, and stood at Braintree, and in 1887 at East Randolph, Vermont.

Several other well-bred Morgan stallions were owned, or stood at stud in Montpelier in the early days. One was the chestnut Wood's Comet 682 (Billy Root 9 x The Crane Mare). Another was Morgan Chief 34, foaled 1832, by Woodbury Morgan 7. His dam, Empress, was supposedly a daughter of Justin Morgan I. This horse went to New Jersey when he was twenty-two. White Mountain Morgan Jr. 828, a beautiful gray grandson of Sherman Morgan 5, was bred by C. B. Martin, North Montpelier, and foaled in the 1840s. His breeder took him to Illinois in 1853. The Churchill Horse 1081, an excellent son of Black Hawk 20, was about twenty-four years old when brought to Montpelier. His dam was the great road mare, Dolly Nichols. Another Black Hawk son, Gifford Black Hawk 1396, was owned by I. W. Brown, Montpelier, about 1872. He was twenty years old and had been a first premium winner at the Vermont State Fair. Abraham 1473 (Daniel Lambert x Polly Cook by Black Hawk) was an elegant horse, sire of many race-winning trotters. Foaled in New York, he later stood with his sire at the Cream Hill Stock Farm, Shoreham, Vermont. He was sold to Massachusetts, then purchased in 1884 by Lowe and Brigham, Montpelier, with whom he remained until his death in 1892. His legs were somewhat faulty; still, he was a striking individual, and an outstanding sire.

One of the Morgan mares of the later period was George F. Sibley's gray Kate, foaled at North Montpelier, in 1874. She was by the Wheeler Horse (Plow Boy), a son of Morrill 55. Her dam was Fly, by the Hammett Horse, by Black Hawk 20; second dam Old Fly, by Hale's Green Mountain Morgan 42. Another Kate, this one a full sister to Biggart's Rattler, was the dam of Bartlett's Morgan 360, by Young Gifford Morgan 359. This stylish, golden chestnut stallion was bred by C. W. Bancroft, foaled in 1853. Bancroft was engaged in the mercantile business, and was active in civic and church affairs. When he died in 1856 his Morgan stallion was sold to New York State, where he sired good stock until his death at the age of twenty-three.

From these sketches it is evident that Morgan horses, right from the beginning, were the choice of men of affairs: the town builders, civic leaders, successful merchants, doctors and lawyers. Men who could afford what they liked chose a Morgan. This was not a horse fit only for those who had to settle for less than the best. Morgans kept breeding on and up because they were so good there just had to be more of them; not only in Montpelier, but in all the other Vermont hamlets and towns, and in other states, wherever men moved who knew what a Morgan horse was: a horse worth having!

References:
Battell, *The Morgan Horse and Register, Vols. I and II*
Hemenway, *History of Montpelier, Vermont, 1780-1882*
Walton's Daily Journal, Montpelier, Vermont, February 24, 1862
Miller, *Photographic History of the Civil War, Vols. II and X*

The Morgan Story
1969

Figure (Justin Morgan), woodcut. Artwork courtesy of the National Museum of the Morgan Horse.

The history of the Morgan Horse is an exciting one. To begin with, the Morgan is the oldest existing light horse breed of American origin. Secondly, the Morgan Horse actively participated in the post-Colonial development of the United States. Last but not least, Morgan stock played an important part in the foundation of several other light horse breeds on this continent.

The Morgan story begins in 1789 – the year George Washington accepted the presidency of the newly formed United States. That was the year that a small bay colt was born in New England - a colt, eventually named Justin Morgan - that would revolutionize the concept of the horse in America.

Justin Morgan was brought from Massachusetts to Vermont as a two-year-old stallion, by the frail singing master for whom he was named. Mr. Morgan had a large family, and very little in worldly goods. As a result, he often leased out the young horse for farm work. Local opinion of the bay stallion was not very high at first, because whcn full grown he was still comparatively small. But Justin Morgan had tremendous muscular development and strength, and a great heart. No amount of work and drudgery appeared to be too much for him. His subsequent owners all subjected him to hard use; however, he was still sound in every respect when he died from an injury when thirty-two years old.

He had grown to be a beautiful animal, and quite different in appearance from any horse that people had ever seen. He had excellent, flat-boned, clean legs, with a long forearm, short cannon, and well-sloped pastern. His step was springy and elastic, and he carried himself with much pride and grace. His body was compact, close-coupled, deep and short-backed. His neck, with its heavy crest and thick mane, was well arched, and very distinctive. His head was lean and bony, with good round jowls, large, intelligent, wide-spaced eyes, and a fine muzzle set off by big flaring nostrils.

Justin Morgan's disposition brought forth complimentary comments, too. He had a great deal of spirit and animation, yet he was gentle and easy to handle, and seemed to love the companionship of human beings. He was, in all ways, an exceptional horse.

Although no exact record of his pedigree was retained, it was said that Justin Morgan had been sired by an English Thoroughbred named True Briton, and that his dam was a Wildair mare of Arabian extraction. Who his parents were was actually of little importance, however, for their son was something exceedingly rare – a mutant, a new kind of horse, and the sole founder of a breed.

As his sons and daughters began to arrive and to mature, it became apparent that Justin Morgan was a very prepotent sire. His offspring so resembled "the Morgan horse." Like their sire, the Morgan offspring stood out in a crowd. They too pranced gaily in a parade, and seemed to know they were "something special." Hitched to sulky or wagon they too could out trot almost anything. And, like their sire, they had the stamina and courage to see them through the hardest day's work. Their dispositions, unless ill-treated, were uniformly kind. It was the same with the third generation, and the fourth.

So the fame and the legend of Justin Morgan grew. His progeny spread across New England to the western frontier and north into the Canadian provinces.

When news of the gold strike in California reached New England, many Vermonters rode and drove their fine Morgans across the United States, joining the great westward migration of 1849 and the early '50s. In the West they found a ready market at high prices for their Morgans, and men like Rollin Jones, Sylvester Rockwell and Benjamin Fry were soon importing them in numbers, bringing some across the plains, and shipping others. Copper kings and railroad barons drove fine four-in-hand teams of matched Morgans. Morgan trotters enhanced the name of the breed on California's new racetracks. Offspring of the Morgan stallion, St. Clair 48, caught the eye of Governor Leland Stanford, and the nucleus for his great band of trotters at Palo Alto Stock Farm was a group of mares by St. Clair and his sons.

It was like that in other parts of the country, too. The best trotting stock in Maine came from a Morgan, General Knox 65. In Kentucky, a Morgan stallion, Blood's Black Hawk 89 (by the famous Black Hawk 20, grandson of Justin Morgan) and Pilot 104 were tremendously important sires of harness horses and outstanding show stock. Morgan names are to be found 'way back in the founding history of the American Saddlebred, Tennessee Walker and Standardbred. Even the Missouri Fox Trot Horse and at least some of the Texas Quarter Horses had Morgan progenitors.

As hardy pioneers moved westward, settling new territories, breaking and clearing land, planting and building, Morgan Horses went with them, always doing more than their share of the work. During the Civil War a regiment of Vermonters earned a military reputation mounted on Morgans, and the courage of those horses under fire was a great boon to the Union cavalryman. Many heroic Morgans died on the battlefields of that war. Rienzi, a Morgan, gained immortality through Thomas B. Read's stirring poem of General Sheridan's ride from Winchester.

For many years a high-quality breeding program was carried on at the United States Government Morgan Horse Farm near Weybridge, Vermont. Government range and livestock experiment stations, and remount stations used Morgan stallions to upgrade the quality of local stock. In the 1920s and '30s, Texas A & M College raised purebred Morgans, with which they won acclaim at

Houston and Dallas fairs. For years Morgan breeding programs were carried on by several Midwest Indian schools. Many outstanding Morgans have been raised through programs at the universities of Vermont, Massachusetts, New Hampshire and Connecticut.

In the period between the two World Wars the popularity of horses as utility animals drastically waned, and their numbers diminished rapidly. During those years dedicated families of breeders from New England to California kept the Morgan from extinction.

Because of his combined qualities of beauty, endurance, versatility, longevity and good temperament, the Morgan Horse is no longer in danger of extinction. On the contrary, the demand for good Morgans has increased steadily during the last twenty years, and classes for Morgan horses are now included in the programs of many horse shows across the country. The future looks just as bright as was the past for the descendants of Justin Morgan.

Owners agree that "Once you own a Morgan, there *is* no other horse!"

The Marguerite Henry book, Justin Morgan Had a Horse, was first published in 1954. It had nine printings by 1972, and was also made into a Walt Disney movie in 1972. Photo courtesy of Jan Gingold.

California's Morgan Sires
1969

The history of the Morgan horse in California began in 1849, with the arrival of St. Clair 48, a dappled-brown pacing stallion from Illinois. St. Clair, noted for speed, and for the quality of his offspring, was the Sacramento area's most popular stallion, siring between 600-700 foals, before his death in a stable fire in 1864. It was said that St. Clair could pace faster than any stallion in California. His daughter, Lady St. Clair, had the fastest five miles on record, and his grandson, Occident, was the first horse to drop below 2:17 for a mile at the trot. Occident's sire, Medoc 597, was one of the first Morgans identified as California-born in Vol. I of the *Morgan Horse Register.*

Morgans were as popular in California in the 1850s, 60s and 70s as were their eastern counterparts. Many fine stallions were brought West during that period, including Keokuk 107, Redfield's Vermont 121, McCracken's Black Hawk 131, Bur-

St. Clair (AMHR #48), a popular Morgan stallion of the California gold rush days, was such a fast pacer that he went unchallenged in the Sacramento area in the 1850s. He was the maternal grandsire of several record-setting pacers in California, and it is believed that the pacing characteristic came down to him from the Narragansetts, through his Canadian dam. The drawing is an artist's conception, taken from contemporary descriptions, as there are no known pictures of this horse. Illustration by Leslie Houlton 1968. Courtesy of LaVonne Houlton.

gess' Sherman Morgan 843, Easton's Dave Hill 1267, and Vick's Ethan Allen 1564. In 1854 a Morgan horse from Vermont, named George Morgan, won a $5,000.00 twenty-mile match race to sulky at San Francisco, in which over $30,000.00 in side bets changed hands. Race records of the era reveal that Morgan trotters and pacers were among the fastest in the state. One of them was Primus 1714, a phenomenal trotter who contended with the best horses across the country. One of the two fastest four-year-olds that had ever appeared in public, Primus was the sire of Magdallah, foaled in 1873, one of the fleetest horses of her day on the Pacific Slope. Morgans were consistent premium winners at halter and on the track at state and county fairs in the early days. For example, David Hill 2nd 1092, a bay grandson of Black Hawk 20, won First Premium at the California State Fair in 1864, and also in 1866 and 1868 when shown with ten of his get.

By the 1870s even faster stock was being imported from Kentucky – sons of the earliest Standardbred sires. In many instances these horses were bred to mares of Morgan descent. Governor Leland Stanford used daughters and granddaughters of St. Clair 48 as foundation broodmares for the famous band of trotters he developed at Palo Alto Stock Farm. Records were set by many Stanford-owned trotters. St. Clair was the maternal grandsire of Fred Crocker, Wild Flower, Bonita and

Manzanita, all of which held world records for two-year-olds in the 1880s. Wild Flower set a record of 2:21 that stood for seven years.

Men of great wealth like William Chapman Ralston, Ansel I. Easton, Darius Ogden Mills and Alvinza Hayward favored Morgans as road horses, and their matched pairs and four-in-hand teams were a common sight on the streets of San Francisco and other Bay Area cities. These sleek and lovely horses wore silver-trimmed harness, and were stabled in stalls lined with mahogany and rose-wood paneling.

Meanwhile, on the huge ranches of the Central and Upper Sacramento valleys, Morgan blood helped improve the quality of utility and stock horses for men like James Ben Ali Haggin, Jesse D. Carr and General John Bidwell. All three men liked trotters, although Southerners Carr and Haggin later switched to Thoroughbreds. Carr owned Redfield's Vermont, a remarkably good trotter, and sire of trotters. His son Vermont Jr. 3496 went to Australia. Bidwell, a leader of the first overland party into California in 1841, purchased the 26,000-acre Rancho Arroyo Chico in Butte County. By 1855 the ranch carried 12,000 cattle and 1,588 horses, plus other livestock. Bidwell's John Morgan reportedly sired the best of stock. The general bred and raised Black Prince 179, whose sire was a black Morgan stallion that caught Bidwell's eye on a trip across the plains around 1855.

In all, about forty years passed before the Morgan star set for a time on the West Coast. The introduction of Thoroughbred running stock and Standardbred trotters changed the tone of racing in the state, and automobiles killed the need for carriage horses. The old-time Morgan breeders were gone, and by the final decade of the nineteenth century raising and importation of Morgans in California had all but ended.

Luckily, as the twentieth century dawned, Richard Sellman began to build his great band of Morgan horses at Rochelle, Texas. It was Reginald O. Parsons who re-introduced the breed to California in 1920, with Baldie's Boy 7117 (Headlight Morgan x Baldie Antoine), and a carload of broodmares and fillies, sent by Sellman to Parsons' beautiful Mountcrest Ranch near Hilt, Califor-

Headlight Morgan. Photo courtesy of NMMH.

nia. Seven of the broodmares were in foal. One of the colts born the following spring was Mountcrest Sellman 7289 (Joe Bailey x Kitty E.), first "native son" of the present century. Baldie's Boy only sired five fillies in 1922-23.

Close behind Parsons in bringing Sellman mares and stallions to California came Roland Hill, who had Redwood Morgan 7217 (Headlight Morgan x Bonnie A.) sent out in 1922. Hill's major need was for stock horses with good conformation, stamina, cow-sense and disposition. Redwood Morgan sired four registered foals in 1923. He was then sold, and had just two more registered colts in 1931: Blackhaux 7973 and Cuyamo 7974. Hill's next stallion was Pat Allen 7344 (Allen King x Patrona),

bred by J. C. Brunk in Illinois. Pat Allen, bred to mares Hill had acquired from Richard Sellman, was the sole sire of California Morgan foals in 1924 and '25. In 1926 he sired nineteen registered foals, and Mountcrest Sellman had his first offspring, Mountcrest Wonder 7547.

In 1924 Hill purchased the yearling colt Querido 7370 (Bennington x Artemisia) from the U.S. Government Morgan Horse Farm in Vermont. In 1925 he obtained the Brunk-bred stallion Pongee Morgan 7427 (Allen King x Galva) from L. M. Huff of Kansas.

Roland Hill was the biggest of California's Morgan breeders. From 1923 to 1954 he registered 558 of them. With over sixty broodmares at his disposal, Hill still had advance sale orders for Morgan horses for two years ahead. Probably his best cross was that of Querido on daughters of Sonfield 7952 (Mansfield x Quietude), the latter purchased in Connecticut in 1939.

From this start, Morgans rapidly gained in popularity, and soon many more names were added to the breeders' roll. Some of them, and their major stallions were: William Randolph Hearst (Uhlan 7564, Mountcrest Sellman 7289, Katrilan 8121, Hacienda Chief 8273), Mary H. Smith (Hedlite 7977), Mr. and Mrs. E. W. Roberts (Blackman 8622), Orris C. Foster (Ken Carmen 7815, Montabell 8117), Jack Davis (Red Vermont 7893), Dr. Clarence C. Reed (Gay Mac 7988), Warren J. Halliday (Redman 8056), Schultz and Kuck (Ryder 8712, North Fork 8082), Sid Forsyth Spencer (Antman X-8318), W. T. Carter (Cortez 8455, Gold Dollar 8006), Dr. Ina M. Richter (McAllister 7896), Stanley Hunewill (Dude Spar 8227), T. R. Rex (Monte L. 8423), and Merle H. Little (Sheriff Morgan 9436, Sun Down Morgan 7388, Lippitt Morman 8211).

The following list shows the numbers of registered California foals by Morgan sires, from Vol. V of the *Morgan Horse Register* (1922-1937):

Querido	137 foals	1927 thru 1937
Pat Allen	50 foals	1924 thru 1926
Pongee Morgan	32 foals	1927 thru 1929
Mountcrest Sellman	32 foals	1926, 1932 thru 1937
Don Juan	12 foals	1932 thru 1937
Uhlan	11 foals	1932, 1933, 1937
Winchester	6 foals	1934, 1935
Redwood Morgan	6 foals	1923, 1931
Red Wings	6 foals	1937
Baldie's Boy	5 foals	1922, 1923
Blackhaux	4 foals	1934, 1936, 1937
Master G.	3 foals	1930
Master G or California Allen	2 foals	1929
Berchwood	1 foal	1928
Bender	1 foal	1929
Raven Chief	1 foal	1933
Eprus	1 foal	1935
Silver Ranger	1 foal	1936
Total	311 foals	

"Wild Bill" Elliott's famous black horse, Thunder, known the world over in the Red Ryder movie series, was actually a Morgan stallion, Anndy Pershing 8390 (General Pershing x Ann Bartlett). Anndy was foaled in Iowa, and owned after Elliott by film star Allan Lane. He too sired some California Morgans in the '40s.

The 1950s and '60s saw even greater interest develop, as more and more people sought the "right" horse for pleasure and show use. Morgans, always noted for beauty, stamina, good temperament and versatility, filled the needs of California's diversified population. Morgans can be found out on the trails, in both pleasure and competitive endurance rides. Some are on working stock ranches, for cattlemen have long appreciated Morgan agility and "cow-savvy." Some are to be seen in the high country, packing out deer and elk. Many Morgans are beloved pets on suburban ranchettes, where each member of the family has his turn at riding.

The Morgan horse has been an active participant in the California way of life for 120 years now. He adapts to change, and grows with the times. We feel he is definitely here to stay. And each one of us who breeds one today is helping to mold the future of the Morgan horse in the Golden State. What we do now will be history tomorrow.

Montabell 8117 (aka Montabell Gift). Photo courtesy of NMMH.

Morgan Stallions in California: El Don
1969

El Don 9239 (Donald Allen x El Lu), a 24 year old Morgan stallion owned by Dianna Foit, Escalon, California. Photo courtesy of NMMH.

Among the older Morgan stallions in the Northern California area is El Don 9239, owned by Dianna Foit of Escalon, California. El Don was foaled in 1945, in Modesto, and has spent his entire life within a radius of about fifty miles from his birthplace. His sire, Donald Allen 8358 (Tehachapi Allen x Dorothy D.H.) was bred by Elmer Brown of Halstead, Kansas. El Don's dam, El Lu (El Cortez x Red Oak Lu) was a granddaughter of Romanesque and Red Oak.

El Don is another of those Morgan stallions that was rarely used at stud until he got older. He was sold by his breeder, H. J. Jacobsen, to Ted A. Davis of Modesto, as a two-year-old. Davis used him primarily as a parade and pleasure mount. El Don has only one offspring, El Cindy 08698 (dam Cindy) listed in Vol. VII of the *Morgan Register*, and just one, Geny 09160 (dam Addy A.) in Vol. VIII.

El Cindy, foaled in 1952, produced a good number of offspring: Dancin, El Dandy, Bonnie's Morgan, Knox Cin, Knoxdale Jester B., Knoxdale Bo-Dee, Knoxdale Danygirl, and Knox's Cindianna were some of them. Dancin 11905 (by Dannie Lu) was the High Point Morgan English Stallion of the Oregon High Point System in 1965. He is the sire of a number of California and Pacific Northwest Morgans. His son, Redcin 14065, won six of the high point awards given by the Oregon Morgan Horse Association in 1966.

Dancin's sire, Dannie Lu, is by Dapper Dan, and Dapper Dan sired Bonnie's Morgan, whose dam was also El Cindy. These two closely-bred Morgans, Dancin and Bonnie's Morgan, produced Knoxdale Phantom, thus insuring another generation in double lines for El Don, through his first offspring, El Cindy.

In 1959 El Don was purchased by Dianna Foit, who was then living in Sonora, California. Since then he has sired over twenty foals out of Dianna's mares, and a number of them have been shown with good success. In 1968 El Don's son, Mercury Floodlite 14068 (dam Fleda) was Champion Morgan Stallion at the Madera and Mariposa County fairs. Flirtation, by El Don, won the blues for yearling Morgan fillies at the Sonora and Madera County fairs, and another daughter, Donna Inez, was Grand Champion Mare at Sonora in 1968. El Don won the Get of Sire class at Mariposa that year, too. Mercury Floodlite's first foal, named Reflection, was born last year, and a black filly out of Wink and chestnut filly (dam Risquee) have arrived so far this year.

So here again is a California stallion that got a pretty late start as a sire, but is making up for it by proving that his offspring can make it in the winner's circle.

General Morgan and Black Bess
1970

In May, when the anthers of its blossoms give the blue grass a distinctive steel-blue tint, the Kentucky woodlands come alive with white blossoms of the red-haw, purple trillium, spring beauty, columbine, dogwood and ferns. Warblers and mockingbirds sing in the tulip trees, and the air is fresh and clear.

On just such a lovely day, over a century ago, John Hunt Morgan must have set out from Lexington to exercise his favorite horse – the beautiful mare Black Bess.

If you could have seen them, you would have been impressed. Morgan was a superb equestrian, tall and straight, yet easy in the saddle, arresting in appearance; and the mare was so exceptional she evoked much praise from all who saw her.

Before the war began, Morgan was captain of the "Lexington Rifles," a volunteer militia company later incorporated into the Kentucky State Guard. In September 1861, an order was issued for disarming of the Guard. Morgan was determined to save his guns for the South, at all cost. With Federal troops camped at the fairgrounds nearby, and with many Union soldiers and sympathizers in the city, cunning was needed to spirit the guns away. After dark on September 20, Morgan and a few of his men removed the guns from the armory, placed them in two wagons, and drove away from Lexington, out the Versailles Road. Meanwhile, a dozen or so men marched noisily back and forth inside the armory to give the impression the "Rifles" were holding drill practice. Morgan rode far enough with the "gun thieves" to make sure they were safely away; then he returned to Lexington.

Excitement was great the next day when the mysterious disappearance of the guns became known. Charges and countercharges were hurled, and Lexington was placed under military rule after street brawls developed. Just ahead of his ordered arrest, Morgan rode south with the rest of his men to rejoin those escorting the gun wagons.

This escapade was typical of John Hunt Morgan. He was quick to see what needed doing and equally quick to strike and be away. He had no formal military training, yet he soon revolutionized the use of cavalry. Discarding the saber, he armed his men with light rifles and side arms. Instead of the massed charge of old, he dismounted the troopers, fighting them as infantry, with their horses held nearby. He originated the cavalry raid deep inside enemy lines to disrupt communications, destroy bridges, capture supplies, and deter troops from their purpose by making them pursue him. "Jeb" Stuart, Nathan Bedford Forrest, and other Confederate cavalry leaders were quick to adopt Morgan's methods, which created a highly mobile, innovative striking force capable of independent action.

Captain Morgan was soon promoted to colonel and then to brigadier general. His daring, successful exploits made him the darling of the South – the "Thunderbolt of the Confederacy." Conversely, northerners feared and hated the raider, calling him "king of the horse thieves."

Black Bess was completely identified with Morgan's early career. When Morgan rode into town mounted on his sleek, elegant mare, people gathered around to pet her, feed her sweetmeats – which she loved – and, if possible, to pull a hair from her mane. Contemporary descriptions of Black Bess paint a picture of exquisite equine beauty.

In this mare, we are told, were combined faultless conformation, femininity and immense power. She stood just under fifteen hands and was glossy black with no white markings. She had a head "as beautiful as a poet's dream," with fine, large, wide-set eyes and a muzzle "small enough to have picked a lady's pocket." She had a flawless throatlatch, excellent neck, and very well proportioned shoulders and girth. Her back was short and broad, her quarters tremendously well developed and muscular. Her legs were clean and trim, and she had flint-hard dainty hooves – "almost as small as a clenched fist."

Black Bess had speed, courage, grace and stamina. She was a horse to match a horseman's dream. She had been singularly endowed with the best characteristics of both her Canadian sire and her Thoroughbred dam. Bess was also blessed by Nature itself, for the Bluegrass Region rests on limestone and shale deposits over half-a-billion years old. This limestone base gives to the grass and water a high content of phosphorus and calcium, which builds light, solid bones, strong tendons, and elastic muscles. Canadian stallions added much to the bloodstock of Kentucky in that era, especially through old pacing Pilot, a Dancereau stallion from Quebec. The Dancerean horses, all black, were noted for extraordinary energy and power. Black Bess had need for that kind of stamina, for Morgan would often ride miles to see his wife at the end of a long day's march.

John Hunt Morgan lost Black Bess shortly after the battle of Shiloh. Although he had other fine mounts, including the handsome gelding Glencoe, none ever captured his or the public's hearts as the black mare had done.

Morgan's men had successfully routed a Federal force at Lawrenceburg, Tennessee, at the end of April 1862. Again the townspeople made such a fuss over Black Bess that Morgan had to put her in the stables before her shining mane all went for souvenirs. Four days later, the raiders were attacked from the rear. In the excitement Black Bess broke the curb of her bridle, and Morgan was unable to pull her up or re-form his men. Soldiers close by tried to hold her by the reins, but she broke away and ran for some distance before Morgan could get her under control.

The retreating Rebels rode on to the river where luckily they found a ferryboat tied. Boarding quickly, they left their horses on the shore. Although his men wanted to take Black Bess, Morgan refused, saying that if time permitted he'd send back for all the horses. Sergeant Tom Quick wouldn't have it that way, and when the far shore was reached he grabbed a canoe and began paddling back to get the mare. By then, though, the Yankees had reached the river, and a volley of shots sank his canoe.

The bluecoats rounded up the Confederate horses, and the southerners later learned that a Yankee was taking Morgan's mare around the country, showing her at "two-bits a look." Basil Duke, Morgan's brother-in-law, felt that her spirit must have been broken, else "she would have kicked the brute's brains out."

Morgan's career also took a downward turn the following year, culminating in his capture and imprisonment after the famous "Ohio Raid" – said to be the longest continuous cavalry ride by such a large body of men in the history of warfare. Within a few months General Morgan escaped, made his way south, and rejoined the Confederate forces, now limping down to defeat. It wasn't easy to win battles any more; men, horses, and equipment were wearing out. But Morgan tried, from January through August, until he was betrayed and killed in September 1864 during an "obscure engagement in a small east-Tennessee town."

The Mysterious Narragansett Pacer
1971

PART I

In the book entitled *History of the New World Called America*, published in Dublin, Ireland in 1775, it is said of the Rhode Island colonists "they have a breed of small horses, which are particularly hardy. They pace naturally…with such swiftness and for so long a continuance as must appear almost incredible to those who have not experienced it."

The historian was describing the earliest light horse breed developed by the American colonies – the Narragansett Pacer. However, after existing for some 200 years, the pure breed quite abruptly became extinct.

Artist's reconstruction of the vanished New England breed, Leslie Houlton 1968. Courtesy of LaVonne Houlton.

Brief references are made to the Narragansett Pacer in contemporary literature about horses, but the full story of this vanished breed is scattered in bits and pieces throughout old histories, out-of-print studbooks, and New England genealogies. Consequently, the old "Rhode Island horse" has attained an aura of mystery in modern times.

Because of the Narragansett Pacer's valuable contribution to some of our existing breeds, we should solve the mysteries of where he came from, what he did, and why he became extinct. A thumbnail history of the various breeds of horses brought to the two Americas in earliest times is essential to solving the first question concerning our colonial equine hero.

The first horses to be transported to the New World were Spanish Jennets, brought over by Christopher Columbus on his voyages of discovery. After his first voyage in 1492, he brought over a number of stallions and broodmares in 1493. The Spanish Jennet, a small pacing horse of primarily Libyan extraction, was one of the most popular breeds of the Middle Ages. Nearly every ship from "home" brought horses to the colonies along the Spanish Main for the next few decades.

The Spanish breeds were all related to some degree. The Jennets and their northern cousins, the Galicians and Asturians, were natural pacers. Others of the period were the Andalusian and the wonderfully even-tempered Barb from Tripoli.

In the early 1600s, when France, England, Denmark and Holland all sought to break Spain's monopoly in the Caribbean, Dutch ships also transported horses for sale to the Spanish colonists. Holland's best breed was the Friesian, or so-called "Dutch horses" – fine, black animals – medium-sized, compact and strong, with excellent legs, great endurance, and "devilish" dispositions. Because of their swift, slashing trot they were also called *Hart-dravers* (fast trotters).

The French were next to bring horses across the ocean, beginning in 1604 when M. L'Escarbot, a lawyer, took horses from Normandy and Brittany to Acadia. Colonists took some of these horses to Quebec in 1608. The Bidets of Brittany had been known for excellence for years. They traced back to Libyan stock and were rather small horses, usually black, renowned for great hardiness and endurance. The Norman Horse was one of the large destriers (war-horses) that for several centuries carried northwestern Europe's armored knights.

Percheron Postiers, small post or coach horses from Perche, France, were brought to Canada in 1634 by Robert Giffard and one hundred farmer-colonists. These horses were a cross of the old heavy horse of Europe on fine Libyan stock brought up from Spain.

A very fine stallion, sent to Quebec in 1647, and twelve excellent horses from the stables of King Louis XIV, brought over around 1665, were most probably Limousin horses – a breed called "the glory of Old France" and one which filled the royal stables in this period. Highly esteemed as saddle horses, they had their origin in the 8th century A.D., and distinctly showed Barb characteristics. Nearly all the ancient, excellent breeds in France derived from oriental stock that traced to the Libyan horse of antiquity.

Horses from England were introduced into Virginia as early as 1609. Although the initial group all perished during the "starving time" that year, more soon followed, and by 1620 Virginia's horses were considered to be of fine quality.

Horses first appeared in the New England regions in 1625 when the Dutch brought a few Flemish draft horses to New Amsterdam. In 1629 Francis Higginson brought twenty-five mares and stallions from Leicestershire, England, to the Massachusetts Bay Colony. That same year marked the arrival of seven more mares and one stallion at Salem. A few stallions shipped aboard the Mayflower and the Whale landed safely at Charlestown Harbor in 1630, though most of the livestock had died en route.

In 1635, twenty-seven Flemish mares and three stallions were brought to Salem by two Dutch ships. These horses of Flanders were the product of an early cross of the old European heavy horse on Libyan stock from the Mediterranean. The Flemish stock left but little trace of its existence after a few years in America. The patroons of New Amsterdam, of course, preferred their fast Dutch Hart-dravers for transportation purposes.

Since the cost of shipping a horse from England to the New World was quite high (ten pounds in 1630), and the voyage rigorous, only young, healthy stock of good blood was considered worthy of export.

The earliest New England stock, used primarily as saddle horses, represented quite a variety of European breeds, most of which bore significant inheritance from their ancient Libyan ancestors. From England came a "duke's mixture" which blended the old, black English war-horse with stock from the low countries and with horses of North African blood.

Other horses from the British Isles were the fine Barbary Horse, well known in England since Elizabethan times, and the exceptional black Irish Hobby. The Hobby dated from the 10th century A.D., and was considered to be the best of the English breeds up into the 17th century. Its earlier names were Haubini and Astercones – the latter because they came from Asturia with Spanish colonists. The Asturian was a pacer, and the Irish Hobbies were also greatly prized as saddlers because they had "so gentle a pace."

The Libyan horse, from which so many of Europe's breeds derived, had its origin in the area of North Africa between the Nile and the Atlantic Ocean, where Libyan tribesmen had developed a fine mastery over the horse as early as the 14th century B.C. The Libyan is considered to be one of the finest breeds ever known. These horses were uniformly bay in color and marked by a star on the forehead.

They had extreme speed, great endurance, a high degree of beauty, and exceptional docility. Their breeding was kept pure for hundreds of years under the careful attention of tribal kings. The mobility of the desert tribes brought about the introduction of Libyan horses to Egypt, Greece, Arabia, Spain, and other lands at a very early time.

Hannibal stationed more than two thousand Libyan stallions with his cavalry on permanent duty in Spain in 219 B.C. In the Andalusian region the pacing Spanish Jennet evolved from Libyan stock crossed on native mares, and was later improved by infusions of the same blood through Arab and Berber horses brought in by Moorish invaders. The Jennet retained the beauty, docility and remarkable endurance of the Libyan horse, as well as its color and relatively small size.

In the north of Spain the Libyan blood was diluted through crosses with the old striped dun of the sierras and with large German stock brought in by Vandal and Visigoth raiders. Here developed the two pacing breeds – Asturian and Galician.

The common characteristics of the various European pacers – gentle nature, strength, endurance, great swiftness, and an easy-to-ride amble or pacing gait – were identical to those of the Narragansett Pacer of Colonial America.

The best European breeds traced to the ancient Libyan, and individuals of those breeds of oriental derivation were brought to the Americas right from the start. The first horses taken to Rhode Island were apparently offspring of the animals that had been imported to the Massachusetts Bay Colony less than a decade before.

Quite logically then, the foundation stock of the Narragansett Pacer was a mixture of the Dutch, Irish and English breeds mentioned above. The pacing characteristic was set in ancient Libya, replenished in Spain, diffused throughout the European continent, and eventually transported across the Atlantic Ocean to re-establish itself in a new world's new breed.

PART II

Colonial New England had a variety of horses, and among them the pacing gait was quite common. Before 1660, English nobles kept two kinds of horses – the huge destrier, or war-horse, that was led until ridden in battle or when engaged in tournaments, and the "ambler" or pacer, used for riding from place to place.

Then King Charles II's tremendous interest in flat racing fostered a complete change in the concept of the "ideal" horse in England. Following the king's lead, England's horsemen took up the breeding of running stock.

The change was so dramatic that it was said that by 1700 scarcely a pacer could be found in all of England. While some had been brought to New England in the early part of the 17th century, a good many more pacers undoubtedly found their way there when the British fashion changed.

Rhode Island colonization began in 1636. William Coddington founded Portsmouth, the second settlement, in 1638. That year the Portsmouth proprietors voted to distribute land among themselves at the rate of one acre of meadow for each cow or sheep and one and a half acres for each horse.

The Narragansett Bay region was ideally suited to development of a large plantation system, where a temperate climate, warmed by the Gulf Stream, and fertile soil rich in iodine and bromine, promoted growth of unexcelled meadows and hay crops. The lower coastline of the bay, especially at Point Judith Neck, formed a perfect range with natural barriers for containment and development of a specific breed of horses.

Horses soon became a prime product of this area. Their environment promoted good health and fertility. Stock increased so rapidly that within a dozen years or less, horses were being exported from Rhode Island to Massachusetts, New Amsterdam, and even to far-off Barbados, nearly one thousand leagues away. Barbados, settled by the British in 1625, had established trade with New England and Virginia by 1634. In 1640, Barbados obtained cane plantings from Brazil and sugar became her greatest export product.

Columbus had taken sugar cane to Santo Domingo in 1493. By 1515 a wealthy physician there had brought in, at his expense, sugar masters and technicians from the Canary Islands. A trapiche, or horse mill, was built for extracting juice from the cane. The trapiche was a very primitive piece of machinery consisting of two or three "cylinders" made from large peeled logs. These rollers were geared to a long shaft that was turned by horses.

As cane production increased throughout the Caribbean, demand grew for more and more horses to turn the trapiches and pull carts to and from the mills. Horses for these cane mills were among Rhode Island's first exports to the West Indies, and Newport became the principal port from which they were shipped. A description of the Barbados in 1648 stated, "…they want (lack) rivers to turn their sugar mills, so that New England sendth them Horses and Virginia Oxen, to turn them, at excessive rates."

The first Rhode Island lawsuit, in May 1656, concerned horses claimed by William Brenton that William Coddington was about to ship to Barbados. Coddington was one of Newport's commissioners to the General Assembly and a past-president of the assembly. Brenton, also active in colony affairs, served as a member of the Court of Commissioners from Providence and later was president of the General Assembly.

The town of Providence set taxes in 1664, payable in "wheat, peas, or pork, at 3 pounds 10 shillings per barrel, or horses or cattle equivalent."

Around 1660, Peleg Sanford & Brothers established themselves in Barbados as factors for Boston and Newport merchants. In this capacity they received horses, sheep, and farm produce from Rhode Island to exchange for West Indian sugar, rum, molasses and cotton.

By 1670 new blood was being added to the old Narragansett stock. Captain John Hull, one of the original purchasers of the Narragansett Tract, raised horses of his own breeding on farms in Boston Neck and Point Judith. He urged his partners to help concentrate choice stock there to produce the best possible horses for West Indian export.

The last decades of the 17th century saw great expansion of New England's merchant fleet. In 1676 Massachusetts alone had 430 ships in trade. Soon after, Bristol, Rhode Island, had fifteen ships trading with the West Indies and on the Spanish Main. By 1686 Colonel Nathaniel Byfield shipped Narragansett Pacers to Guiana on the Bristol Merchant – an odorous voyage, for the cargo contained red onions as well as horses.

Now, comfortable horses were in great demand both in the colonies and the sugar isles, for they made excellent pleasure mounts. So extensive was the market for pacers that other horses were taught to pace. As early as 1690 pace-trainers came into vogue, especially around Ipswich, Massachusetts.

Their methods were "trammeling" and "cross-spanning." Logs were placed across training roads at certain intervals to induce a pacing gait. An early chronicler reported, "the way in which a horse was learned to pace was by fastening his two right and two left feet together with leather straps, so that the two former might step together, and then the two latter." These methods were in use for about eighty years.

Until the eve of the Revolutionary War, the Atlantic sea-lanes teemed with ships, and horses by the hundreds were transported down the coast to the Caribbean. In 1716, for example, a Captain Hutton shipped forty-five horses to Barbados. A fleet of six ships left New London, Connecticut, in 1724, bound for the West Indies, carrying horses tethered on deck. Brigs in those days could carry forty-nine horses per cargo, and sloops (which normally made two trips per year) held up to thirty-five hobbled on deck, with other cargo stored below.

William Robinson (1693-1751) was a resident of the Narragansett area. He served as a member of the legislature from South Kingston in 1724, 1726, 1734, and was deputy governor of Rhode

Island, 1745-48. In 1751, the inventory of his estate listed "30 horse kind." Governor Robinson's horses were the very finest of their day, descendants of a pair of Spanish Jennets he imported from Andalusia around 1735, or possibly before. Robinson had undisputed claim to bringing about the greatest improvement in the Narragansett breed through use of his exceptional Jennet stallion on Rhode Island mares, and through the outstanding offspring and descendants of his imported Jennet mare and stallion.

A second excellent outcross was provided through the blood of an imported stallion, Old Snip, from Tripoli, which added further endurance and stamina to the breed.

Governor Robinson was related by marriage to Robert Hazard, a successful Newport merchant-farmer who shipped one hundred Narragansett Pacers annually to Cuba and the West Indies. Hazard was a partner in two Newport privateers, the 110-ton sloop Success, fitted out at Newport in 1744, and the 170-ton brigantine Prince Frederick, which made her maiden voyage on December 2, 1745.

In 1744 Rhode Island fitted out her most famous ship, the 90-ton sloop Prince Charles of Lorraine, which mounted ten carriage guns and had a crew of eighty men. Three Newport men and Simeon Potter of Bristol owned her. Potter, just twenty-four years old, was given command of the new vessel, which sailed on September 8, 1744. The Narragansett Pacers that Captain Potter took to the sugar islands that year were traded for molasses and mahogany planking. One of his ports of call was Cayenne, capital of French Guiana, which did a busy trade in Rhode Island horses. The Prince Charles returned to Narragansett Bay on April 27, 1745, after an astounding series of adventures.

Between 1741-56 little Rhode Island, just forty-eight miles long by thirty-seven miles wide, kept more ships at sea than any other colony. In the period from 1765-1775, New England alone exported 37,000 horses and other livestock. An interchange of racing was also common by mid-century between Rhode Island and Virginia. Races were held twice a year on the hard, sandy beaches of Newport and Narragansett.

Sportsmen gathered from far and near to watch these pacing contests for which the winner always received a silver tankard. George Washington (whose mother rode a pacer when she was a child) favored the Narragansett Pacer, and is known to have raced at least one of them. Some of the breed's best individuals went to the southern colonies where racing was very popular.

Narragansett Pacers were the fastest pacing horses in the colonies. They could pace a mile in just a fraction over two minutes and easily covered three miles of uneven, rocky ground in seven minutes – an average of 2:33 for the mile. Long trips in short time were of common occurrence.

The Narragansett Pacers were ideal saddlers for more reasons than just speed. They were noted for ease of motion, which propelled the rider in a straight line without any side-to-side or up-and-down joggling. Such comfort in the saddle made long trips possible in the sparsely settled colonies. These pacers were extremely sure-footed, an added blessing in an un-cleared land. They were tough, hardy animals, noted for great stamina and endurance. That they were favorite mounts for women attests to their calm, tractable natures.

Narragansett breeders liked colorful names for their pacers, choosing such sobriquets as: Peacock, Grand Turk, Revival, Jolly Farmer, Whirligig, Rainbow, Smiling Ball, Free And Easy, and Feather.

New Yorker Rip Van Dam purchased a Narragansett pacer in Rhode Island in 1711 for $160. The horse was sent almost immediately to Philadelphia where the consensus was that, while high-priced, he was "no beauty." Van Dam's pacer had a playful, nervous temperament. He never stood still, and he had a taste for beer, wine and hard cider!

53

Colonel Wadsworth of Hartford, Connecticut, owned Whirligig, a full-blood Narragansett Pacer of "exceptional carriage, spirit, and movements" that stood at stud in the 1780s. Whirligig was famous in his day, and news that he had been sold for a "vast sum of money" created quite a stir throughout the country.

Whirligig's offspring included Young Rainbow, said to equal his sire in grace and agility, and Young Kitt, a spirited, dark-sorrel stallion that could trot and canter as well as pace rapidly – unusual for a purebred.

Smiling Ball, taken to Connecticut in 1785, was a descendant of Old Snip from Tripoli. He paced exceedingly fast, and was unbeaten in races.

Free And Easy, a full-blood Narragansett Pacer, was advertised at East Windsor, Connecticut, 1785-87, at the low price of "$1.00 the single leap, $2.00 the season, to encourage those having likely mares of the same breed to bring them, that the breed so valuable may not be lost." He was a good-looking, well-proportioned stallion, strong and active, the pride of his owner.

Hannah Robinson owned a "splendid Spanish Jennet or Narragansett Pacer, named Selim," whose sire and dam had been imported from Andalusia by her grandfather, William Robinson.

A bright bay stallion with black points was advertised at Kensington, Connecticut, in 1793 as "the only one in the world of the Narragansett breed unmixed." This horse, King Philip, was purportedly the sole remnant of his breed by 1800. During the War of 1812 the captain of a British man-of-war had agents searching throughout the Narragansett area for a Narragansett Pacer to give his wife. But not a single full-blood pacer was to be found.

There has been much conjecture about why this breed became extinct. One school of thought held that Narragansett breeders exported so many pacers that they depleted their stock. However, the canny Yankee traders would hardly have been guilty of such poor judgment.

Others felt that improved roads and the corresponding switch to coach and carriage killed the popularity of the Narragansett Pacers. Yet it seems there would still have been loyal breeders and at least a limited market for such easy-gaited saddle horses. It would then have taken longer than twenty-odd years for these pacers to die out.

The breed established by the Vermont stallion, Justin Morgan, at the close of the 18th century also faced the problem of obsolescence a few generations later. Faithful breeders, however, nurtured their small purebred bands of Morgan horses and today Morgans are found in large numbers throughout the United States, and there are many in Canada as well. This should also have been true of the hardy, popular Narragansett Pacer, had it not been for some drastic happening within a short period of time.

A great and sudden change did, in fact, take place, and the answer to this riddle is clearly spelled out in the pages of Rhode Island history.

PART III

According to *The Book of Rhode Island*, distributed by the Rhode Island State Bureau of Information in 1930, "until the Revolutionary War, the production and exportation of horses in Rhode Island was a great agricultural enterprise, which served as a means of developing the state's maritime trade." Shipbuilding had begun at Newport in 1646.

By 1700 the colony included nine towns and had more than seven thousand inhabitants. The period between 1700 and 1760 was one of increased commerce and privateering. Many Rhode Island residents owned plantations in the West Indies from which they derived part of their income. When the infamous "triangular trade" developed, ships brought in sugar and molasses, the latter for conversion to rum. Hogsheads of rum were then shipped to the coastline stockades of Africa and traded for slaves, which in turn brought a lucrative profit in the marts of the Sugar Islands. At the peak of West Indian commerce in 1763, about one hundred fifty Rhode Island vessels engaged in this trade.

England's Sugar Act of 1764 imposed a tax of threepence per gallon on molasses brought from the Indies to the colonies. In protest, colonists organized a boycott of British goods and encouraged illegal manufacture of rum. This act and its predecessor, the Molasses Act, were eventually repealed; but other levies soon followed and the taxed and hampered colonists found their resentment of the mother country growing.

In July 1769 the British ship Liberty, hunting smugglers, was wrecked and burned near Newport. When the crown's revenue cutter Gaspée ran aground in the waters off Rhode Island in 1772, she was seized and burned, to England's great outrage.

In December 1773 the tax on tea led to the Boston Tea Party. Acts passed by King George III next blockaded, closed, and sealed the Boston port. British troops were quartered in the town. From this point on, all steps led to war. At the Continental Congress in Philadelphia in 1774, Rhode Island, Connecticut, and New Hampshire were called upon to supply regiments of minutemen for the Continental Army.

In the spring of 1775 the Fishery Act completed the breech by excluding New England's colonies from the Newfoundland fisheries. This act robbed them of income from codfish and whales and restrained them from trade with the British Isles and West Indies. Hard on its heels came the first skirmishes of the Revolutionary War at Lexington and Concord.

Many Rhode Island farmers rushed off to Boston to join the Continental Army under General Washington. Others went with Benedict Arnold on his expedition against Quebec. This was the same Arnold whom the British called a "horse jockey," mocking his skill as a horseman. He had done a profitable business shipping horses from Canada to the West Indies in his own New Haven-based ships.

Newport was a prime target for the British since it rivaled New York, Boston and Philadelphia in affluence. Nine thousand troops were sent to occupy the town, and from 1776 through 1780 Rhode Island was in a state of siege. In December 1776 a British flotilla bottled up Narragansett Bay. A British ship blocked the mouth of Bristol Harbor.

Rhode Islanders suffered greatly during the war. They saw the town of Newport brought to ruins. Bristol, a port of promise, was burned. Other towns were ransacked, their inhabitants threatened and harassed. Many, deprived of all means of livelihood, fled from the colony. All the trees on the island of Rhode Island were cut for firewood, and the best of the farmland was occupied and devastated by the Redcoats. In the summer of 1778 the British laid waste all the countryside around Newport and Conanicut. They filled in wells, drove off livestock, and confiscated equipment. A summer storm destroyed all the crops and most of the livestock around Bristol.

That winter was the coldest in Bristol's history. The harbor was solid ice, and sentries froze to death at their posts. The Continental paper dollar depreciated so fantastically that by 1779 John Kolb complained "an ordinary horse is now worth $20,000; *I say twenty thousand dollars!*" Late in 1779 the British abandoned Newport, and a French fleet of eleven ships and an army of four thousand men moved in to defend the area. They too lived off the land. General Jeremiah Wadsworth sent his dispatch rider, Private Levi Pease (later the famous "Stagecoach King"), to Rhode Island to buy up stores for the commissary department and horses with which to remove the French artillery from Newport.

Just as the colony and her inhabitants were ruined, so too was the Narragansett Pacer, a casualty of the Revolutionary War.

With her farmland laid waste, her trade potential destroyed, her currency inflated out of value, and her livestock and equipment nearly gone, Rhode Island – especially in the Narragansett region – suffered a depression from which it took years to recover.

It is very doubtful that between 1776 and 1781 any attention whatsoever was paid to horse breeding. It is highly unlikely that more than a handful of foals were born during those years. A good percentage of the strong, mature horses had been siphoned off for use by both armies.

In the poverty years just after the war nearly all the remaining stock of Narragansett Pacers was sold to neighboring states. Those that were left in Rhode Island were the ones too old and worn down to find a market anywhere. Consequently, by 1812, the British captain and a Virginia breeder's agent were unable to find a purebred left, though they scoured the state.

Many of the pacers were bought up by neighboring Connecticut horsemen. Newspapers of the 1780s and '90s abounded with ads both offering and seeking horses of "the true Narragansett breed." Many of them were purchased as "shipping horses" for export and resale. Their crossbred descendants were bred to other breeds until the original mold was lost.

At about this time the French Canadians of Quebec had developed a penchant for fast pacing horses. Their own native stock, although extremely hardy, swift, and energetic, did not exhibit the pacing characteristic. By 1795 a man named King, residing in Williston, Vermont, had begun a lucrative business with the nearby Frenchmen. King bought up as many of the Narragansett Pacer mares as he could find – most of them "weak and rickety." Good business dictated that these mares would bring more if sold in foal. Justin Morgan, foundation sire of the Morgan breed, was standing at stud in Williston in 1795, and it is safe to assume that some of these pacing mares carried Morgan offspring in utero to Quebec.

King made numerous trips to southern Quebec each year, taking six or seven Narragansett mares at a time and disposing of them on a swing through Fairfield, St. Caèsairé, and St. Hyacinthe. It didn't take other New England horse traders long to discover this new market for pacing stock.

Louis Dansereau of Contre Coeur, P.Q. was one of the French Canadians who eagerly snapped up pacing mares, and from these he developed a remarkable strain of black pacers. The foundation mare of the Dansereau line was a black pacer, about fourteen years old, obtained from a Yankee trader. Dansereau bred this mare around 1817 to Voyageur, whose pacing dam was bought, when carrying him, from a Yankee trader. The result of this mating was a black pacing mare, Jeanne d'Arc, who produced an outstanding group of black pacing stallions. The Dansereau strain was largely inbred, and from it came the pacers Pilot, Pilot, Jr., Columbus, Petit Coq (Beppo), and others.

Pilot was bred by Louis Dansereau, foaled in 1823, and arrived in Kentucky in 1831. In the ensuing twenty years Pilot sired some of the finest pacing and trotting horses ever to be developed in Kentucky. Other great Canadian pacers to go to Kentucky were the original Copperbottom – fastest pacer in his day – foaled in 1809; Tom Hal, a horse with extraordinary speed; and Davy Crockett. All came from southern Quebec where the Narragansett mares from Vermont had gone. They had uniformity of type, pacing characteristics, and flashing speed.

The Canadian pacers had caught up the flickering torch all but dropped by the vanishing Narragansetts and carried it to new, bright glory on the race tracks of Kentucky.

It has been said that the bloodlines of every horse that paces today can be traced to the Narragansett Pacer, but there is no way to prove this.

Some of the earliest Morgan stallions were bred to mares of Narragansett blood. Although the pacing characteristic has been bred out over the years, a number of the old-time Morgans did pace, and very rapidly. St. Clair 48, a pacing stallion from Illinois, was brought to California in 1849. He was sired by a Morgan stallion and was out of a black Canadian mare. St. Clair was popular at stud, siring between six hundred and seven hundred foals in California, several of which were fast pacers.

In the Middle Basin of Tennessee, as early as 1790, plantation owners had crossed several breeds of horses to perfect an ideal saddler for long rides through the fields. Among the types used in formation of the Tennessee Walking Horse were Canadian pacers and Narragansett Pacers. One of the Narragansett stallions was the peerless Free And Easy, the same horse advertised in Connecticut in the late 1780s and brought to Tennessee and North Carolina for breeding purposes. General Andrew Jackson was one of the horsemen interested in the arrival of Free And Easy.

Of the Canadian pacers that left their mark in the propagation of the Tennessee Walker, Copperbottom was undoubtedly the greatest. From him descended the outstanding family of Mountain Slasher F-59. Others of note were the blue roan Tom Hal, foaled in Canada in 1802, and the famous Pilot, Jr. These same early sires were also important in the foundation of the American Saddlebred and the Standardbred. Tradition says that the famous Hiatoga family of pacers had its origin from a Narragansett Pacer.

Another breed that may still carry a trace of the old Narragansett blood is the Paso Fino from Puerto Rico. The island was discovered by Columbus in 1493 and colonized from 1506 on. Martin de Salazar took Spanish Jennets and Andalusians there in 1509.

During the 16th century raids from French, British and Dutch freebooters frequently harassed the island colonies under the crown of Castile. As Spain's power declined and the corsairs' raids increased, she found it more and more difficult to supply her colonists. The exportation of horses to the islands had all but ended in the first half of the century, as those colonies had enough stock built up to serve their needs. By 1569 there were just two hundred Spaniards left on Puerto Rico, most of whom were poor, and much of the land had reverted to wild tropical growth.

St. Clair 48 was such a fast pace he went unchallenged in the Sacramento area in the 1850s. Illustration by Leslie Houlton. Courtesy of LaVonne Houlton.

In 1596 George, Earl of Cumberland, wrote the following, during a visit to Puerto Rico: "About their horses, none of which I have seen by much so tall and goodly as ordinarily they are in England; they are well made and well mettled, and good store there are of them, but methinks there are many things wanting in them which are ordinary in our English light horses. *They are all trotters*; nor do I remember that I have seen above one ambler and that a very little fiddling nag."

If the pacing characteristic had all but vanished from the native Puerto Rican stock by 1600 and not been reintroduced, today's Paso Fino might have been a trotter. The most likely horse to have brought the "pace" back to Puerto Rico was the Narragansett Pacer that was peddled through all the islands of the Caribbean in great numbers throughout the 17th and 18th centuries. The Puerto Rican horse of those times, of course, still had the pacing gene in his blood, but it had become recessive until made dominant again through the Narragansett Pacers, with which they shared a common ancestry.

Of all the modern pacing breeds, the Paso Fino probably most resembles the extinct Narragansett Pacer in size, appearance, gait and way of going.

The "flower of Rhode Island horses," once the proudest product of New England, has vanished into the mists of history. Yet this was too old and noble a blood to die completely. His faint echo may still be heard through the ringing hoof beats of hundreds of pacers of today.

Morgan Breeding Stallions of the West
1975

Red Vermont 7893 *Jubilee King (Penrod x Daisette) x Daisy Knox (Knox Morgan x Daisy de Jarnette)*

Dark chestnut, with strip; left hind sock white. Foaled January 1934. Bred by Joseph C. Brunk, Springfield, Illinois. Sold as a yearling to Grace B. Woods, Walpole, New Hampshire. Purchased 1940 by Jack and Harriet Davis, Arcadia, California. Red Vermont made Morgans quite popular in Southern California because of his impressive appearance, style and manner. He wasn't a big horse, but he stood up and looked big! Red Vermont was especially handsome in the silver mounted parade equipment that Davis found so much use for. Owned by the Davis family for the rest of his life, Red Vermont died in 1958, leaving a whole galaxy of "Vermonts" to carry on for him.

Red Vermont 7893, cover of the Western Livestock Journal's Horse of the Month, undated. Courtesy of Golden West Region 7.

Jack Davis had a divided heart where horses were concerned. Palominos were extremely popular in the 1940s, and Davis had some beauties. He owned two gorgeous golden stallions, the full brothers El Moreno and Beau Brummel, both show winners and very popular sires. Because of this association, Red Vermont found himself a sire of registered Palominos. Jubilee Gold, one of his earlier California foals, was double registered (X-8430 AMHR; 6551-M PHBA). He was a very handsome parade-type horse of excellent Palomino color. Another fine son was Golden Vermont (7523 PHBA), foaled at San Bernardino in 1944.

Red Vermont's pedigree credentials were of the best. His sire was the renowned Jubilee King, his dam the good Brunk mare, Daisy Knox. Both his sire's dam and his dam's dam were from the Jubilee de Jarnette line. Jubilee de Jarnette was twice a winner at the big Madison Square Garden Show, and had wins at many other shows when shown double with his dam, the incomparable Lady de Jarnette. Coming from such a family, it was only natural that Red Vermont would not only be a winner, but would in turn sire show-quality stock. A daughter, Verdonna Vermont, was Grand Champion Mare at the Golden West National Morgan Horse Show a few years ago. She has been a fine broodmare for the James Wagoners of Modesto.

Jack Davis' son, Gene, carried on the Davis Breeding Farm, later located near Lodi, and campaigned two Red Vermont sons, Monty Vermont and Domino Vermont and their get to many wins in Northern California shows.

58

A Red Vermont daughter, Belle of Vermont, was the dam of the stallion Eco Jubilo, owned by Mr. and Mrs. Sam Overstreet. Bred to a Red Vermont daughter, Bonnie Heather, Eco Jubilo has sired such show Morgans as Jubilee Jazz and Serena Suzette.

Leo Beckley's great show stallion, Montey Vermont, was out of a Red Vermont daughter. He in turn has sired many fine Morgans in the Pacific Northwest, such as Moco Vermont, Schauer's Forecast, Beckridge Montaco and many others. Also in the Northwest are the Red Vermont daughters Fairland's Trixie, Mardy Vermont (dam of Nimbus) and Georgette Vermont, dam of Keystone's Gigi, Keystone's Georgette, Keystone's Gorgeous and Keystone's Annette.

Starlite Vermont, owned by Barbara Rovira in Crestline, California, was the dam of Irish Belle Monte and Sir Guy Vermont. At the Charles Sutfin's Willow Glen Morgans a few years ago, Shron Vermont produced Willow Glen Rocket, and Tono Vermont (Allen Vermont x Shron Vermont) became the dam of Willow Glen Erin.

There are many who still remember the show ring performance of the good gelding, Morgan's Jubilee Vermont. And in the 1940s Sunny Vermont won quite a few halter classes, as did Allen Vermont, Vermont Doll, and other family members.

JoAnn Stewart and Pat Swift, Woodside Morgans, at Olema, California, started their breeding program on a foundation of Red Vermont stock: Vicki Vermont, Vanity Vermont, Annabelle Vermont, Nimbus and Victoria Vermont. In Idaho, the good Neeley-owned Sireson 9704 (Red Vermont x Birdie Kellog C. K.) added more names to the family roster. Although he had quite a few more daughters than sons, Red Vermont was fortunate in that many of his sons made fine sires: Easter Vermont 9804, Allen Vermont 8944, Bricktop 8592, Redmont B. Morgan 9124, Lucky Vermont 9533, Sunny Vermont 8705, Homestake 10637, Domino Vermont 11179, Monty Vermont 9707 and Sireson 9704 attest to that.

Sonfield 7952 *Mansfield (Bennington x Artemisia) x Quietude (Troubadour of Willowmoor x Ruth)*

Dark chestnut with star and snip. Foaled May 11, 1935. Bred by the United States Department of Agriculture, Middlebury, Vermont; owned by Dr. W. L. Orcutt, West Newbury, Massachusetts.

Sonfield was a fortunate stallion, born under the luckiest of stars. First off, he was fortunate in his parentage. His sire, Mansfield, was one of the greatest Morgan stallions of modern times, and his name turns up in several lines in innumerable pedigrees today. Sonfield's dam, Quietude, counted among her produce the illustrious sire, Upwey Ben Don and the incomparable mare Upwey Benn Quietude. Truly, Sonfield was of noble birth. In appearance, he resembled his sire and his great-grandsire, General Gates, a good deal, though he was perhaps a bit more rounded through the barrel than they were. He had an especially fine head, and his general "look" was easily discerned in his get and even in their descendants. He did have one conformation fault — he fell off in the croup — but seldom transmitted it to his offspring. Even when he did his sons and daughters were of such overall quality that a "Sonfield croup" rarely hurt them in the show ring.

Sonfield's "luck" seemed slow in coming. He was sold in New England, and again when he was two. Meanwhile, across the continent, the biggest Morgan breeder of them all was trying a number of stallions to find the right "nick" for his mares. Roland Hill was the breeder, and the stallion he needed to replace was Querido 7370, a full brother to Mansfield. Hill's young mares were Querido daughters, out of mares of the old Sellman breeding. The several stallions he tried weren't giving the results Hill desired, so he turned to New England and that fountainhead of performance and endurance Morgans, the General Gates line. In the four-year-old Sonfield he found what he sought. The transfer to Hill was recorded December 1, 1939, and a whole new chapter of Morgan history was about to be written.

Sonfield's first foals arrived in 1941 – three fillies and seven colts, including two that became noted sires: Rosefield 8568, who sired many of the Morgans at the J. C. Jackson Ranch in Montana, in addition to his fifteen earlier California foals for Dean Witter's Lone Pine Ranch, and Sheik F. 8567, who remained in Central California. So many of Sonfield's colts were gelded to provide good cow horses for Hill's vast Horseshoe Cattle Company operations in California, that it was left to just a few to carry on for him in the male line: Linden Sonfield (a consistent show winner in his time, who died in 1974 at the age of thirty-one years), Ryder, sire of a number of foals in Siskiyou County in the late '40s, Harvest Field and Ivon Field, especially.

Roland Hill was obviously pleased with that first group of Sonfield foals. He then bred twice as many mares to the stallion who crossed so well on his Querido daughters, and got eighteen foals in 1942. Sonfield sired thirty foals the following year. During ten breeding seasons Sonfield sired 177 foals, all under the ownership of the Hill family and the Horseshoe Cattle Company. He did not stand to outside mares from 1940-1949. His last four California-bred offspring (1951) were from outside mares. In December of that year Sonfield was transferred to the late Mr. Hill's brother,

Sonfield 7952 with Jean Hill. Photo courtesy of NMMH.

Russell, who kept him through 1955. By now Sonfield was twenty years old. He had had an illustrious career at the stud, and sired more foals than any Morgan stallion in California for a century. Their accolades in the show ring alone could have let him rest on his laurels. When Sonfield mares were offered for sale eager breeders had their checkbooks ready. Luckily, he had sired even more fillies than colts, so there were over ninety of them. Here are just a few: Alma Sonfield 06713, a grand champion mare of the '40s; Analin 07969, dam of Quiet Son De, Deanne and others; Addy May Field 07929, dam of the champion gelding Castle Star Reporter; Anita Blossom 06722, dam of Honey Bun, Toy Ann and for-

mer National Junior Champion Mare, Blossom's Lass 013320; Iva Sonfield 05721, dam of the versatile stallion Kings River Morgan; Kitty Field 06718, herself an N.C.M.H.C. Show Grand Champion Mare at age 16, and dam of the fine performance mare, Scarlet Ribbons 010855; Bay Blossom 07928, dam of Impala Blossom, who in turn has produced several winning fillies.

A popular T.V. ad says "You're not getting older; you're just getting better." So it was with Sonfield, whose star was still on the rise when he was purchased in 1957 by Mr. and Mrs. Leo Beckley, Mt. Vernon, Washington. In the decade left to him, Sonfield sired many more outstanding Morgans: Panora Field 011278; Beckridge Sunfield 15944 (who returned the sire line to California); Skyfield 13052, a Canadian champion; My Gay Pixie 011742, another Canadian; Sunnyvale Valentino 14364 (winning performer in Oregon, and at the 1974 Grand National Morgan Horse Show);

Sandora Field 012351; Norfield 12842; Albafield 011639; Arana Field 12841; * Sonfield's Sammy 13053, a fine sire, and others.

Many of us have known of a stallion, beautiful and well-bred, who through some quirk of ownership or fate never had a real opportunity to prove his worth as a sire. That was not Sonfield's fate. For him, fortune smiled all the thirty-two years of his life. Bred to greatness, owned by the largest breeder, with a court of outstanding broodmares, and given the chance for a second career in his later years, blessed with good health and longevity, the fabulous Sonfield fulfilled the destiny he so richly deserved. Over 250 registered sons and daughters, and many, many descendants provide living testimonial to his greatness.

I didn't know about Sonfield's Sammy when I wrote the article, - he lived up on the Rogue River at Hidden Valley, and was just gorgeous - dark liver chestnut, beautiful head and all, and I could pick every one of his offspring out of the field. I bred Blossom's Lass to him, and got a drop dead gorgeous filly I named Viking Quietude. I had the great misfortune to lose this young mare that everybody loved to a dried wisp of deadly nightshade. lh

Redman 8056 *Mountcrest Sellman (Joe Bailey x Kitty E) x Red Dot (Pongee Morgan x Rodota)*

Dark red chestnut, with an irregular strip, and a brown spot on his right side; both hind stockings white. 15.2 hands, weighed 1100 pounds. Foaled April 26, 1936.

Mountcrest Sellman was bred by Richard Sellman, Rochelle, Texas, who sold his dam, Kitty E. to Reginald H. Parsons, Mountcrest Ranch, Hilt, California, in foal to Joe Bailey. Mountcrest Sellman was one of the first colts foaled in California in the re-born Morgan era. He was purchased in January 1936, to head up millionaire William Randolph Hearst's Morgan breeding program, under ownership of his Piedmont Land and Cattle Company. Red Dot was a Hill-bred mare, foaled in 1938, purchased by Hearst as a yearling.

Redman's grandsire, Joe Bailey, was by Headlight Morgan 4683, a son of Ethan Allen 2nd 406. Through Kitty E., Pongee Morgan and Rodota, Redman traced primarily to Daniel Lambert 62, twice through that peacock of the Morgan world, Jubilee de Jarnette 3854.

Bred by Hearst, owned by C. J. Ferrari, San Francisco, Redman was sold to R. L. Welborn, Campo, Cali-

Redman 8056. Photo courtesy of the National Museum of the Morgan Horse.

fornia as a two-year-old. Welborn bred three foals from him: Red Leaf X-05786 in 1940, Red Ann 05684 in 1941, and Blackman 8622 in 1942. The dam of the last two was Gojea 04610, a fine brown show mare, foaled in 1929, bred by J. C. Brunk of Illinois. Gojea was brought to California in 1934. Welborn sold Gojea to E. W. Roberts, Hi Pass, California, on April 2, 1942, and it was at the Roberts Ranch on June 23, 1942 that Redman's greatest siring son, Blackman 8622, was foaled.

Redman had excellent Morgan type, and was a consistent model winner in California shows. Among his wins were 1st – Morgan stallions at the Orange County Fair, and 1st at the Coronado National Horse Show in 1941. There are certain horses who carry themselves with particular pride – as though they know they are Something Special. Redman was like that – handsome, strong, sleek-coated and proud, very competent under saddle – to know him was to admire him . . . and to never forget the way he was.

E. W. Roberts bred two mares to Redman in 1943. One of the foals from those breedings was Red Gates 8954, another of Redman's good siring sons. In 1944 Roberts bred eight mares to Redman, getting two good colts and five nice fillies. The colts were ill-starred. Purchased by the Chinese government, they were part of a Morgan band of fourteen mares and twelve stallions that steamed out of San Francisco Bay one dark September night in 1947 aboard the "Philippine Transport." Red Rex 9321 was fatally injured trying to jump an iron fence shortly after reaching the Chinese mainland. Red Lancer 9320 went on to the Sung Ming Military Stud, Yunan Province, together with ten Morgan mares and another stallion. He was to be crossed on Mongolian mares, and his sons from Morgan dams were to be bred to Mongolian mares. Whatever became of him and his progeny is lost in the folds of the Red Chinese curtain.

In the 1930s and early '40s many large-scale western ranchers turned to Morgans as the mounts most suitable for stock and range work. One such was Warren J. Halliday, who was ranching near Bishop. His first Morgan mare, Tabby Hawk, was a Querido granddaughter, out of the Brunk-bred Gojea. Since Redman was bred entirely in the lines that had made the famed Sellman ranch a major source of outstanding Morgans throughout the West, he was an ideal choice for Halliday's breeding program, and was purchased by him in the spring of '42. Warren carefully selected nine more broodmares over the next three years, of Hill, Sellman or Brunk breeding.

In 1945 the Halliday family, Redman, and his band of mares, moved from the Owens Valley to Blue Heaven Ranch, 632 lovely acres of meadow and hay land nestled in Scott Valley at the base of the Siskiyou Mountains, a mile south of Etna, in Northern California. While this move took Redman out of circulation to outside mares for some years, he sired many fine colts and fillies in the Siskiyous. Redman daughters found ready places in broodmare bands throughout the state and in the Pacific Northwest. One of his daughters, Etna 06593, became the dam of Marjorie Hambly's great stock and trail mare, Keystone's Rome Beauty 010290. In all, Warren Halliday got twenty-nine foals from Redman. The horse was not used at stud during 1950 and 1951. After one brief change of ownership, he was purchased in 1952 by Dr. Ina Richter, Kedron Farm, Solvang, who raised eleven foals from him.

Mrs. Sid Spencer bred one of his 1957 foals, Billy Rebel 11904, a well-known sire in Oregon, owned by Jean Blewett. The aging Redman was transferred late in 1958 to Gene and Shirley Mathews of Santa Ynez, and his last three foals were born in 1959. Redman, a truly outstanding Morgan was coming into his twenty-seventh year when he died. Bred to just a few mares each year during seventeen breeding seasons, his progeny totaled thirty-one colts and thirty-one fillies.

The final proof of a stallion is in his ability to breed on. Without even considering the production records of his daughters or other sons, the contribution of Blackman and Red Gates alone to the breed are enough to warrant the Seal of Approval for excellence to Redman. One could talk all day about Blackman's get. Here are just a few of the well-known names from his line: Bikini, Blackman Allen, Harold Roberts, Baacamanto, Belle Romanesque, Jeanne Allen, Kathleen B., Lady Gay, Lois Morgan, La Mesa, Margaret Collins, Slower Nell, Justina Allen. Red Gates gave us such outstanding Morgans as Ann Bolin, Bea Nickerson, Gojean, Poco Aljoy, Otto McClure, Red Cal, Gay Gypsey, Diamond Star, and Red Allen. Better still the Redman family was one that could successfully be bred back up to itself, and E. W. Roberts did this repeatedly. The good performer Diamond Star 10739, for example, was by Red Gates, out of Aabaca, by Blackman. Another consistent ribbon winner, Justina Allen, was by Nathan Allen, out of Justina Morgan, who were both by Blackman. Red Cal was by Red Gates, out of Baja Cal, by Blackman, and so on. What Roberts really did was concentrate anew the old true-type, capable Morgan blood that had been melded years before by Richard Sellman, through a descendant of his stock, Redman 8056.

Montabell 8117 *Mountcrest Sellman (Joe Bailey x Kitty E.) x Jinglebells (Querido x Texanita)*

Dark chestnut, flaxen mane. Connected star, strip and snip. Left hind stocking and inside right hind pastern white. Bred by William Randolph Hearst, San Simeon, owned by Orris C. Foster, Calabasas, California. Foaled April 28, 1936.

Montabell was a paternal half-brother to the stallions Redman, Antman, Kenelm Morgan and Cloverman. Their sire, Mountcrest Sellman, was acknowledged as one of the best horses of his time, and was the first California-born sire of prominence in the 20th century. Mountcrest Sellman's sons resembled him, and each other, to a large degree, being good-bodied, up-headed, stylish

Montabell (also known as Montabell Gift) 8117. Photo courtesy of NMMH.

animals. They made fine parade and show horses. From the Mountcrest Sellman line have descended such fine stallions as Blackman, Bikini, Red Gates, Poco Aljoy, Baacamanto, Blackman Allen and others. A lot of Mary Smith's Hedlite mares and stallions came from Mountcrest Sellman daughters. By the end of the 1950s Mountcrest Sellman's descendants numbered over five hundred registered Morgans.

Although registered as Montabell, Mr. Foster, who used "Gift" as a distinguishing suffix on most of his horses, always called him Montabell Gift. In Volume VI of the book *Here's Who! In Horses of the Pacific Coast* for 1949, Mr. Foster announced that "Monty's" colts could be found in all ten of the western states. Since all the recorded transfers of Montabell's Morgan offspring to that time were to California owners, it appears that the stallion saw quite a bit of service to mares of other breeds. Orris Foster did have a dream. He wanted very much to re-establish Morgans as harness horses for the racetrack. Although he didn't succeed, he came close with Jim Dandy Gift (Montabell x Kathleen C., a Standardbred mare). This chestnut gelding made his track debut at Bay Meadows June 4, 1947. Through some mix-up he had been worked fourteen miles that very day, and everyone thought he'd be too tired to come close to winning…and he was unplaced in his first two starts. Mrs. Foster insisted that her husband place a bet on the third race anyway, and that $2.00 bet made Foster $78.00 richer when long-shot Jim Dandy Gift crossed the finish line ahead of the field. He placed 2nd and 3rd in later races at the meet, and at Santa Anita he won five of his six starts, with a trotting record of 2:05.5 for a mile. Jim Dandy Gift was owned by Dr. L. A. Cleveland, Reseda, California.

Orris Foster was also a member of the Palomino Horse Breeders Association, and "Montabell Gift" became a sire of registered Palominos. Two that Foster bred were Sparkler Gift (2884-M) and Sunset Gift (2420-M).

Montabell sired a few Morgan foals each year (except 1949) from 1939-1951. He had no off-spring for the next four years, then only four more foals from 1956-1959. One of his sons, Calabasas Gift 8320, went to Oregon in 1950, after siring six foals in California. He returned to this state a few years later, and in 1966 Forrest Jones of Termo, Lassen County, had five mares and a stallion all sired by Calabasas Gift, who was owned by Millard Ulch of Susanville at the time these Morgans were bred.

Dick Nelson, now with Mohican Morgans in Missouri, owned Oh-Cee's Gift 010940 (Montabell x Jane Abbey) and raised several good foals from her, including Querida Mia, Rojo Mac and Vacquero Mac. Princess Firefly (Montabell x Princess Joaquin) is the dam of Dusty Silverton, Serena Fireflight, Serena Firelight and others. Another daughter, Nellie Gift, was the dam of Abra-ham Lincoln Gift 8758, and Poco's Queen was out of Julie Belle Gift 07186.

Sheriff Morgan 9436 will be long remembered in Southern California, where he was a consis-tent ribbon and trophy winner in a variety of classes, first for the Riding family, and later for junior exhibitor Danny Weinberger – those two went together like bread and jelly. Sheriff Morgan's dam was Anita Belle Gift, by Montabell.

Montabell himself was a show champion. Among his wins were Grand Champion Stallion at the Los Angeles National Horse Show in 1945 and the Ventura County Fair in 1946. His offspring did well in halter and performance classes. While not so widely known as some of the California sires, Montabell added to the luster of the breed in this state.

Lippitt Morman 8211 *Mansfield (Bennington x Artemisia) x Lippitt Kate Moro (Moro x Croydon Mary)*

Chestnut, small star, narrow strip, snip; right hind stocking white; fifteen hands, 1120 pounds. Foaled May 30, 1939. Bred by Robert L. Knight, Rhode Island. Mr. Knight sold Lippitt Morman as a two-year-old, and bought him back the following year. He was purchased in August 1943, by W. A. LeBoeuf of Bellevue, Quebec, who conditioned the stallion for endurance competition. Lippitt Morman became the first stallion ever to win the Green Mountain Horse Association's 100 Mile Trail Ride in Vermont, winning both his division and the sweepstakes award in 1946. This three-day ride is designed to prove the stamina of horses, with the award going to the animal judged to be in the best condition at ride's end.

Roland Hill purchased Lippitt Morman in February 1947, and kept him until October 1948, when he was sold to contractor Merle H. Little, El Rancho Poco, Monrovia, California. Oddly enough, Hill only got two foals from Lippitt Morman those two seasons: Angel Morman 07648, out of Angel D. in 1948, and Morman's Angel 07926, out of Angel A., in '49. Both dams were by the Sellman stallion, Moleskin, a grandson of Headlight Morgan 4683.

During the 1950s Lippitt Morman sired thirty-seven foals - thirteen for Mr. Little, and the oth-ers to outside mares. From one of the outside breedings came the good broodmare Coffey Choice, dam of the handsome, typey Morgan stallion, Red-Jo-Allen C, owned in Oregon. Another good Lippitt Morman daughter was Princess Victoria, dam of Triton El Capitan, herd sire at the Point Reyes National Seashore Park Morgan Horse Farm. Mrs. Sid Spencer's fine mare, Morman's Red Lady, dam of Sir Rust, Wenonah and others, was a Lippitt Morman daughter. So were Morman's Flame, Mornaquin and Kedron Beatrice, the dam of the lovely show mare Lorwin Kahlua. Lippitt

Morman sired more fillies than colts, and is best remembered as a broodmare sire. His get were uniformly good performance horses.

Lippitt Morman was a full brother to that nationally famous versatile Morgan, the late Lippitt Mandate (in the early days Lippitt Mandate was touted as the full brother of Lippitt Morman!). He was lucky to land in the stable of Merle Little, who was one of the leading show winners on the West Coast – his tack room overflowed with trophies, ribbons and win pictures, and Lippitt Morman had garnered his share. In 1949, for example, he was Champion Morgan Stallion at the Ventura County Fair, Los Angeles County Spring Fair, San Fernando Valley Fair, and Riverside County Fair. He won pleasure horse classes, parade horse classes and trail classes, too. Little, his wife and two daughters rode in the Tournament of Roses parade as a quartet, mounted on Morgans – one of them was Lippitt Morman.

Lippitt Morman 8211. Photo courtesy of NMMH.

One of Lippitt Morman's best offspring was Little Joe Morgan 11369, a top competitive trail ride horse. Marjorie Hambly rode him to a first in the six-day High Sierra Trail Ride in '62. He won the Lightweight and Sweepstakes at a N.A.T.R.C. Class A Ride at Calistoga in '63; won the Lightweight and was second in the Morgan division of the N.A.T.R.C.-sanctioned Hesperia ride in '64, and was first in a Class A ride in Scottsdale, Arizona that year. He won the N.A.T.R.C. award for Champion Lightweight Competitive Trail Ride Horse at the Cow Palace in 1964. He had other talents in his background too, having been trained to do circus tricks, and had been raced, and roped from.

Many of Lippitt Morman's get were familiar to the winner's circle at Southern California shows: Kedron Woodstock, Poco's Monej, Sister Poco, Doctor Morman, Red Arrow Sunday, Mornaquin, Susie Belle, and Lazy Sue, to name some. They showed in every kind of class – English and western pleasure, pleasure driving and combination, trail, reining, parade, Australian pursuit race, gymkhana events, and at halter.

Lippitt Morman: a versatile stallion from a versatile family, with a string of versatile progeny to prove he was entitled to a niche in California Morgan history.

Gay Mac 7988 *Mansfield (Bennington x Artemisia) x Dewdrop (General Gates x Ellen)*

Very dark bay; star, left hind sock and right hind heel white; 15.2 hands, 1130 pounds. Bred by the U.S. Department of Agriculture, Middlebury, Vermont, foaled May 3, 1936. Purchased as a weanling by Dr. W. L. Orcutt, West Newbury, Massachusetts, who sold him to Clarence C. Reed, M.D., of Compton, California, April 24, 1942.

Gay Mac's sire was the General Gates grandson, Mansfield. His dam, Dewdrop, was a daughter of General Gates. Thus Gay Mac was doubly endowed with the qualities for which the General Gates line became famous: excellent conformation, performance ability, fine disposition, and a special kind of beauty. It was said that Gay Mac showed an almost perfect resemblance to General Gates.

Impeccably bred, of near flawless conformation, a proven sire of quality foals, Gay Mac was still denied the full opportunity at stud that his birthright called for. While he sired sixty foals between 1943-1950, they were the produce of only twenty mares, seventeen of which were owned by Dr. Reed. His total "outside" service consisted of four foals from three mares. Almost without exception these twenty mares traced to General Gates through their sires. Over half of them were Querido daughters, three were by Sonfield. Others traced to General Gates through Red Oak and Linsley.

Gay Mac's first California foals arrived in 1943 – two colts and five fillies – something of an omen, as he consistently sired more fillies (38) than colts (22), in small annual crops that never exceeded thirteen foals.

Gay Mac 7988. Photo courtesy of NMMH.

Dr. Reed had purchased his broodmares from Roland Hill. He carefully selected a sire from the Morgan breed's leading performance line to provide top quality cow-horses for his 2,600-acre San Clemente Hereford ranch. Gay Mac was also his personal mount, and the pair covered many miles of trails, looking at the cattle, overseeing ranch operations. Most of the Morgans Reed raised saw duty on the vast ranch. About 1948 Dr. Reed announced purchase of the picturesque 3,000-acre Rahling-Brown Ranch in Siskiyou County, near Yreka, California. Around this time a dozen Gay Mac offspring were sold to Oregon owners. Others went to Washington, Idaho and California breeders, so that today Gay Mac descendants are found throughout the Pacific states.

Probably the best luck that Gay Mac had as a sire was that one of Reed's mares was Bessie Ro 04978 (Querido x Roboss), who produced Bess Gates, Flika, Ro Mac, and one other colt by Gay Mac. The two full sisters in turn were the dams of Dapper Dan 10696 and Muscle Man 10697, two popular and prolific stallions in Central California, whose offspring are carrying on the tradition of beauty, ability and disposition. Ro Mac sired a number of fine show and stock horses in Southern California, and their descendants may now be found in Missouri, at Mohican Farms.

Through one of his outside breedings, to Jipsey Allen, Gay Mac sired Gay Jipsey 06753, who was to be the dam of Steve Reeves' stallion, King's Ransome 13413, and Lady Gay 08216, dam of El Dorado King, California Lady, California Jypsey, Miss California, California Prince – all many times winners at halter. Viking Coronado (El Dorado King x Blossom's Lass), a young park saddle stallion with three crosses to Gay Mac through his sire and dam, shows a marked resemblance to that stallion. In the Pacific Northwest, Gay Mac daughters provided more show winners – Sandea, being the dam of Beckridge Sunfield, Sandora Field and Sanson Field. Laurinda was the dam of Elizabeth Equals' chestnut gelding Gay Equitation and the Canadian mare My Gay Pixie. Gay Mac descendants have exhibited winning ways down through the generations. Still, one must wonder how much more Morgan history he might have written had the handsome, intensely bred Gay Mac been granted more extensive use at the stud.

Monte L. 8423 *Major R.M. (Romanesque x Dorothy D.H.) x Jumina (Jubilee King x Allana)*

Copper chestnut with small star, left hind pastern white, 15.1 hands, 1100 pounds. Bred by Mr. and Mrs. James M. Lemon, foaled March 23, 1941 at Sheridan, Wyoming. Sold as a yearling to Mrs. George Suplee, Wheatland, Wyoming. The Suplees kept one of his sons, and sold Monte L. in January 1946 to J. C. Jackson, Harrison, Montana, who used him at stud that year. In February, 1947, he was purchased by T. R. and Frieda Rex, and taken to Southern California, where he was bred to four mares: Lana and DeNette, owned by the Rexes, E. W. Roberts' Lucyayr, and Maryellen Roden's Dolly S.

Monte L.'s first California foal crop included a real winner – the famous Rex's Major Monte 9996 (dam Lana) – as well as Rex's Don-Nette, Black Monte and Ramona Redwing.

Monte L. 8423. Photo courtesy of NMMH.

Monte L. only stayed in California for seven years, during which time he sired twenty-nine foals: eighteen colts and eleven fillies. Four of his offspring went to Hawaii; one son, Le Monte, went to Washington, and later to Alaska. He was the sire of Lady Monte, a bay mare owned in British Columbia. One Monte L. daughter, Monte Gay 08696, sold young to Vermont, and was sold again to Michigan in 1960, where she and her daughters became the dams of many of the Pinehaven Morgans. Monte Gay was still producing foals in the early '70s.

T. R. Rex rode Monte L. in parades, and in groups with other stallions and mares, and he was always well-mannered. His foals were said to bear a striking resemblance to him in size, manner and conformation. At halter Monte L. did very well. In 1947 he won three championships and four blues. The next year he was Grand Champion Stallion at the Riverside County Fair at Indio, and Grand Champion Stallion at the San Diego National Horse Show at Del Mar. He was in the ribbons in a class of thirty stallions at the Los Angeles County Spring Fair. He placed high in the ribbons at a half dozen big Southern California horse shows in 1949. Two of his yearlings were also shown that year. Rex's Don-Nette was third, yearling mares, at Del Mar and Indio. Rex's Major Monte captured the blue for yearling stallions at the Hemet National Horse Show, San Diego National Horse Show at Del Mar, Riverside County Fair, and the San Fernando Valley Fair. "Major Monte" kept right on winning. Through 1957 he had won thirty-five blues out of forty times shown.

Monte L. was bred along blue ribbon lines. His dam, Jumina, was a Brunk mare, by Jubilee King, out of an Allen King daughter. His sire, Major R. M., traced to General Gates 666 through both his sire and dam. Major R. M., a fine looking stallion of great power, was the epitome of Morgan versatility. Bred by Elmer Brown of Kansas, he went to Wyoming as a yearling, where he was owned by Mr. and Mrs. Lemon until purchased in 1945 by Joe and William Maycock, Gillette, Wyoming. Major R. M. stood 15.1 hands and weighed 1175 pounds. He was a top working horse in competition against all breeds, with wins at halter, calf roping, team tying, stake turning, parade, novelty racing, steer jerking, western pleasure, and as a rodeo pick-up horse. Having made quite a name for himself in Wyoming, he attracted the attention of J. C. Jackson, who bought him in 1950 and took him to Harrison, Montana, where the horse was to be used extensively at stud. Just a year later, though, Major R. M. had the great misfortune to get a leg so badly tangled in a fence that he had to be destroyed.

Mr. and Mrs. Rex raised eight foals from Monte L. After the death of Mr. Rex his widow married Frank Waer, and the Waers raised four more Monte L. foals before selling him to Mr. and Mrs. E. W. Roberts, of Hi Pass, California, who bred fourteen Monte L. foals in all.

A son, Waer's Black Rascal, sired Hedlite's Mickey Waer 11361, a well-known Oregon sire, owned by Mr. and Mrs. Howard Splane of Applegate. The Splanes also own Midnight Black Joy (dam: Linn's Black Beauty, by Monte L.) and Midnight Jubilee, by Black Monte, by Monte L. Linn's Black Beauty is also the dam of Dapper Dinah, Gimma, Yankee Melody, Dapper Dante and other very good California Morgans. Waer's Cameo, Waer's Polly D. and the outstanding Waer's Lady Be Good are full sisters by Rex's Major Monte (Monte L. x Lana), out of Waer's Miss Moffett (Monte L. x Gontola).

In 1953 Mr. and Mrs. Roberts sold Monte L. to the Deseret Livestock Company of Salt Lake, and in 1957 he became the property of Fred B. Shepherd of Morgan, Utah. Although his California sojourn was fairly brief, his contribution to the breed here was great. His descendants can be found today through the state, the Pacific Northwest, the Inter Mountain region, Michigan, and even in New England. He was a fine individual, and a sire of note.

The Morgan Horse in California, 1849 – 1959
1975

The Morgan Horse is no "Johnny-come-lately" to California and the West. Morgan hoofbeats have echoed the length and breadth of the state since 1849. Except for a brief hiatus around the turn of the century, the breed's California residence has been continuous. The first Morgan stallion to arrive was a true pioneer - a '49er. He crossed the plains with a wagon train of gold seekers; helped a team of oxen haul a heavy wagon up over the Sierras and down into the mining camp called Hang-town; toiled and drudged in the streets of the infant but burgeoning city of Sacramento – unsung, but high of courage. Then came the halcyon days, when he was taken out of work harness, pampered and stabled, hitched to a racing cart, applauded and acclaimed as he won many mile heats and races at the pace on the kite or egg-shaped tracks of the day.

His name was St. Clair 48. His progeny numbered nearly seven hundred, including many of the fastest, most noted trotters, pacers, sires and broodmares of the age. His death in a stable fire in 1864 was lamentable enough to rate him a eulogy in the *Sacramento Union*. His grandson, Occident, was the first horse in racing history to trot a mile in under 2:17, and he set a new world record by doing so – just one of many records set by descendants of St. Clair.

Burgess' Sherman Morgan 843 reached Sacramento in 1850. This two-year-old gray grandson of Sherman Morgan 5 set the tone for those who followed, for he won the blue in every fair he was exhibited in. Morgan stallions swept the show rings of the 1850s and '60s, garnering awards against all comers. They were the apples of their owners' eyes, and their owners, by and large, were men whose names are familiar in the pages of California history: William Chapman Ralston, Darius Ogden Mills, James Ben Ali Haggin, A.B. Spreckels, Ansel Ives Easton, and many others of lesser wealth and smaller fame.

By 1889 at least a hundred well-bred Morgan stallions and a number of mares had been brought to California. A high percentage of them were offspring or descendants of Black Hawk 20. The fabulous little chestnut mare, Lou Dillon, was a granddaughter of Fly, whose sire and dam were both by Black Hawk. Fly and her full sister Gypsy came by the overland trail to San Francisco in 1872. Fly was owned by the Santa Rosa Stock Farm, one of the largest stud farms ever established in the state. Bred to the Standardbred Milton Medium (4782), Fly produced Lou Milton, dam of Lou Dillon, the first horse in history to trot a mile in less than two minutes, with a world record of 1:58½ in 1903. She was purchased for $12,500.00 two years later by Cornelius K.G. Billings, a New York multimillionaire.

Lou Dillon is typical of what became of Morgan blood in the last decades of the 19th century. There had been many Morgan breeders in the early days – J. G. McCracken in Sacramento, Ansel Easton and his Black Hawk Ranch in San Mateo County, Gen. John Bidwell at Chico, Leland Stanford at Palo Alto, and others. Californians were a strange breed, though, always looking for the new excitement, the new challenge. Change was always the order of the day, and change to Western breeders meant embracing the new, swift Standard-breds, many of which already had Morgan antecedents. As the old purebreds succumbed to age or accident, their progeny and descendants were swallowed up in the breeding programs of the new speed-seekers. You'll find their names in innumerable pedigrees in the old *Wallace's Trotting and Pacing Yearbooks* (the author has tracked down nearly eight hundred California Morgan/Standardbred crosses in them), but with one tenuous exception you can't trace them back from modern Morgan pedigrees. Except for the occasional family pet, like the mare Ed Roberts' family brought with them by rail in 1909, pure Morgan imports had ceased by about 1890, and the Golden West was not to see their like again for thirty years.

Before we can re-introduce the Morgan, we must go to Texas where one man, Richard Sellman, was diligently working to preserve the old time Morgan. Sellman was a wealthy Marylander who moved to Rochelle, Texas in the late 1800s, and founded the 40,000-acre Mountain Vale Ranch. The ranch held thousands of cattle and sheep, and soon became noted throughout the country for its excellent Morgan Horses.

Sellman deplored the rage for cross-breeding, and he wanted to save the distinctive, typey pure-bred Morgan at its best. His ideal was Hale's Green Mountain Morgan 42, and most of the stallions he purchased met that standard. His purchases were Major Gordon 4924, Major Antoine 4776, Gold Medal 4847, The Admiral 4871, Headlight Morgan 4683 and Red Oak 5249. Sellman considered Major Antoine to be the best broodmare sire ever used on the ranch. His daughters had excellent breed type, fantastic dispositions, and were especially good in the legs and feet, and they passed these characteristics on through their offspring.

Major Antoine, Gold Medal, The Admiral and Red Oak traced tail-male to Sherman Morgan 5. Major Gordon and Headlight Morgan went to Woodbury Morgan 7. Major Gordon had very fine action, was stylish and large – sixteen hands, 1260 lbs. The Admiral, by Jubilee de Jarnette, combined beauty, speed, soundness and development. Major Antoine and Gold Medal were three-quarter brothers, sons of a fine show stallion, Meteor Jr., out of daughters of a noted trotting sire. Red Oak, a show-winning, very popular stallion from Vermont, was by General Gates. Headlight Morgan was one of the finest stallions of any era. Handsome, well-muscled and powerful, possessed of an excellent disposition, and just eight generations removed from Justin Morgan 1, he was awarded a silver trophy in 1900 by the Morgan Horse Club of America, as the best living representative of the original Morgan type. He was Grand Champion Stallion at the Kansas State Fair seven times.

Those were Richard Sellman's breeding stallions, and this was his breeding program: Sellman used many sons of his six major stallions later in his breeding program, and did purchase a few other studs. He grouped mares into family units. In the first half of the program, daughters of Major Gordon were bred to Major Antoine, The Admiral and Gold Medal. The Admiral was used on the Major Antoine mares. Sellman crossed some of The Admiral's daughters back to him or to one of his sons, but most of them were bred to Headlight Morgan. Still later he bred mares by Headlight Morgan to Red Oak and his sons, and so on. Over the years an easily distinguished "Sellman type" of Morgan was developed. The Headlight Morgans were especially distinctive, and over sixty years later it was said that "Uncle Dick" Sellman would still recognize them.

In all, Sellman registered 689 Morgans. In the period 1905-1925, he had foals from 273 broodmares. He liked to sell mares in their family units, and preferred to select a stallion to accompany them. The first Californian to import Sellman stock was Reginald Parsons, who bought Baldie's Boy, by Headlight Morgan, in May 1920 and welcomed a carload of mares that December at his beautiful Mountcrest Ranch near Hilt, in Northern California. Five of the mares were in foal to Joe Bailey, a Headlight Morgan son, and two carried foals by Dot, by Morgan Chief. Three colts and four fillies came in the spring, and one of the Joe Bailey colts was Mountcrest Sellman, whose ongoing influence on the breed deserves special note.

Parsons' business interests claimed most of his time within a few years, and by 1927 he had sold most of his Morgans to Northern California and Southern Oregon people. He kept several horses for ranch use, and maintained Mountcrest Ranch for many years after.

One of the mares that stayed in California was Balkitty 04437 (Baldie's Boy x Kitty E. by The Admiral). She was purchased by Joe Silva 1926 as a three-year-old. Silva lived about thirteen miles northeast of Ager on the old Beswick Road in Siskiyou County. Balkitty was still quite attractive when she was old, and Silva registered two foals she had in her twenties: Copco Joe, by King Shenandoah, and Copco Silva, by North Fork. Byron White, who also lived on the Beswick Road, closer to Ager, later owned the two colts.

North Fork 8082 was a marvelous horse, a picture Morgan. Chestnut, medium-sized, proud and handsome, his wavy forelock hung to his nostrils. He'd pose, head high, looking through that fall of mane to the far beyond. Put foot in the stirrup though, and be prepared to move out – North Fork was a working cowhorse, and he loved his work. He was by Don Juan, out of Roverta. His breeding was Government, Sellman and Brunk. Bred by J. Sheldon Potter, he was purchased in 1939 by Schultz, Kuck & Schultz, of Yreka. Young J. D. "Jiggs" Kuck had started the saddle stock movement in the northern county when he decided that registered Morgans could work his father's Herefords in timber and rimrock as well or better than cold bloods could. The Kuck Ranch, founded in 1860, had five thousand fenced acres and a thousand-acre leased range on top of Willow Creek Mountain, northeast of Montague. The ranch carried five hundred head of cattle. Jiggs bought North Fork and two mares from Roland Hill - Oretia A., by Silver Ranger, and Tabette, by Querido. Their third mare was Georgette, by Mountcrest Sellman, obtained from Reginald Parsons. The three mares gave them nineteen foals, by North Fork, and later by Ryder, a Sonfield son obtained from Hill in 1944. Within a decade from their small start, the Kuck Ranch registered twenty-nine foals, most using the prefix "Siskiyou," from the three mares, their daughters and a North Fork mare purchased from her breeder. Jiggs' Morgans got small-boned, heavily muscled attractive foals, agile as mountain goats from being raised among brush, timber and lava rock. They worked cattle over the lava beds with no hesitation, and showed natural "cow savvy." Neighboring ranchers were quick to buy up Kuck & Schultz Morgans, and to breed their best grade mares to North Fork. E. R. "Ed" Titus, for example, was not a Morgan breeder, but the best working horses on his 1,200-plus acre Cold Creek Ranch on Beswick Road out of Ager were the ones with Morgan blood. And when he had a big Hereford roundup and long cattle drive to take to the railhead at Ager, he borrowed North Fork to ride as he headed the operation.

Cattle raising on a large scale and Morgan horses were going together all over the state. That in fact was the reason for the Morgan revival in California. In 1944 R. E. Spence said in an article on the Morgan Horse in the West, "Wherever you find people with time and money on their hands, there you will usually find the greatest improvement in livestock, especially horses and cattle; for these people want the best, have the money to buy what they want, and the time to experiment and improve. For this reason the Californians have done much, and it is notable that they have taken strongly to the Morgan Horse." The reasons were clearly stated by their owners. Cattle ranchers preferred Morgans for their ability to take and keep a rein, their level-headed temperament, balanced quarters, natural headset and durability. J. Sheldon Potter said the prime reason for his Morgan breeding operation had been the impossibility of buying good stock horses suitable for the conditions demanded by his ranch near Merced. Sid Forsyth Spencer raised Morgans for use on her

Arroyo Grande cattle ranch. Mary Smith of Camarillo also bred Morgans for ranch use, as did Dr. C. C. Reed and E. W. Roberts. Vail & Vickers of Los Angeles County purchased the Morgan stallion Mahan Field 9297 to breed to their range mares, for producing cow horses for their extensive Santa Rosa Island Ranch, where they carried over ten thousand cattle. Red Flash was bred to grade Thoroughbred-type ranch mares, too, for a number of years. William Randolph Hearst maintained a large stable of saddle mounts for the pleasure of his guests at San Simeon, but also used horses, including Morgans, on his extensive ranching properties in California and Mexico. Roland Hill, the dean of Morgan breeders in the West, and largest breeder in the United States, used registered Morgans in his far-flung Horseshoe Cattle Company operations. Mares were not broke to ride; they had to prove themselves as producers of superior "using" horses. Hill's ranch near Elko, Nevada, used about a hundred purebred Morgan geldings. One visitor who went on spring roundup at the ranch noted that there were eight Morgans with one wagon outfit. In two months of work, he said, there was not one "bronc for breakfast" incident in the whole remuda.

Out of this need for good working horses by men who liked to go to a horse show and bring back ribbons too, there developed a class of Morgans so strongly bred that their type and talents are still evident in show Morgans of today. Star-Vue Cassiopeia 017508 is an excellent example. Her pedigree reads "California" all the way. She has three crosses to Monte L., two to Mountcrest Sellman, and one each to Red Vermont, Querido and Blackhaux. "Cassiopeia" captured the Western Pleasure Championship and Ladies' Western Pleasure Championship, and was Reserve Champion in Amateur Western Pleasure at the 1973 Grand National Morgan Horse Show. Bueno Mac 19181, 1974 Grand National Reserve Champion Stock Horse, is another true example of the "old" California breeding. He goes to Sonfield, Sundown Morgan, Pat Allen, twice to Gay Mac, and three times to Querido.

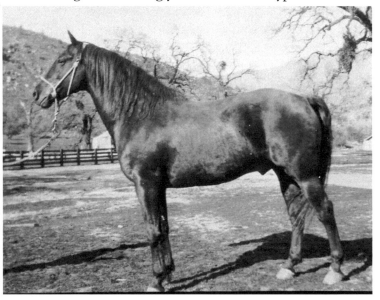

Querido 7370 (Bennington x Artemisia) sired 156 Morgans. He was owned between 1924 and 1937 by Roland G. Hill, who then sold him to parties in Hawaii. Querido was noted as a great broodmare sire. Photo courtesy of NMMH.

The three biggest Morgan breeders of the earlier period were Roland Hill, E. W. Roberts and William Randolph Hearst. Between them these three made California the largest Morgan breeding state in the Union. Together they had registered 898 foals. Roland Hill was the biggest breeder of all, with 530 registrations of his own. Lumping together the Hill family and Horseshoe Cattle Company registrations with the original mares and stallions Roland purchased, you come up with six hundred Morgans.

Hill had imported five stallions in the 1920s and '30s: Redwood Morgan 7217 (1922, from Sellman in Texas), Pongee Morgan 7427 (1925, from J. C. Brunk, Illinois), who was later injured and had to be destroyed; Querido 7370 (1924, from U.S. Morgan Horse Farm, Vermont); Winchester 7683 (1930, U.S. Morgan Horse Farm); and El Cortez 8076 (1937, Elmer Brown, Kansas). He later owned Sparbeau 7734, sent out to California about 1934 to another owner, from Brown in Kansas. In the earlier part of his breeding program he tried sixteen different stallions. His foundation mares came mostly from Richard Sellman in the early 1920s, and later he obtained mares from Brown and Brunk. Hill's last great import was Sonfield 7952.

Edward W. Roberts was second, with 240 registrations. He had a 160-acre ranch at the top of the Tecate Divide at Hi Pass, near San Diego. His first sire was Monterey 7476, by Mansfield, who got nineteen foals in California. In 1946 Roberts had three stallions, forty-two broodmares and many two-year-olds and yearlings at the ranch. The younger stallions were Blackman and Governor Pico, both out of the well-known dam, Gojea. Roberts had long familiarity with the breed. His family had brought a favorite Morgan to California with them in 1909. He selected his breeding stock with considerable care. In 1946 he purchased the entire stud of Charles F. Ayer in Colorado. He crossed Linsley mares on Redman, and Blackman on Querido mares. By 1951 Roberts had about two hundred head of Morgans. Other Roberts mares came from Elmer Brown, Roland Hill, W. R. Hearst and Dr. C. C. Reed. The mare band traced mainly to Headlight Morgan, Red Oak and the General Gates line. Roberts' goal was to establish an individual strain, established on the selection of individuals, through successive generations, from the best of his breeding. He bred only pedigreed stock of fashionable background, culled the poorer ones to sell as "grades," and his rigid program has benefited a lot of present day Morgan breeders.

William R. Hearst registered one hundred Morgan foals. His broodmares were obtained from Hill and carried the old Sellman breeding. His stallions were Mountcrest Sellman, Uhlan and Hacienda Chief. From Uhlan 7564 (Bennington x Poinsetta) descended the fine line of Katrilan – Katrilan Prince, Trilson, Dapper Dan and Muscle Man, as well as a number of other very good Morgans. Hearst was also responsible, through the urging of his stable manager, Jack Sturm, for the Morab breed's inception. Hearst registered twenty of these half-Morgan, half-Arabian foals between 1933-1941. The outstanding sire Antman x-8318, by Mountcrest Sellman, was one of them. Hearst used the finest Arabian bloodlines in America to produce these "Morabs," and the goal was to breed an extremely short-coupled, compact horse, of fine appearance, hardiness and good temperament. According to Jack Sturm, these Morabs were broke to ride, drive and jump, and were shown successfully in all three categories, some being driven in pairs.

Rex's Major Monte 9996 (Monte L. x Lana), a very popular sire and show horse, bred and raised by Frank and Frieda Waer. Photo courtesy of NMMH.

Other breeders of some size in this period were J. Sheldon Potter (61), Dr. C. C. Reed (59) and Merle Little (46). Sid Forsyth Spencer and her late husband together had fifty registrations through 1959. Coming along somewhat later and building fast were W. T. Carter, Millard Ulch, the J. Clark Bromileys and Frank and Frieda Waer, each utilizing different lines of California sires, and building identifiable breeding programs of their own. One must at least also mention the names of the Davis Breeding Farm, Dr. Ina Richter's Kedron Farm, Warren Halliday, Dean Witter, F. A. and Nellie Fickert, Mary Smith and August

Schmidt, each of whom had registered over twenty foals prior to 1960, all of whom had some impact on the California Morgan of today.

Let's tip our hats to the Morgan stallions who were the "Pioneers" in the 1920s: Baldie's Boy (1920), Raven Chief and Redwood Morgan (1922), all from Texas, Querido (1924) from Vermont, Pongee Morgan (1925) from Illinois, and Eprus (1927) from Washington.

Some mention has been made here of Morgan contributions to other breeds – Arabians, Standardbreds and Palominos. Ken Carmen and Choice Master were also found in Palomino pedigrees, and the Pongee Morgan daughter, Sunbeam Maid 04525 was not only dam of the Palominos, Princess Rosalita (7105 PHBA) and Sunshine Princess (7106 PHBA) but of the registered Quarter Horse mare Rocket (22,298 AQHA). In fact, in the period from 1940 to the mid-1950s over seventy registered Quarter Horse foals born in California carried Morgan blood to a greater or lesser degree. All this Morgan ancestry was carried through maternal and paternal mare lines in the AQHA pedigrees. Several of the mares were registered Morgans: Sunbeam Maid, Kitty Pongee 04529, Helen Field 06205, Katrina Field 07049, Emily G. Field 06204, and Tabie Field 06002. Some were "grade" mares sired by registered Morgans: Red Vermont 7893, Red Wings 7965, Sparbeau 7734, Gold Dollar 8006, Don Juan 7623, Choice Master 7810 and others. A number of the mares descended from the Sellman stallions Headlight Morgan and Bobbie Burns 6180. Quite a few were identified by breed only ("Morgan mare" or "by Morgan Horse"). Sonfield was the maternal grandsire of four Quarter Horse fillies – Helen May (35,102), Lady Katrina (35,103), Lucky Emily (35,104) and Tabie Traveler (35,105) - foaled in 1950 at Rocklin, California, bred and registered by Roland Hill's Horseshoe Cattle Company.

Last of all, that one little link between the California Morgans of the 19th and 20th centuries comes to us through the full sisters Dulcet x-05342 and Laydee x-05689. Their second dam was a chestnut mare with four white stockings, bred by James Ben Ali Haggin, and used on the Jesse D. Carr and J. B. Haggin Kern County ranch. The mare was said to be part Morgan, and undoubtedly was. Carr owned the fine Morgan stallion Redfield's Vermont 121, and raised stock from him beginning in 1871. Vermont's sire was a grandson of Black Hawk 20. Haggin owned Bismarck 1864, a grandson of Black Hawk 20, and bred Morgan stock. A number of Carr & Haggin mares were sired by one or the other of these stallions, and used either at Salinas, Sacramento or in Kern County. It is almost certain then, that Dulcet and Laydee's granddam was a not-too distant California descendant of the Black Hawk family.

Government Bloodlines . . .
Their Influence on California Morgans
1975

When interest in the Morgan Horse was revived in the Far West in the early 1920s, Californians turned to two major sources for the type of horse they needed. The first was Richard Sellman's Mountain Vale Ranch in Texas; the second was the U.S. Government Morgan Horse Farm in Middlebury, Vermont. From these two places – and from other breeders carrying the same bloodlines – Californians brought to the state many Morgans that were descended almost exclusively from General Gates 666. A secondary male line was that of Troubadour of Willowmoor 6459.

Roland Hill started it in 1924, with the purchase of eleven Sellman mares that were daughters of Red Oak 5249 (General Gates x Marguerite 01635). These mares, Redoasy 04213, Roaka 04156, Robona 04194, Roboss 04179, Robsart 04180, Roda 04154, Rodota 04815, Rogata 04189, Rokit 04177, Rotila 04160, and Red Oak Lu 04316, played an important part not only in Hill's breeding program, but also in the programs of many other Californians who later purchased breeding stock from him.

Red Oak pictured in 1914 in Middlebury, Vermont.
Photo courtesy of the National Museum of the Morgan Horse.

In the '30s Hill bought two young Red Oak grandsons in Kansas and used both as sires. They were double-bred to General Gates through their sire, Romanesque 7297, and through their dams, who were both by Linsley 7233, by General Gates. These two colts, Joaquin Morgan 7947 and El Cortez 8076, were bred by Elmer Brown at Halstead, Kansas, as was another Hill purchase, Sparbeau 7734, whose sire was Linsley.

Senor Morgan 8647, foaled in Arizona in 1942, and owned by Merle Little, was out of the mare Bonnie Sue 05436 whose sire was by Linsley, dam by Romanesque, and second dam also by Linsley.

Monte L. 8423 (Major R. M. x Jumina) was another Western stallion linked to Red Oak through his sire, a son of Romanesque. Monte L. was in California from 1947-1953, under successive ownership of T. R. Rex, Mr. and Mrs. Frank Waer and E. W. Roberts.

Four other stallions Roland Hill brought West traced to General Gates through the Bennington line. He purchased Querido 7370 (Bennington x Artemesia) from The Morgan Horse Farm as a yearling in 1924. Winchester 7683, by Mansfield, out of Narissa, by Troubadour of Willowmoor, was also purchased as a yearling in 1930. Hill's third stallion from this line was Sonfield 7952, by Mansfield, out of another Troubadour of Willowmoor daughter, the great mare Quietude.

The last of the quartet was Lippitt Morman 8211 (Mansfield x Lippitt Kate Moro), famed as the first stallion ever to win the Vermont 100-Mile Trail Ride. Hill was impressed by Lippitt Mor-

Senor Morgan, winning stallion for Merle Little in the 1940s. Photo courtesy of NMMH.

man's heavyweight win in 1945 and sweepstakes win in 1946, and purchased the horse in February 1947. Hill only bred two mares to "Morman" and sold him to Merle Little in 1948. Under Little's ownership this full brother to Lippitt Mandate 8331 had a fine career in the show ring, at the stud and as a Rose Parade entry.

Two other double-bred General Gates line stallions that came to California were Gay Mac 7988 and Monterey 7475. Gay Mac (Mansfield x Dewdrop, by General Gates) was foaled at The Morgan Horse Farm at Weybridge, Vermont in 1936. Dr. Clarence C. Reed purchased him in 1942 as herd sire and personal mount at Reed's large San Clemente cattle ranch.

Monterey was also by Mansfield. His dam, Scotanna, was by Scotland, a very elegant trotting stallion sired by General Gates. Monterey was foaled in Connecticut in 1925, and owned by The Farm. He had two owners in Montana before Kathleen M. Daly brought him to California in 1944. She sold him two years later to Mr. and Mrs. E. W. Roberts, Hi Pass, California.

Another Morgan stallion of major importance to the breed in California was Uhlan 7564 (Bennington x Poinsetta, by Troubadour of Willowmoor). Foaled at The Morgan Horse Farm in 1927, Uhlan was purchased by William Randolph Hearst, San Simeon, in 1930, who kept the horse for seven years. Uhlan even found his way into early Texas Quarter Horse pedigrees, through his half-Arab daughters from Hearst's ranch in Mexico. He was later owned in Nevada.

The Government Remount Service stallion Revere 7422 (Mansfield x Folly, by Bennington) sired a dozen or more Morgans in northeastern California in the 1940s and left sons to carry on for him in that region.

The vast majority of Morgans foaled in California from the late 1920s through the 1950s and even later traced to one of the above stallions in the male line, and had several of the others (plus a Red Oak mare or two) in their five-generation pedigrees.

As an example, the typical "California" pedigree

Gay Mac, sire of many champions.
Photo courtesy of the National Museum of the Morgan Horse.

of Blossom's Lass 013320, owned by Viking Morgan Ranch in Modesto, has three crosses to Querido, two to Sonfield and one each to Uhlan, Joaquin Morgan, Gay Mac, Red Oak and Troubadour of Willowmoor.

There were two other stallions that also carried Government lines. Eprus 7557 came to California in 1927. His dam, Pomona 04230, was by Troubadour of Willowmoor, out of Helen 01014 by General Gates. General Ben 7733, bred by Elmer Brown, was brought to California from Kansas in 1938 by Leila Mae Davis. He was by the Bennington son Rockwood 7423, whose dam was Carolyn 02868, and second dam by Borden's Ethan Allen 3rd 3987.

Even the many descendants of Headlight Morgan 4683 that came to California in the twenties can claim a kinship to "Government" lines, since his sire, Peter's Ethan Allen 2nd 406 was the paternal grandsire and maternal great-grandsire of the great old broodmare Artemesia 02731.

All of the above Government line families helped to mold the West Coast Morgan, as we know it today, and each of the sire lines made its own distinctive contribution.

Of the Red Oak daughters, three come immediately to mind: Rodota, Roboss and Red Oak Lu. Bred to Pongee Morgan, Rodota produced Red Dot 04577, who became the dam of Redman 8056, one of the best stallions ever bred in the state. A show champion and model class winner, he also shone as a sire, giving us the great stallion Blackman 8622, as well as Red Gates 8954, and Billy Rebel 11904, who carries on the male line. Among his best daughters were Etna 06593, dam of Keystone's Rome Beauty 010290; Wenonah 09860, one of Mrs. Sid Spencer's good mares; Gertrude Mae 09794, broodmare and riding horse for years at "Echo Hills," home of Dr. and Mrs. H. P. Boyd of San Rafael; and Gayler K. 06749, dam of Miss Tayler 08201, one of the foundation mares for the late W. A. Lorenzen's "Impala" Morgans. Miss Tayler was the dam of Impala Claudia 011319 and Impala Nobleman 13626 – both of them helped Mr. Lorenzen come home from the fairs with a hat full of ribbons many times. Blackman contributed many fine broodmares to the California scene: Ann Bregman 08461, Jeanne Allen 08211, Lois Morgan 08206, Luccia 07700, Margaret Collins 08459, Nell Knox 07702, Slower Nell 08200 and Elizabeth Blackwell 06796 among them. Bikini 9366, Blackman Allen 10147, Harold Roberts 10328, and Baacamanto 9980, sire of the great roadster Welmore Zorro 15104, owned by the Schlehubers of Alpine, California, were also Blackman's get.

Roboss, by Red Oak, was the dam of Bessie Ro 04978, whose two daughters, Bess Gates 06482 and Flika 06187, produced the noted stallions Dapper Dan 10696 and Muscle Man 10697.

Red Oak Lu had sixteen foals. One was Brown Knox Lu 06476, whose daughter Lulin 07968 was the dam of Dannie Lu 11277, a popular central California sire in the '50s. Another daughter, Lula Lee 04704, produced Starlight Lu 05250, dam of Eco Lujo 11715 (sire of Eco Jubilo 13056), Echohaux 11308, Eco Lucida 011285, and others, bred by the H. P. Boyds. A third daughter was El Lu 05847, whose son El Don 9239 is the sire of the nice mares Donna Ines 013975 and Donna Lee 013092, owned by Dianna Foit of Escalon.

The champion stallion, Monterey. Photo courtesy of NMMH.

Not all fifteen of the General Gates line stallions mentioned earlier were destined to become great California breeding sires. Eprus, Winchester and Senor Morgan only had a handful of foals, and left no outstanding sons to carry on for them. Joaquin Morgan and El Cortez are best remembered for their daughters. General Ben had very limited use in the stud. Monterey got eighteen foals between 1945-1949 – he was twenty-four years old when the last three arrived. Monterey is also best remembered for his daughters in California – he had some good ones, and they were well-placed. Belle Gales 07935 and Monterey Belle 07120 were purchased by F. O. Davis and taken to Vermont in 1956. There, Belle Gales was the dam of Windcrest Belle 010100 and Windcrest Gigi 010591, both by Upwey Ben Don. Monterey Belle produced Windcrest Monterey 11924 and Fairlea Don Juan 13084, a fine show gelding, both by Upwey Ben Don. Monterey Belle was sold to New Mexico in 1959, and was later owned by Robert Morgan of Red Fox Stables, Gilroy, California, for whom she produced Triton Mystique 015202. Another good Monterey daughter was Jean Mary 07697, dam of Ramona Brave 12033, Ramona Dawn 01826 and several others for Richard Mears in Southern California. She also went to Red Fox Stables, where she produced Triton Genie 015207.

Lippitt Morman sired thirty-seven foals during the 1950s, and many of them gained repute in the show rings of Southern California, where they excelled in all kinds of events. One of his sons, Little Joe Morgan 11369, was a top competitive trail ride horse, much in the manner of his noted sire. Lippitt Morman, too, is well-remembered for his very good daughters – Coffey Choice, Mornaquin, Morman's Red Lady and Kedron Beatrice, to name a few.

Monte L. left good sons and daughters both to carry on his line in California and the Pacific Northwest. The beautiful Rex's Major Monte 9996 was the blue ribbon prize in Monte L's first California foal crop. He could hardly have done better. Owned by Frank and Frieda Waer, Orange, California, Rex's Major Monte has had an illustrious career in the show ring, and has sired many outstanding halter and performance horses. The Oregon stallion Hedlite's Mickey Waer 11361 is Monte L's grandson, Waer's Lady Be Good a granddaughter. Monte Gay 08696 is the dam of a number of "Pinehaven" Morgans in Michigan. There are Monte L. descendants in New England, Alaska and Canada, too.

Sparbeau got a lot of fillies, and only seven colts in the 1930s. Three of his sons carried on his male line from Linsley. The Hunewill family of Bridgeport built their large band of Morgans on a foundation of Dude Spar 8227 and his sons crossed on mares by Joaquin Morgan and Sonfield. Many Westerners will find "Spar" horses in their Morgan pedigrees, either through Dude Spar, Danspar 8161 or his son Benbeau (whose dam was Laura Kali by Querido), Francisco 8396, herd sire for J. Sheldon Potter in the '40s, or the many fine Sparbeau mares.

Revere stood for service to Northern California and Western Nevada mares in the 1940s. He has a number of descendants in the West, many by Ringling's Revere 8313, whose dam was also by Revere. Oscar Burrough's Windswept Ranch at Orland had the mares Reverie 06702 (Revere x Trixie Spar), Elm 08656 and Rie 09370, both by Ringling's Revere, out of Roelm Morgan (Kenelm Morgan x Roboss) in his broodmare band some years ago. Roelm Morgan was by Kenelm Morgan out of Roboss. Millard Ulch of Susanville used a lot of Revere stock in his breeding program. Forrest Jones of Termo had many Revere mares, and his stallion Stormy H. 11753 was by Sunshine R. 8315 (Revere x Golden Revere).

Probably the best present day line from Revere came through his son Winnemucca 8312, sire of Duke 10183. Duke's claim to fame and insurance for the Revere clan of Morgans was his son California King 11383, sire of a whole string of show quality Morgans, including Mr. America 12938, owned by Roy and Janie Coats of Delhi. In still another line the continuity of the Revere strain is insured - again beginning with Ringling's Revere, down through his son General Revere 10527 to Kandy King 11307, the sire of King P. 12280, a very good horse owned by Don and Joyce Straw, Alamar Morgans, Auburn, California.

The Revere line did well in competition. Winnemucca was Reserve Champion Stock Horse at Salt Lake City, Utah, some years ago. At the Lassen County Livestock Show in 1949 eleven Morgans were in the ribbons. Six of them were by Revere, and one by Ringling's Revere. The Reveres took first in every halter class except four-and-over mares, winning six blues, champion stallion, and one second.

In 1930, California millionaire William Randolph Hearst purchased Uhlan, foaled at the U.S. Morgan Horse Farm in 1927. Hearst owned a number of Morgan mares from the Hill ranch. Uhlan's dam, Poinsetta, was the second dam of Marionette, who produced U.S. Menmar. Lightly used at the stud, Uhlan only sired 17 Morgan foals over a ten-year period - seven colts, ten fillies. Actually, he could have gotten by with just one son, Katrilan 8121, to carry on his name, but all of his sons made fine sires in the West. Pico Chief 8046 and The Senator 8042 both sold to livestock companies in Arizona. Jack London 8041, Uhlan-Ro 8134 and Enowe 8606 were sold to California livestock concerns. Piedmont Apache 7915, too, had a cattle company background. His first foal was Sonoma 8141, Phil Morrison's beloved old stallion, sire of many well-known Morgans in the Pacific Northwest.

Hearst kept Katrilan and got twenty-four foals from him. In 1942 Princess Allen 04635 (Querido x Tab) foaled a sharp, dark chestnut colt, which was named Katrilan Prince 8667. Some years later, Katrilan Prince sired a liver chestnut colt called Trilson 9892, thus assuring immortality to his grandsire's line. Poor Trilson only lived for seven years. A thoughtless farrier lost his temper one day and threw a rasp, which punctured Trilson's stomach and caused his death. The loss to the breed is hard to contemplate, for from his little handful of foals he had already sired two future grand champion stallions, get of sire winners and sires extraordinary – Muscle Man 10697 and Dapper Dan 10696, both out of full sisters by Gay Mac 7988.

Mr. and Mrs. J. Clark Bromiley of Winton have always owned Muscle Man. Among his get are the versatile El Mejor 14918, a consistent high point winner, owned by the Philip Piazzas of San Jose; Castle Star Reporter 20569, a grand champion gelding, owned by Barry Leonardini of San Francisco, and Blossom's Lass 013320, a former National Junior Champion Mare (Golden West National, 1965), and dam of Viking Coronado 21054, N.C.M.H.A. 1973 Reserve High Point Park Saddle Horse. The list of Muscle Man get and their winnings is most impressive, both at halter and in performance classes.

Sonfield (Mansfield x Quietude) is pictured here at the age of 25. Photo courtesy of NMMH.

Dapper Dan's record is equally impressive. His daughter, Dapper Dolly 09773, was a natural stock horse, and P.C.H. and J.A. Class "B" Champion before her untimely death. Kelly's Pretty Nino 013963 won kudos as an A.H.S.A. Park Harness Champion. Black Brandy 16963 was top ten in four western pleasure classes at the 1973 Grand National Morgan Horse Show.

The offspring of these two descendants of Uhlan have come out of the ring with ribbons in just about every kind of performance class there is. At the Northern California Morgan Horse Association's big annual All-Morgan Show, Muscle Man won Get of Sire class in 1962, Dapper Dan won it in 1963 and 1964, and at the second Golden West National Morgan Horse Show in 1966 Muscle Man won again, with three beautiful daughters, all liver chestnut, and very much alike.

Querido and Sonfield wrote their own history in the West – Querido with 150 foals, Sonfield with 161 under ownership of Roland Hill. Both gained the reputation of siring broodmares of exceptional quality. And both had fine sons to carry on the male line as well. The use of Sonfield on Querido daughters gave the West many superb Morgans, the mares being especially fine. Alma Sonfield 06713 (Sonfield x Angel B. by Querido) had a great show record in Southern California in the late '40s. Linden Sonfield (x Sallie Ann by Querido) was undefeated at halter for several years. From fourteen shows (to 1949) he had won twelve championships, one first, and was California State Horse Show Grand Champion. An article in the September 1949 issue of *The Morgan Horse* magazine, speaking of Querido and Sonfield, stated, "In halter and performance classes, and in open competition throughout the state, the horses carrying these bloodlines many times have held the championship spot…year after year the get of Sonfield win…"

Querido left a number of sons to continue his line. Don Juan 7632, Master G. 7585, Red Wings 7965 (went to Oregon), Silver Ranger 7813 (went to Texas), Choice Master 7810, Tejon Prince 8105, Pepper 8016, Peerless A. 8017 (sold to Nevada), Master Billie 7998 and Tehachapi Allen 7910 (went to Kansas) being the most important. His many daughters became foundation mares in many breeding programs. North Fork 8082 and Millbrae 7871 were two of Querido's good grandsons.

Sonfield, too, left several good siring sons: Linden Sonfield 8907, Ryder 8712 in Northern California, Rosefield 8568, purchased by the Jackson Ranch in Montana, Sheik F. 8567 and Candy Joe Field 9995. Two Sonfield sons that were bred by Leo Beckley in Washington are now standing in California – Beckridge Sunfield 15944, owned by Woodside Morgans at Olema, and Sonfield's Sammy 13053, owned by Mr. and Mrs. Zola Bauer at Covelo. Sonfield's daughters became the treasures in many California breeders' barns.

Gay Mac, a near photocopy of General Gates, bred in the best of Government lines, was also brought to California for use on a large cattle ranch, "Rancho Capistrano," owned by Dr. Clarence C. Reed of Compton. Dr. Reed purchased several mares, Querido and Sonfield daughters, from Roland Hill, to breed to Gay Mac, and over several years Gay Mac sired sixty foals, the produce of twenty mares, all but three of them owned by Dr. Reed. A few of his sons were sold as stallions, but most of them were gelded for use as cow horses on the 2,600-acre ranch. The Gay Mac daughters made exceptionally fine broodmares. Flika 06187 and Bess Gates 06482 were the dams of Muscle Man and Dapper Dan. Gay Jipsey 06753 produced King's Ransome 13413 and Lady Gay 08216, dam of Eldorado King 13603, Miss California 09547 and several other well-known Central California champions. Gay Berta 06858 spent almost half her life as a producer of registered Quarter Horses before being "rescued" by the Richard Nelsens, then of Atascadero. She won a halter championship at age sixteen, and had a number of good Morgan foals – Bueno Mac, Saranita Ro, Panzarita Ro among them. The Nelsens also owned the Gay Mac son Ro Mac 9409. If you see a "Ro" or a "Mac" Morgan in Missouri these days, chances are it's a descendant of Gay Mac. Others of the Gay Mac line have gone to the Pacific Northwest and British Columbia.

In 1947 Earl Krantz, then with the U.S.D.A., wrote "In the East, U.S. Morgan Horse Farm animals have been successful on the bridle path, in the show ring, in the endurance rides of the early '20s, and now in the trail rides. In the West they are principally using stock horses. The lead that Farm horses have taken in such uses is most impressive." He then speaks of the Linsley, Red Oak, Querido and Sonfield lines in Morgan stock horses of the West. They were all MORGANS, East and West, similarly bred, differently used…

The wonderful thing about Morgans is that they've always been so adaptable…filling whatever the need might be, in their time and place: farmer's helper in a rocky New England clearing; cavalryman's steady steed in a Civil War skirmish; trotting crack for a Sunday sportsman; sleek, pampered carriage horse in a mahogany-lined, silver-fitted, crystal chandelier-lighted stable "down the Peninsula"; carter's drudge; child's companion; show ring peacock; and cowboy's treasure – Morgan Horses have been there, and done it all!

In the years between the two World Wars, when California's vast ranges fed hundreds of thousands of beef cattle, Morgan Horses again fulfilled the needs of their particular time and place. Critical stockmen tried them, and the Morgans were not found wanting. Smart and steady, agile, responsive and enduring - "cow horses" in the truest sense of the term - Morgans could, within a few short years, be found on almost every big cattle spread in the state. Morgan sires were chosen to improve the mixed saddle stock on many Pacific ranches.

Westerners today are justly proud of the "California" pedigrees of their Morgans. Those old stallions, mares and geldings proved themselves in a tough arena, and their blood was just as blue as that of the New England antecedents from which they sprang.

Roland Hill and his California Government Morgans
1975

In his time Roland Hill was called "the Dean of Morgan Horse breeders in the West." It was a title he had certainly earned for a number of reasons. He was one of the first men to bring Morgans back to California in the 20th century, and he created a lot of interest in the breed. Many ranchers started bands of Morgans from Hill's stock. He became an active member and officer in the Morgan Horse Club (as it was then called). And, of course, his own band of Morgans had to be considered not only in terms of quality but of quantity. Hill was the biggest breeder in California – in the West – in the entire country.

To illustrate, Volume V of *The Morgan Horse Register* listed 346 stallions, mares and geldings for California. Of these, 260 were owned by Roland Hill or his Horseshoe Cattle Company. Another 68 were the produce of Hill mares owned by others, and three more were from granddaughters of Hill mares. That's almost 96 percent of all the Volume V California bred or owned Morgans.

The California breeders of this period (1920-1939) who established their programs on Hill mares were William Randolph Hearst, August Schmidt, Duval Williams, J. Sheldon Potter, L. W. Rutledge and Jean Hill. The other two California breeders, Reginald Parsons and Frederick A. Fickert had Morgans who were "kissing cousins" of the Hill stock, since the whole lot had originated with Richard Sellman's Texas Morgans. (In the whole of Volume V there was only one totally unrelated California Morgan, and he had an X-number and an American Saddlebred sire). Carrying this a bit further, of those 346 Morgans, 301 were sired by Hill-owned or bred stallions, or their sons, and 35 more were from related Sellman stock, leaving only ten who didn't share a common heritage – and seven of this last group had top quality Arabian sires (from Hearst's short-lived "Morab" program).

Between 1923-1955, Roland Hill, his brother Russell, daughters Jean and Margaret, and the Horseshoe Cattle Company registered 606 Morgans. Adding in the stallions, colts, mares – some with foals at side – he purchased, the total Hill package exceeds 700 Morgans. Hill-bred Morgans were the produce of 93 broodmares, and were sired by twenty or twenty-one owned stallions, or descendants of owned stallions.

To understand the composition and consequences of the Hill breeding program you need a clear picture of what comprised his foundation stock, which can only lead into an analysis of Richard Sellman's breeding program.

Sellman's breeding plan was so concise and constant that you can almost quote his pedigrees without looking them up.

At the beginning, Sellman had a group of nineteen mares. One was of untraced ancestry; two were by an imported Cleveland Bay stallion, another by a Yorkshire Coach Horse. The rest were purebred or part-Morgans. Sellman bred them all to Major Gordon 4927, a big (16 h., 1300 lbs.), black, stylish and high-stepping stallion by Young Octoroon 1715, out of an untraced mare of some quality. There was a lot of speed behind Major Gordon. Young Octoroon's dam was by old Joe Brown, a son of Davy Crockett 603, of the fast Canadian Dansereau family. Young Octoroon's sire's dam was Brinker's Drennon 607, by Davy Crockett. His grandsire's dam and second dam were by Bulrush Morgan 6. Tail male, Major Gordon went back in eight generations to Justin Morgan through Woodbury.

The next step in Richard Sellman's breeding plan was to breed Major Gordon's daughters to one of his sons of Meteor Jr. 4458, a fine Morgan stallion who had won five county and state fair first premiums, 1897-99. Meteor Jr. traced to Black Hawk 20 through both his sire and dam. Sellman had two of Meteor Jr.'s sons: Major Antoine 4776 and Gold Medal 4847 were ¾ brothers, out

of daughters of General Lee 936, who also went right back to Black Hawk. Major Antoine traced almost entirely to Sherman Morgan 5, while Gold Medal also had a line to Woodbury Morgan 7, through his second dam.

Most of the Major Gordon mares were mated to Major Antoine, the rest to Gold Medal. The mares from that cross in their turn were bred to The Admiral 4871, who was a mix of the Sherman, Woodbury and Bulrush lines. His sire, Jubilee de Jarnette, was a descendant of Black Hawk, tail

The Admiral (photo 1910). Photo courtesy of NMMH.

male, and also through his sire's dam and his dam's sire. The Admiral's dam was a brown mare by Winnebago Chief 263, and his second dam was a chestnut daughter of Monogram 1655. These two stallions both descended from Bulrush Morgan 6 through the Morrill 55 line. The mares in Winnebago Chief's pedigree were mainly from Sherman, though one was a Woodbury granddaughter. The mares in Monogram's papers traced to either Sherman or Bulrush.

By the time The Admiral's daughters were of breeding age, Sellman had a band of uniform, extremely well-bred Morgans on his ranch in Rochelle, Texas. The next stage in the program was to breed these fine mares to another outstanding stallion — one that also went straight back in the male line to Justin Morgan. The sire selected was Headlight Morgan 4683 (Peter's Ethan Allen 2nd 406 x Lady Stratton, by Vermont Morgan 462), who was rich in the blood of old Hale's Green Mountain Morgan 42 on both sides of his pedigree, and had seventeen crosses to Justin Morgan!

A bit later, many of The Admiral's daughters were bred to sons of Headlight Morgan, and Headlight's daughters were mated to the highly regarded stallion Red Oak 5249 (General Gates x Marguerite, by White River Morgan 482), who was a good combination of the old Sherman and Woodbury lines. In over forty years of breeding Morgans, Sellman's program was designed to produce outstanding horses for cattle and ranch work, with a policy always of breeding "the best to the best," using only typey, "old-time" Morgans of the finest family lines.

During 1922 Roland Hill made four purchases of Sellman stock, securing one stallion, sixteen mares, two yearling colts, two foals and a gelding. Six of the mares were in foal to Joe Bailey 7119 (Headlight Morgan x Polly B., by The Admiral). Two of the mares, Jenavive K. 03921 and Sophomore 04071, were by Headlight Morgan, out of daughters of Major Antoine. Alkali 04077 and Camille 04097 were by Alkadaza 6606 (Headlight Morgan x Lulu Antoine by Major Antoine), out of mares by The Admiral. Addy 04083, Angelina 04100 and Texanita 04201 were by Texas Allen 6650 (a grandson of Headlight Morgan) and their dams were by The Admiral. Madcap 04066, Lucia 04073 and Wooddot 04076 were daughters of Woodrow Wilson 6290 (Headlight Morgan x Dot M. by Gold Medal), all three the produce of The Admiral mares. Tab 04214 was by Texas Allen out of Birdie, by Major Antoine. Kitty C. 03306 and Lulu G. 03406 were by Sunny South 6765 (The Admiral x Jewess, by Ethan Allen 3rd 4406), and their dams were also by The Admiral. Lucca 04072 was by Bald Eagle 6250 (Headlight Morgan x Puss, by Gold Medal) out of Bonnie B. by The Admiral. Nancy G. 01898 was by Golden 5691 (Gold Medal x black mare by Major Gordon), out of Nancy Gordon, by Major Gordon.

The last mare in Hill's 1922 purchase was Melissa 03892, whose dam was by Major Gordon. Melissa was sired by another of Sellman's stallions, Morgan Chief 6884, who traced to Winnebago Chief 263.

Sellman's breeding pattern is obvious in all the above pedigrees, and Wooddot's can be used as a typical example. Her sire, Woodrow Wilson, was by Headlight Morgan, out of Dot M., a Gold Medal daughter. Her dam was Dot N., by The Admiral, 2nd dam Dot M. by Gold Medal, 3rd dam by Major Gordon, 4th dam a mare of Morgan type.

To carry on his program Sellman had recommended Redwood Morgan 7217 (Headlight Morgan x Bonne A. by Major Antoine; 2nd dam by Major Gordon) as the right stallion to go with Hill's mares. Roland Hill, feeling this was breeding too close, only used Redwood Morgan on four mares in 1922, and sold him the following spring. It was said Hill later regretted this, as some of his outcross efforts weren't too successful in terms of the kind of horse he wanted to raise. This brings us to why Hill needed horses, and why he selected Morgans in the first place.

Roland Hill was born in 1884 in California's Tehachapi Mountains. It fell to him to take over the family ranch at age sixteen, following the death of his father. Cattle, many of them Mexican, were raised and sold. Roland and his younger brother, Russell, often rode south to participate in rodeos and roundups held at General Truxton Beale's huge El Tejon Rancho. Here the boys learned a great deal about range management and the training required to finish a good reined cow horse.

Surrounded by vast cattle spreads, Roland Hill dreamed big dreams. In 1915 a partnership was formed, called the Tehachapi Land and Cattle Company, operating in Kern County. The company bought land and cattle herds, started a feedlot and fell victim to the 1929 crash. After a few lean years when about all he had left was his band of horses, Hill formed another partnership, and the Horseshoe Cattle Company went into business on 40,000 rented acres, with some 5,000 head of cattle near Chowchilla. After one year on this ranch many of the Morgans came down with sleeping sickness.

The Hill family moved to Gustine about 1938, to an even larger rented ranch, which was sold a few years later, necessitating moves to the Gilroy and Tres Pinos areas.

Tired of fixing up rented properties that were sold out from under them, Hill and his partner purchased the 195,000-acre TS Ranch near Battle Mountain, Nevada. Hill also bought a smaller ranch near Rocklin, California. The California range carried five hundred head of cattle, while eight thousand could be maintained on the Nevada ranch.

A lot of horses were needed to work operations of such magnitude, and the requirements for a good cow horse were pretty specific. Roland Hill liked a "stocky" horse. By that, he meant one that was broad-chested, deep through the heart girth, with well-developed, muscular hindquarters. Strong, dense-boned, clean legs and good hooves were a must. A good cow horse has to be quick and agile, able to work well off his quarters – "supple" and "catty" are descriptive terms. Endurance was required too, to last out a tough day on the trail. Last but not least, a sensible disposition is essential to the good stock horse.

In Hill's own words, "a well-reined Western horse is so well in hand at all times, and at any speed that he can be stopped and turned in his tracks, no matter how fast he is running, with scarcely any pull on the bit. A good rope horse is so well-reined and knows his work so well the rider hardly uses the reins at all. Horse and rider work as one."

In the 1920s Hill hadn't been able to find the right cow horses in California. But in Rochelle, Texas, someone had been turning them out for years. The best ones had Headlight Morgan on top of their pedigrees, Major Antoine on the bottom, and they were purebred, registered Morgans. Headlight Morgan was an excellent sire for stock horses. He was very deep and wide in the chest, had a very large heart girth, excellent feet and legs, and was powerful and strong in the quarters — qualities he passed on to his offspring. The daughters of Major Antoine produced Morgans with excellent breed type, and the very best of feet and legs. The offspring from this cross inherited marvelous dispositions from both sides of the family.

Following his initial purchase of Sellman stock, Hill returned to Texas and got fifteen more mares in 1924. Ten of these were out of The Admiral's daughters. Two had dams by Major Antoine, another's dam was by Headlight Morgan, and one dam each by Gold Medal and Major Gordon. Two of the mares, Hegira 04173 and Hemala 04186, were by Headlight Morgan. Semmes 04187 and Sonna 04176 were by Sooner 7059 (Headlight Morgan x Nannie L. by The Admiral), which doubled their lines to The Admiral. The other eleven mares were daughters of Red Oak 5249, by General Gates 666.

In 1928 Hill purchased Headstar 04093, a Sellman-bred daughter of Headlight Morgan that F. A. Fickert had brought to California in 1922. Still later, he got four intensely bred mares from W. P. Thornhill of Miami, Texas. These were Betty Skinner 04987, her daughter, Dan's Betty 05005, Bessie Dix 05087 and Betsy Dix 05004.

Betty Skinner's dam, Nellie Skinner 03580, was a granddaughter of Headlight Morgan. Betty's sire was Dan 7095 (Headlight Morgan x Kate B. by The Admiral). Bred back to her own sire, Betty Skinner produced Dan's Betty, and Pacheco 7978, also owned by Hill. Bessie Dix and Betsy Dix were full sisters by Dixie 7970, out of Cavey 04988. Dixie's sire was Dixie Dan 7096 (Headlight Morgan x Mollie A. by Major Antoine), and his dam was Nellie Skinner, 2nd dam Lady Skinner by Headlight Morgan. Cavey was by Dan 7095, out of Nellie Skinner.

Blossom's Lass (with family friend Gina Keener), a fine example of the "Blossom" family, from the crossing of Querido daughters and Sonfield granddaughters. Photo courtesy of LaVonne Houlton.

The four Thornhill mares and the colt were about as "pure" Sellman as you could get. And they were the last purchases of Sellman stock that Roland Hill made. He got the two good mares, Miga 04800 (Winterset x Potena) and Kathleen McCavlin 05012 (Barney Hudson x Miga), at the C. G. Stevenson Estate sale in Kansas, 1941, and purchased Vigella 06039 (Vigilant x Sirenelle) from Dr. W. L. Orcutt in 1943. These were his only outcross broodmares.

Richard Sellman had built up his family of Morgans so carefully and so well they were only strengthened by linebreeding. His Morgans were highly regarded and eagerly purchased throughout the West. Hill had the mares, but dropped the Sellman line breeding, and was then left with trying to find his own "perfect nick."

Mr. Hill first got the high-powered, Brunk-bred Pat Allen 7344 (Allen King x Patrona) and raised fifty foals from him. Also Brunk-bred was the beautiful Pongee Morgan 7427, a sorrel with flaxen mane and tail, white sox and a blaze. Pongee was by Allen King 7090 out of the good mare Galva 04250. He only got thirty-one foals before an injury necessitated his being put down. From Elmer Brown in Kansas, Hill got Hiebert's Challenge 8076 (El Cortez), by the Sellman-bred Romanesque 7297 out of Viola Linsley 04789. Joaquin Morgan 7947 was also by Romanesque, and came from Elmer Brown, as did the Senator Knox son, Brown Knox 8360 and the Linsley son Sparbeau 7734.

In all, Hill used twenty-one stallions in his breeding program, with various degrees of success. Some were sons of his older stallions. He got a lot of good ranch geldings, and some fine mares and colts – many of which he sold, but it was not until he went back to line breeding, through his two top Government-bred stallions, Querido 7370 and Sonfield 7952, that he found his own magic formula.

Querido 7370 was purchased from the U. S. Morgan Horse Farm, Weybridge, Vermont in March 1924. He was bred to the Sellman mares and their daughters for thirteen years, and then sold to Hawaiian interests. During those years with Hill he got 150 foals. The Querido offspring came with innate "cow savvy" – they made excellent mounts for ranch use, and were the strong, "stocky" kind that Hill liked. Querido was a full brother of the great Government stallion Mansfield, and to replace him in the stud Hill selected Mansfield's son, Sonfield 7952, whose dam was Quietude 04271 – also the dam of Upwey Ben Don and Upwey Benn Quietude. Sonfield sired 161 foals during Hill's ownership.

It was when Roland Hill began to cross Sonfield on his Querido mares that beautiful things began to happen. The family of Camille 04097 makes a shining example. A lovely group of "Blossom" mares sprang from her Querido daughters and Sonfield granddaughters. Their names and bloodlines are cherished among California and Pacific Northwest breeding establishments today. The "Angel" mares from Angelina, the "Kitty's" from Kitty C., the "Mala's" from Hemala are other fine examples of the Querido-Sonfield cross.

Hill mares and stallions that were sold and entered other breeding programs have had lasting influence on the breed, too. Red Dot 04577 (Pongee Morgan x Rodoata), owned by William R. Hearst, became the dam of the great Redman

Silver Ranger 7813 (Querido x Tab). Photo courtesy of NMMH.

8056, by Mountcrest Sellman 7299 – a grandson of Headlight Morgan. Jinglebells 04582 (Querido x Texanita), also owned by Hearst, was the dam of Montabell 8117, also by Mountcrest Sellman. Tehachapi Allan 7910 (Querido x Tab) became a sire for Elmer Brown in Kansas, was in the Remount Service for several years, and later was owned in Colorado.

Silver Ranger 7813 (Querido x Tab) became a sire of note in the Texas Panhandle, being highly regarded by Quarter Horse breeders as well. Choice Master 7810 (Querido x Hemala) sired a number of good ones in the West, as did Don Juan 7623 (Querido x Addy), Red Wings 7965 (Querido x Tab), Dude Spar 8227 (Sparbeau x Sallie Ann), Linden Sonfield 8907 (Sonfield x Sallie Ann), Rosefield 8568 (Sonfield x Rose Mala), Ryder 8712 (Sonfield x Angel A), Silver Dan 8226 (Joaquin Morgan x Dan's Betty), Tejon Prince 8105 (Querido x Addy), Francisco 8396 (Sparbeau x Hemala),

Sheik F. 8567 (Sonfield x Princess Sabab) and others. The stallions Blackhaux, Cloverman, Cuyamo, Ben Gates, Gold Dollar, Hedlite, Kenelm Morgan, North Fork, Millbrae and a host of others all came from Hill-bred stock.

Alma Sonfield 06713 (Sonfield x Angel B.) was one of the outstanding show mares of the 1940s, with many wins and championships to her credit. Kitty Field 06718 (Sonfield x Kitty Joaquin) won the Mares 4 and Over class at the Northern California Morgan Horse Club's annual shows in 1961, in a class of seventeen, and beat out twenty-two younger ones as well, for the Grand Championship – she was sixteen years old at the time. She also won the Produce of Dam class that day. At the C.S.H.A. Blue Ribbon Horse Show at Sacramento in 1949 two-year-old Candy Joe Field (Sonfield x Roseta Mala) was Champion Stallion. Silver Dan 8226, purchased from Hill as a yearling by Wilbur White of Folsom, developed into an exceedingly handsome show stallion and was undefeated in the ring for a dozen years. Linden Sonfield 8907 was also unbeaten for several years.

Alma Sonfield 06713 (Sonfield x Angel B.). Photo courtesy of NMMH.

From one county fair alone Roland Hill is said to have taken home $1000.00 in prize money won by his Morgans. While at Tres Pinos the Hills, mounted on six Morgans, won the family class, with Roland proudly mounted on Sonfield, who took the blue in hand at the same show.

It's an established fact that for many years, in both halter and performance classes, in open competition and breed classes throughout California the horses carrying the Querido-Sonfield lines, derived from Government, Sellman, Brunk and Brown Morgans, have many times taken the championships, and are still doing so.

The influence of all the Hill family stock on present day Morgans in California and the West makes a tale too long to tell here.

In addition to the breeders mentioned early in this article, many more drew heavily on Hill Morgans to establish their own programs – Warren Halliday at Bishop and Etna; Schultz, Kuck and Schultz at Yreka; L. G. Montgomery of Mare Island; Dr. C. C. Reed, for his big San Clemente cattle ranch; E. W. Roberts of Hi Pass; W. L. Linn at Turlock; W. T. Carter of Sanger; the Bromileys in Tuolumne County; Dean Witter's Lone Pine Ranch and the Hunewills of Bridgeport, to name just a few.

Hill raised well over a hundred geldings for ranch use by the Horseshoe Cattle Company hands. It took three years of very careful training and work under an expert reinsman to "finish" a stock horse to its full potential. Consequently, most of the broodmares were never broke to ride. They were expected to prove themselves as superior producers of working stock. Some of the mares were trained as young horses, though. Red Tawn 04531 (Querido x Texanita), for example, was well-started, and saw a year's hard cattle work before being sold to the Hearst Ranch.

So popular were Hill's Morgans that he would have advance sale orders for two years ahead. For quite a few years he registered more foals annually than any other Morgan breeder in the United States. He took an active interest in the affairs of the Morgan Horse Club, and was a member of the national board of directors from 1931 to 1949. He was also a highly respected Morgan and Stock Horse judge. In 1949, after having seen Morgans from the West Coast to the East he said, "I think Mansfield and his line are the best producing family in the breed today." He certainly helped prove that belief in the West. Few of the big cattle ranches were without their share of Hill-bred stock. The huge Vail & Vickers Company of Los Angeles, for instance, purchased Mahan Field 9297 (Sonfield x Helen Mala) to sire good using horses for their extensive Santa Rosa Island Ranch, which ran over 10,000 cattle.

The historic old Kuck Ranch in Siskiyou County started its Morgan breeding program in the '30s with Hill stock. So it went.

Roland Hill passed away in 1955 at age 69 following a series of strokes that totally incapacitated him. He had started out to build a good remuda for his ranch work. The results of his program reached far beyond the confines of his range. He found the Morgans to be more than satisfactory for the work required of them. In fact, not long before his death Hill remarked that, in over 30 years' experience with the breed he found the Morgan "the best cow horse I have ever used." The Morgans, he said, "never came to the end of the road."

There's not that much call for cow horses anymore. The descendants of Hill's Morgans haven't rested on those old laurels, though. You can find them in the ring at almost any show on the Pacific Coast – in the ribbons at halter, under saddle, in harness – carrying on a tradition of excellence, disposition and usefulness...and being the best loved horses in the barns of a multitude of westerners.

Dapper Dan: A Legend in his Own Time
1976

In 1958 a well-known horseman saw the bay Morgan stallion Dapper Dan, and was moved to write, "If all Morgans looked like that horse, I'd surely like to have one!"

Dapper Dan is well known and admired throughout the country, and not just by Morgan breeders either. From Dapper's 107 registered get have sprung a great family of Morgans combining the three basic ingredients so important to our breed: beauty, disposition and ability. As his 25th birthday approaches, it seems fitting to tell his story.

Dapper Dan was foaled May 10, 1951 at Sonora, California. His breeder, J. Clark Bromiley, sold him as a two-year-old to W. L. Linn of Turlock. In 1955 Mr. and Mrs. Ed Walter of Modesto purchased him, and later sold him in March 1960 to Frances Kellstrom, also of Modesto. His whole lifetime has been spent in about a 75-mile radius of his birthplace.

Dapper Dan 10696 (Trilson x Bess Gates).
Photo taken at four years of age.
Photo courtesy of the National Museum of the Morgan Horse.

His Pedigree

Dapper Dan is twelve generations down the line from Justin Morgan I. His sire, Trilson 9892, was by Katrilan Prince 8667, by Katrilan 8121, by Uhlan 7564, a son of Bennington 5693. Uhlan (dam: Poinsetta 04232) was bred by the U. S. Morgan Horse Farm at Middlebury and sold to William Randolph Hearst in July 1930. He was a full brother to Bingham 7763, Villager 7617 and Willow 01620, and a maternal half brother to Evadne 04870, Frieda 04962, Doreen 04821 and Grenfel 7990. Uhlan sired seven colts and ten fillies in California. Most of his daughters carried Hearst's "Piedmont" prefix. Uhlan's sons, Pico Chief 8046, Piedmont Apache 7915, Enowee 8606, Uhlan-Ro 8134 and Katrilan 8121 became sires of many good California Morgans. Uhlan was eventually sold to a party in Nevada in his later years.

Katrilan 8121 sired fourteen colts and ten fillies, and his best line was carried through Katrilan Prince 8667, sire of the ill-fated Trilson 9892. Mr. and Mrs. I. E. Hottel of Modesto, California, owned the Hearst-bred Katrilan Prince. He made a good record as a halter stallion. The Hottels rode "Prince" and his half-brother, Trilan 8666, as a matched pair in parades and shows for many years. Katrilan Prince had a wonderfully gentle disposition for a stallion and was always Mrs. Hottel's mount. He was a very handsome, impressive horse, with lots of substance, big, gentle eyes, and the pride of a peacock on parade. When he was sixteen, Prince was sold and gelded, and died within a year. His son, Trilson, had been even more unfortunate.

Trilson was known as "the purple horse," because of the unusual luster of his liver chestnut coat. His dam, Roseta May 06207, was a Sonfield daughter. He was bred and owned by the J. Clark

Bromileys. During his brief show career, he won ribbons at the Amador and Tuolumne county fairs, and in Northern California Morgan shows. Trilson was the sire of only six foals: Trianne 08127 (dam: Bess Gates), foaled in 1950; Tuolumne Rose 08376 (dam: Roseta May), Muscle Man 10697 (dam: Flika), and Dapper Dan 10696 (dam: Bess Gates), all foaled in 1951; Tony Rose 11107 (dam: Roseta May) and Our Girl Friday 08856 (dam: Flika), both foals of 1953. The Bromileys bred all of these horses.

Of his three sons, two were kept as breeding stallions. The third, Tony Rose, was gelded, and used as a ranch horse for many years. The careers of the two stallions, Dapper Dan and Muscle Man, both as individuals and as sires, make it clear that Trilson's untimely death was a great loss to the Morgan breed. He should not have died; a rasp thrown by a disgruntled farrier stabbed Trilson, and caused his death when he was only seven years old.

Dapper Dan and Muscle Man are full brothers in blood. Their dams, Bess Gates 06482 and Flika 06187, were full sisters by Gay Mac 7988, out of Bessie Ro 04978, a Querido daughter. The two stallions often vied for the blue in halter and get-of-sire classes, and if one did not win, the other generally did. Their offspring have been equally impressive in the show ring. "Dapper" and "Muscles" do not look alike, and their respective get are different, so that each has been the founder of a distinctive family.

Having Uhlan, Sonfield, Gay Mac, Querido and Red Oak in his pedigree gave Dapper Dan a definite Government heritage. When Lyman Orcutt saw Dapper as a young stallion he remarked that the colt looked "just like Gay Mac when we brought him out" (to California). He began his show career at an early age, and by the time he was seven, Dapper Dan's show record was stated to be "phenomenal." But there was more to come.

In the Show Ring

By 1959, Dapper's get were beginning to stand out in the show ring. At the Northern California Morgan Horse Club's (N.C.M.H.A.) first show, Linn's Knox 11442 won the High Point Halter and Performance Combination award, with ribbons in five categories. Linn's Linden 09279, Linn's Baby Lu 09535, Dapper Dolly 010673, Deanne 09039 and Dannie Lu 11277, all by Dapper Dan, were also in the ribbons. Linn's Anne 09281 was added to the roster of winners the following year. In 1961 Midnight's Black Joy 011490 won the weanling filly class. In 1962 Dapper Dinah 010674 was Grand Champion Mare; Linn's Anne captured the blues in the stock horse and trail horse classes, as well as five other ribbons.

The N.C.M.H.A. show was held in Antioch in 1963, and was judged by Mrs. Anna Ela of Townshend Farms. Dapper Dan and his offspring had a field day at that show! Dapper won the four and over stallion class and was Grand Champion Stallion. He went on to win the Get of Sire class (Muscle Man's get were 2nd). Dapper Dinah topped the four and over mares class, and was crowned Grand Champion Mare. Deanne was second, four

Dapper Dinah 010674 (Dapper Dan x Linn's Black Beauty).
Photo courtesy of the National Museum of the Morgan Horse.

and over mares. The "Dapper" bunch took 23 ribbons at that show, at halter, English pleasure, western pleasure, trail horse and reining.

In 1964, the N.C.M.H.A. show moved to Sacramento, where Dapper and seven of his offspring were shown. Dapper again won the Sire and Get class, and was Reserve Grand Champion Stallion. Dapper Dolly won the reining class, and Kelly Vermont 13633 was third in the roadster class. Other offspring were in the ribbons in halter, trail and western classes.

Dapper stayed in the ribbons in the Sire and Get class at the 1965, 1966, 1967 and 1968 Golden West National Morgan Horse Shows in Sacramento. Some of his blue ribbon offspring during those years were Daisy Gay 011848, Bercinda Macdan 14569, Dapper Dolly, Bercinda Macdonn 16058, Windswept Imperial 16560, Rhed Fitzgerald 15364 and Viking Cavalier 15808.

Up through 1968 at the annual N.C.M.H.A. shows, 26 of Dapper Dan's sons and daughters had won 122 ribbons in halter and performance, and Dapper Dan had picked up a dozen more of his own.

1968 marked Dapper's last campaign season. He had garnered innumerable ribbons and about forty championships, and now he was seventeen years old. It was time for his get and grand-get to carry on the family name. And that they have done. The show-stopper of the 1970 season was the black mare, Kelly's Pretty Nino 013963 (Dapper Dan x Pretty Lass), who swept the park saddle and harness classes and was named 1970 A.H.S.A. Park Mare of the Year. Dapper Dolly 09773 (Dapper Dan x Redonna Vermont) won reining and stock horse classes and was the leading Pacific Coast Hunters and Jumpers Association Novice Stock Horse, in open competition, until an accident claimed her life in the mid-1970s.

A grandson, Bourbon Prince 15909 (Shawalla Prince x Linn's Anne, by Dapper Dan), won the Golden West National Stock Horse class four years in a row, and retired undefeated. Bourbon inherited ability from both his parents. Shawalla Prince was also an accomplished stock horse, and Linn's Anne had been a well-known performer with a number of High Point awards to her credit.

Viking Cavalier 15808, bred by Viking Morgan Ranch in Modesto, won the three-year-old stallion futurity at the Golden West National in 1968, and won several halter classes in Northern California and Nevada. Now owned by the W. S. Needham family of Walnut Creek, Cavalier has carried Betsy Graves to win hunt seat equitation awards. He has also twice been a member of the trio that won the Golden West Family Class.

The 1972 Golden West National had 22 of Dapper's family entered, and they garnered 73 ribbons, including eleven Firsts, eleven Seconds and fifteen Thirds. One Dapper Dan son, Black Brandy 16963 (dam: Impala Princess) won sixteen ribbons at that show, and he was to win national acclaim three years later.

His Get at Grand National

Black Brandy, Bryson's Jamie Boy 22503 (dam: Lady Fiona) and Dapper's Delight 018847 (Cap's Nugget x Kelly's Dapper Dana, whose dam was Dapper Dolly) all participated in the 1975 Grand National Morgan Horse show in Oklahoma City. The results were most exciting. Bryson's Jamie Boy, owned by Mr. and Mrs. Frank Dodd, Fernley, Nevada, and shown by Marvin Mayfield, made Top Ten in the $500.00 Grand National Morgan Stock Horse class. "Jamie Boy" had won the stock horse class at the Golden West Regional Championship Morgan Horse Show, his first time out, in July 1975.

It's hard to believe what Dapper's Delight accomplished at the Grand National! She was Top Ten, Mares 5 and Over; Reserve Champion Ladies' Pleasure Driving Morgan; Reserve Champion Ladies' Western Pleasure Morgan; Reserve Champion Ladies' English Pleasure Morgan; Champion

Amateur Pleasure Driving Mare; Top Ten in the $2,500.00 English Pleasure Morgan Stake; $2,500.00 Champion Western Pleasure Morgan; and Grand National Reserve Champion Pleasure Driving Morgan in the $2,500.00 Stake. Now, Dapper Dan can't take all the credit for Delight's performance by any means – she had a great sire, too, in Cap's Nugget, but Dapper can claim a share of the glory.

Black Brandy, shown by Trisha Barr for Sunbay Farms, Watsonville, California, was undefeated in all his classes except one, and it took Dapper's Delight to snatch that championship from him. Here's how he fared: Grand National Champion Amateur Western Pleasure Morgan; Grand National Champion Ladies' Western Pleasure Morgan; Grand National Champion Junior Exhibitor Western Pleasure Morgan; and Reserve Champion in the $2,500.00 Western Pleasure Stake.

Just for the record, another "family member" from Oregon, Lin-Kim Leprechaun 22316, was a Top Ten Four Year Old Western Pleasure Horse. His dam, Gay Leaf Danleva, is by Dancin 11905, a Dapper Dan grandson. Muscle Man's honor was upheld at the Grand National too, by his son El Mejor 14918, owned by Mr. and Mrs. Philip Piazza, Jr., of San Jose. El Mejor was consistently high in all his classes, and walked off with the Grand National Championships in Western Trail and Stock Horse.

Stallions Must Breed On

The proof of a stallion is not only in the show ring, but also in his ability to breed on. In this, Dapper Dan has excelled. His many daughters have consistently been good producers, and they are greatly desired by Morgan breeders. Many Dapper sons have carried on his male line. Dannie Lu 11277 was one of the first, and sired some good ones. Unfortunately, he was sold to a Thoroughbred farm, and has been wasted for years as a teasing stallion. His son, Dancin, is a well-known sire in the Pacific Northwest. Linn's Knox 11442 is another son that went to Oregon in the early '60s, and has numerous get there. Kellfleet 14488 sold to Mary Lasiter, and has sired many foals in Colorado, most with the prefix "Royal." Angle's Victor 14316, Linnsfield 11441, Jamaican Ebony 11625, Linn's Black Morgan 11631, Que-Dan 12937, Linn's Black Dan 14691 (by Linn's Knox), D Knox 13684 (by Linn's Knox), Brookwood Dan Pat 14303 (by Dannie Lu, out of Linn's Linden, by Dapper Dan), Special Edition 23858, Kelly's Bay Lad 14347, Kellfield 13456, Dapper's Doozie 15942, Windswept Imperial 16560, Viking Cavalier 15808, Dapper Duke 17485 and Norfleet 17041 are some of those who have sired foals to carry on the line for Dapper Dan.

It was a lucky day for Frances Kellstrom when she got Dapper Dan. He really put her breeding program on the map. It was a lucky day for Dapper, too. He found a permanent home with someone who loved him and did well by him. He has had 54 colts and 53 fillies. His last foal, a beautiful little bay filly, died of pneumonia before she could be registered. It has not been possible to mention all of Dapper's family, and many that were not mentioned are as good as the several that were. No slight is intended against those not listed here! Already Dapper Dan's extended family numbers well over four hundred. That is more than enough to influence the Morgan breed for the good, and to make of a beautiful, gentle stallion the living legend he has become.

Early History of Morgan Mares in California
1977

During the Gold Rush, and in the decades just following, well-bred Morgan stock enjoyed wide popularity throughout California. By far the most desired strains in that era were the "Saint Clair's" and the "Black Hawk's," and several hundred mares descended from these two stallions had a great influence on the history of California's horse business in the 19th century.

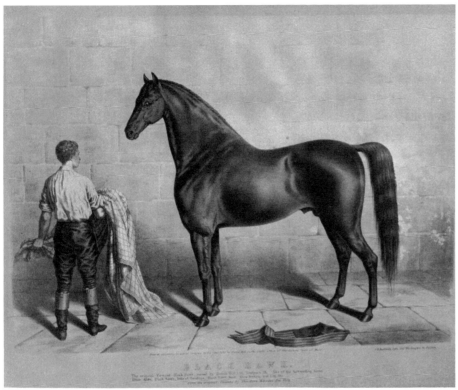

Black Hawk 20 as shown here in a lithograph print.
Courtesy of the National Museum of the Morgan Horse.

Sad to say, there is no unbroken tail-male chain of descent from the Morgan stallions of California's early days to Morgans here today. The Pacific region didn't have little pockets of land where families who had raised pure Morgans for generations continued to do so, as New England did. Instead, led by trend-setting, big-moneyed breeders like Leland Stanford, William Corbitt, and the Whipples, Westerners joined the speed-crazed, record-happy concept that each new horse must be faster than the last one. Classic conformation and purity of blood meant little from the 1870s on. Californians had a different frame of reference. They wanted speed, and pedigree influenced breeding only to the extent that it produced speed. To this end, the speed-breeders brought in trotting-bred sires from the East and looked to their native mares - with Morgan sires and grandsires - who had the stamina and natural gait from which to build their dream trotters and pacers.

California's Morgans were incorporated into the American Trotting Register (Standardbred stock), not because they weren't valued for themselves, but because they were.

A quote from the *American Horse Breeder* in September, 1906 said, "A combination of the blood of Messenger, Morgan and Diomed is the best combination in 40 years of producing speed at all the gaits, and no other combination has yet been discovered that has surpassed it in this respect, especially when the Morgan strain has come through Vermont Black Hawk." The Californians had been proving that since the early days, when fifty-eight of their Black Hawk line stallions sired 133 mares which became dams and second dams of trotters and pacers which raced - and won - all across the country.

93

Another great nick was created by blending the blood of St. Clair 48 with that of Electioneer (ATR 125), Leland Stanford's prolific and remarkable stallion by Hambletonian (10). Two of Electioneer's offspring from this cross set world's records as two-year-olds: Fred Crocker (dam: Melinche, by St. Clair), and Wildflower (dam: Mayflower, by St. Clair). Another two set world records for four-year-olds: Bonita (dam: May Fly, by St. Clair), and Manzanita, out of Mayflower, who had been a winning race mare herself.

An article from their heyday states that, "Among the St. Clairs there was the highest quality exhibited. Every one of the St. Clair mares, and even the granddaughters at Palo Alto (Stanford's farm) closely approximated the same models. His daughters, many from inferior mares, set records in the early days of trotting on the Coast." Lady St. Clair won many 3- and 5-mile heats, and held the honor of the fastest five miles on record. Several of St. Clair's sons are in the Morgan Registers, but you won't find numbers for Melinche, May Fly, Mayflower, Lady St. Clair, Jenny St. Clair, Rachel, Lady Zetler, or his many other fine daughters, though they had more than enough of the original Justin Morgan blood to qualify. So did a lot of others, who traced from Morgan lines other than Black Hawk 20 and St. Clair 48.

It's not always easy to track down the history of these early representatives as their "Morgan" identity was rarely stressed. For example, the California State Fair only had breed classes for Thoroughbred stallions and mares. All others, including Morgans, were shown as "Horses Other Than Thoroughbreds," or as "Roadsters" or "Carriage Horses" or "Horses of All Work" - the western version of the Morgan's storied versatility.

As indicated above, another identity problem exists because many California offspring of registered Morgan stallions were never registered, even though they qualified under the old Rule 1 ("'any meritorious stallion or mare that traces in direct male line to the original Justin Morgan Horse, and has at least one sixty-fourth of his blood"). Quite a few stallions, and a lot of mares were lost to the breed through failure to seek this registration. Over the years priceless Morgan blood dwindled away into "grade" stock, or, largely through mare lines, was absorbed into the Standardbred breed. The 1905 rule changes (Vol. II

Adios (1:57 1/2), a world record holder and leading sire of money winners, tracing through his sire to Beautiful Bells, The Moor 466, and others. Photo courtesy of NMMH.

of the Register) picked up some of this last group, but not nearly as many were eligible. These rules stated that (1) "any meritorious stallion, mare or gelding that traces in direct male line to Justin Morgan, and has at least 1/64 of his blood, provided the dam and sire's dam were bred in approved speed or roadster lines," or (2) "any meritorious stallion, mare or gelding having 1/32 or more of the blood of Justin Morgan, provided the sire and dam were bred in approved speed or roadster lines" were admissible for registration.

One interesting Western product of Rule 2 was the wonderful black mare called Beautiful Bells. She was foaled in San Gabriel in 1872, and raced in 2:29 1/2 at Sacramento in 1878. Leland Stanford purchased her, and at his Palo Alto Farm she earned the title "Queen of Broodmares," producing fourteen outstanding offspring, eleven of them having race records of their own. Her eight sons and six daughters eventually produced 314 horses listed in the 1907 American Trotting Register "Great Table" - 235 trotters and 79 pacers. One of her sons was Chimes (2:30 3/4), who appears in the tail-male pedigree of the greatest pacing sire of all time, the Standardbred Adios. Adios set six world records, was syndicated in 1955 for the then-record price of half a million dollars, and sold for a record fee of $15,000.00. For nine years he was the leading sire of money winners. In the early 1960s, his son, Adios Butler, became the fastest harness horse of all time on both mile and half-mile tracks, and won the first Triple Crown of Pacing. Adios Butler won thirty-seven of his fifty races, and earned over half a million dollars on the track.

Adios Butler (by Adios) became the fastest harness racer of all time. Top and bottom of pedigree both trace to some old Morgan lines. Photo courtesy of NMMH.

Close on the heels of Adios Butler's records came another Adios son, Bret Hanover, who soon surpassed his half-brother's feats. Bret won all of his twenty-four starts as a two-year-old. Between 1964-1966 he went to the post sixty-eight times and won sixty-two heats. He set ten world records and won the Triple Crown of Pacing in 1965. Three times voted Harness Horse of the Year, Bret Hanover earned close to a million dollars, and lowered the time record for the mile to 1:53 3/5, to become the fastest harness horse in the world. Other Adios offspring did nearly as well.

Beautiful Bells was by The Moor 466 (Clay Pilot 465 x Belle of Wabash, by Day's Copperbottom 283). Her dam was Minnehaha, by Stevens' Bald Chief; 2nd dam Nettie Clay, by Cassius M. Clay Jr. 2149. Through her Clay lines, Beautiful Bells traced to Revenge 8 by Justin Morgan 1. Her son Chimes (great-great grandsire of Adios) was by Electioneer (125), who also had the Clay line to Revenge 8 through his dam. Within his seven-generation pedigree Adios had fifteen lines to Rule 2 registered Morgans. His 8th dam was Maggie Gaines, by Blood's Black Hawk 89.

Another interesting example of the Morgan and Standardbred cross was Lou Dillon. A fragile little thing, she apparently raced more on guts than good health. Lou Dillon was foaled in1898 at the Santa Rosa Stock Farm in Southern California. When she first appeared on the trotting tracks her career took off like a Fourth of July skyrocket. Few horses had as colorful and productive a life as she. She became the World's Trotting Champion at Readville, Massachusetts, in 1903. Her fastest time was 1:58 1/2. Cornelius K. G. Billings purchased Lou in 1903 for $12,500.00, and took her to New York. Immensely wealthy, Billings had built the finest stables in the country. After she broke the two-minute mile Lou Dillon went on to break records to bike, sulky and wagon. She was officially retired from racing in 1906. Billings took his record-breaking mare on an extended European tour in 1909, where she trotted exhibition miles. She trotted in Berlin before the German Crown Prince and the Kaiser, and she won the hearts of the Russian people when exhibited at the Imperial Trotting Club in Moscow, and gamely trotted her exhibition miles in a drenching rain. After the tour, Lou Dillon was taken to Kentucky, where she enjoyed notable success as a broodmare, producing a number of fine performers. Still later she returned to the state of her birth to live out her years, dying in 1925 at the age of twenty-seven.

Lou Dillon's story really began in 1872 when a beautiful matched pair of fine Morgan mares was brought overland from Wisconsin to San Francisco. The two full sisters, Fly and Gypsy, were by Black Flying Cloud 168 (Black Hawk 20 x Kate, by Black Hawk 20). Their second dam was a great-granddaughter of Woodbury Morgan 7, making them a very well-bred pair, indeed. Fly became the property of Santa Rosa Stock Farm, where she was bred to Milton Medium, a trotting sire, and produced Lou Milton, the dam of Lou Dillon.

All of Black Flying Cloud's offspring resembled him greatly, being very superior, handsome, and lofty, with a long, slashing gait. Beautiful, and wonderful movers, his get commanded premium prices as high-class carriage horses, with matched pairs selling as high as $5,000.00. On their dam's side, Fly and Gypsy also came from noted road horses, so the Morgan credentials that Fly passed on to her granddaughters Lou Dillon, Alein, and Ethel Mack, and her grandson Redwood (11814) were of the very best.

Redfield's Vermont 121 was a black Morgan stallion brought to California across the plains in 1859. His sire was Independence 1025, by Peck Horse 120, a son of Black Hawk 20. His dam was by Royal Morgan 11, also a son of the great Black Hawk. Redfield's Vermont was a great trotter, one of the best of his time in California, and he also became a prolific and noted sire of fine, speedy stock. He was also the cornerstone of well-bred stock in Oregon, through his sons Mike 1027 and Frank Tollman 2467, and through his many daughters and descendants. Some of the Redfield's Vermont daughters who became fine producers were Ribbon, Susana, Lucy, Blackey, Salinas Belle and Susie. Susie's daughter, Lady Rivers, was the dam of a noted trotting mare named Sweet Marie, who combined the blood of Black Hawk, Mambrino and Hambletonian.

Sweet Marie was a bay mare, foaled at Los Angeles in 1896. In 1904 she was entered in thirteen trotting races, in New York, Rhode Island, Massachusetts, Ohio, Connecticut, Kentucky and Tennessee. She won all but one of them. Some were two-heat races, some three heats, others five heats (each heat was a one-mile distance). Usually Sweet Marie won all the heats in a particular race. At the end of the 1905 season she was the sixth fastest horse in the country. In 1906, when she was ten years old, Sweet Marie raced seventeen one-mile heats and won sixteen of them. In Wallace's Table of Fastest Records for 1906 she held the year's record for fastest mare, stallion or gelding to sulky. Her fastest time was set at Columbus, Ohio, September 21, 1906, a one-mile heat to beat 2:03 3/4 time—she did it in 2:02 flat. In 1907, she won five races against time, but lost one of her two match races. Sweet Marie tried three times in three states to beat her own 2:02 record, but was unable to do so.

Addie Lee (2:36 1/2) was another wonderful producer from the early days. She was foaled in the 1860s. Her sire was Culver's Black Hawk 1026, a son of Redfield's Vermont 121. Her dam, Old Nancy, by Morrill 55, was brought to California some years earlier. Addie Lee had a son by Reavis' Blackbird, named Berlin (3514), who sired fine trotters. She had one daughter, Adalia, by Fred Lowe 605, by St. Clair 48, four offspring by Electioneer (125) and one by General Benton, whose second dam was Morgan. All of Addie Lee's offspring raced or produced racers.

McCracken's Black Hawk 131 was another of the five-mile trotters who sired many fine daughters in California. Notable among them was Sisson Girl 02329, one of only four early California mares to be given Morgan registry numbers (the others were Vidette 02574, Mayfair 01723, and Gladys H. 0879). Other daughters of McCracken's Black Hawk whose offspring produced A.T.R. stock were Flora Temple, Dimple, the Ryan Mare, Old Brown Jenny, Mary, Dolly, Tatum Mare, Lady Emma, Nell White, Gipsey and Fern Leaf.

One of the fastest horses of her day on the West Coast was the chestnut mare Magdallah, foaled in Stockton in 1873. Magdallah raced from 1877-1886 and set a time of 2:23 1/2. She was by Primus 1714, a great-grandson of Black Hawk 20, and himself a phenomenal trotter in his time. Magdallah's second dam was said to be by Hale's Green Mountain Morgan 42.

All of the above are only a sampling of the Morgan stock and their stories. The early Trotting Registers list over 150 trotters and pacers with standard time or better who had St. Clair 48 close up in their pedigrees. Most of the more than one hundred Morgan stallions in California between 1849-1889 had Standardbred descendants. Morgan blood was halved and quartered and diluted yet again over the generations, until the names of their progenitors were off the pedigrees, and all but lost in time. The old mares died, and were not replaced. Their daughters and granddaughters were bred to trotting sires. The old days, when the McCrackens, Easton, Millers, Carr, and Haggin and many others had purebred (or nearly so) Morgans of high quality and typical breed appearance were gone. Their like was not to be seen in California again for nearly a quarter of a century.

Epilogue: There was one mare left over from the old days, who spanned the gap and provided the only link between past and present. Her name is forgotten now, which is too bad. She was a chestnut mare, with four white stockings, and she was bred by James Ben Ali Haggin at the Carr and Haggin Ranch in Kern County, probably around 1910 or so. Jesse D. Carr and Haggin both raised Morgans in the early days. Carr at one time owned Redfield's Vermont 121, and bred a son, Vermont, Jr. 3496, that went to Australia. He also bred and owned Bickford, a racing gelding that was Morgan on both sides of his papers. Haggin's stallion was Bismarck 1864 (David Hill 2nd 1092 x Flora Temple by McCrackens' Black Hawk 131), and he had mares of good Morgan blood as well, some of it of St. Clair 48's line. A dozen or more of Haggin's horses had race records. The two stallions were used on native mares to produce working ranch horses for the Kern County properties and Haggin's Sacramento area holdings as well. Later Bismarck sons were used, and it is likely the unnamed chestnut mare traced to him, through either her sire or dam, since it is known she was part-Morgan. Thus it is fairly safe to assume that the chestnut mare was a distant descendant of the Black Hawk 20 line, and she possibly carried some other Morgan blood as well. In 1928 Duval Williams of Chowchilla bred this mare, who must have been well along in years, to Bender 7489 (Pat Allen x Marietta), a stallion he had purchased the year before from Roland Hill. The resulting foal was a chestnut filly with a blaze and two white hind pasterns, named Lady.

Lady had two registered daughters by Cuyamo 7974 (Redwood Morgan x Jocbo Brownie) - Dulcet X-05342, foaled in 1939, and Laydee X-05689, foaled in 1941. Dulcet produced the following foals: Sunshine Revere 8965, Brown Sugar 06642, Sunshine Sue 06083, Red Silver 9534, and Gingydar 07352. Sunshine Sue was owned by W. T. Carter, and that line lives on today through her offspring, among them being Sundee Gold D. 07399. Laydee also had a number of foals: Shiek F's Ladybelle 06819, Shiek F's Sabrina 06533, Shiek F's Ladybird 07110, Victor Vermont 11827, Vicki Vermont 010377, Sea Star 014894, Vanity Vermont 011618, Valiant Vermont 011170, and Tony Vermont 013412.

Anyone whose Morgans carry one of these names in their pedigrees has a unique living link with California's Morgan history of a century ago.

California Mare Families of the Twentieth Century
1977

Morgan horses were re-introduced into California in the early 1920s by three men who imported stallions and mares from Richard Sellman's ranch in Texas. Sellman's Mountain Vale Ranch was located near Rochelle, in the Brady Mountains, between the Colorado and San Saba Rivers. He had begun breeding Morgans there before the turn of the century, and over the years had developed a large and fine band of uniformly typey Morgans that found a wide market.

Many of Sellman's Morgans, incidentally, also became unsung members of another breed — stock from which, in part, the modern-day Quarter Horse was formed. Many Morgan stallions and some Morgan mares as well were to be found in the background of horses listed upon formation of the A.Q.H.A. registry in 1948 - Headlight Morgan, Romance, Redolent, Jubilee King, Silver Ranger, to name just a few. After all, Morgans had a lot of the qualities the early Quarter Horse men found desirable. Sellman's Morgans had been bred to work cattle in the high country for generations. They had broad chests, strong quarters, excellent legs, and good backs. Their shoulders were well-laid, and they were deep through the girth, muscular and well-balanced. Sensible, agile and enduring, the Morgans had what it took to get the job done. They were fast over short courses, too — Justin Morgan might have been claimed as a "quarter" horse in his competitive days.

These were the kind of Morgans that Reginald Parsons first brought to California in December 1920, with his purchase of a dozen mares (seven in foal) and fillies, and one stallion. Roland Hill began purchasing Sellman stock in 1922, and so did F. A. Fickert.

Eight of Parsons' mares were by The Admiral 4871, two were by a son, and the other two were by Headlight Morgan 4683 and his grandson. Parsons registered only thirteen Morgans, and by 1926 had sold most of his stock. Several of them went to Southern Oregon. The very best thing that came from Reginald Parsons' brief breeding program was the excellent stallion, Mountcrest Sellman 7289 (Joe Bailey x Kitty E.), who gave us the fine sires Antman x-8318, Montabell 8117, Cloverman 8074, Kenelm Morgan 8077, twenty good daughters, and the superb family of Redman 8056, his son Blackman 8622 and all their descendants.

In the summer of 1922, F. A. Fickert of Tehachapi, California, bought the stallion Raven Chief 7116 and thirteen mares from Richard Sellman. Twelve of the mares were by Headlight Morgan 4683 or a son or grandson, and the other was by The Admiral 4871. Most of the mares were out of daughters of The Admiral.

Bred to Raven Chief and his sons, this group of mares produced an influential family, including six good sons that bred on. From Texsky 04087 came Sun Down Morgan 7388 and the mares Red Sail 05311, Mixer 05314, and Ding Dong 05462. Kita K 04019 produced Bear Valley Chief 8174 and Colorado 8173 (Fickert bred Louisa 04075 to Colorado, and the resulting foal was Red Flash 8416, a successful halter stallion in his young days, and a well-liked sire in his sunset years). From Conant K 03925 came Chief of Chestnut 8177 (by Chestnut Chief 8135) and Lucy Belle 05669 (by Colorado). Consuela 04085 was the dam of Tonto Traveler 05340, and Dulcimer 04104 produced Tonto Queen 05330. Other offspring [Sellman-bred dams in brackets] were: Chlorine 05310 [Emma B. 03030]; Eagle 8189 [Favonius 04069]; Chestnut Chief 8135 [Jael 04078]; Alida 06454 and Tonto's Roamer 8196 [Marta 04063]; Glenna 05312 and Dickens 05313 [Mary K 03449]; Carlotta 05309 [Minna K. 03900]; and Copper of Tonto 05331 [Ramona K. 03919].

To bring the Fickert program into more modern focus, let's take one example. Sun Down Morgan sired a mare called Almond Joy 08167. She was the dam of Orron 11756, owned by Jim and

Lea Mueller of Ontario. She also was the dam of Poco Aljoy 11485, sire of Quiet Son De 13181 and of Barbara Rovira's Cinder Miss 010880.

Another small sample from the Fickert band of mares is Glenna 05312 (Raven Chief x Mary K, by Headlight Morgan). She was first the dam of foals by Montabell; her later foals were by Red Vermont. One result of this later cross was Gene Davis' Monty Vermont 9707. Domino Vermont 11179 also belonged to this family through his dam, Nona 06452, who was by Chestnut Chief 8135 out of Mixer 05314.

The John F. Van Leuven's Morgans of River Way also were a part of this Fickert-bred family of Morgans from the Sellman strain. The six Raven Chief sons sired fifty registered Morgans between 1938-1958.

The first *Region VII Directory* lists the mare Tule Belle 09682 as owned by Barry S. Robinson. Her dam, Sunbonnette 06112, was by Sun Down Morgan.

Roland Hill's breeding program was so large and has been so often described that it's hard to say anything new about it. Something of its scope becomes apparent when you realize that 31 of his original mares (from Sellman) produced 240 registered foals.

Addy 04083 had fourteen foals, including the Querido sons Don Juan 7623 and Tejon Prince 8105. Angelina 04100 produced Silver Ranger 7813, and was responsible for a whole line of "Angel" mares. Camille 04097 contributed to the wonderful family of "Blossom" mares, and the "Kitty" line in California began with the Sellman-bred Kitty C 03306. Tab 04214 was a remarkable black mare who had nineteen foals – thirteen of them colts. Her sons included Red Wings 7965, El Caballero 8393, and Tehachapi Allen 7910, all by Querido 7370. Among Tab's daughters were Princess Allan 04635, Tabette 05165 and Tabie Field 06002.

Jaye P Collins 019911 (Muscle Man x Margaret Collins) and LaVonne Houlton. Photo courtesy of LaVonne Houlton.

Hemala 04186 was another prolific broodmare. Except for 1934, Hemala had a foal every year from 1925 through 1943 – eighteen in all, half colts, half fillies. Five of her sons made good as sires, and her daughters Brown Betty 04701, Helen Mala 05199, Helina May 04748, Luala 04427, Mahala 04470, Rose Bud Rose 04570, Rose Mala 04981, Roseta Cortez 06013, and Roseta Mala 05395 were fine mares and producers. Hemala's stallion sons were Choice Master 7810, Czar Morgan 8005, Master Billie 7998, Master G 7585, and Francisco 8396.

Roboss 04179, by Red Oak 5249, was another of the good Hill producers, dam of fourteen foals, including Bessie Ro 04978 and Roberta Ro 05162. Sonna 04176 had three colts and twelve fillies, among which was Sallie Ann 04980, dam of Linden Sonfield 8907, Dude Spar 8227, Analin 07969 and others.

Then there was Red Oak Lu 04316, who had seven colts and ten fillies. She was four years old when her first, the mare Lupat 04418, was born and she had her last foal, Master's Lu 07045 at age twenty-five. Hers tends to be a long-lived line, as evidenced by her daughter El Lu 05847 ("Granny Lu") and grandson El Don 9239, foaled in 1945. Some other Red Oak Lu offspring were Luetta A 05167, Lula Lee 04704, Brown Knox Lu 06476 and Whitefoot Lu 04522.

Another good producer for Roland hill was Marietta 04317, who had 15 foals to carry on her name and line.

The main thing about these early mares from the Sellman band is that, through Roland Hill's program, they produced the great families of "Querido mares" and "Sonfield mares," the very backbone of all the California breeding programs of a few years back, and we, today, are still reaping the benefits.

Rodota 04185 was one of these Hill mares, and in 1928 she foaled a filly by Pongee Morgan 7427 called Red Dot 04577, who became the dam of Redman 8056, by Mountcrest Sellman 7289. Redman in turn sired Blackman 8622, who was outstanding as a broodmare sire. He had fifty-six daughters between 1946 and 1953, and breeders still seek his blood close up on the female line.

Baacamanto 9980, by Blackman 8622. His dam was Angela Sprat 05032, out of Angela K. 04700 (Querido x Angelina). Photo courtesy of NMMH.

One of his daughters was Judy Guy 08460, the grand-dam of Star-Vue Cassiopeia 017508.

Another outstanding Blackman daughter is Margaret Collins 08459, who always has been bred to Muscle Man 10697, and produced a fine group of Morgans. Now both twenty-six years old, Muscle Man and Margaret Collins are the proud parents of a 1977 foal!

The Blackman daughters Belle McLinsley 08212, Lela Linsley 07930, and Memphis Belle 07121 were sold to F. O. Davis of "Windcrest" fame. Liz Taylor 08463, by Bikini 9366, a son of Blackman, became the dam of Windcrest Harmony 12383, Windcrest Play Boy 12096 (sire of Big Bend Top Joy 012805 and Green Trim's Topmiss 012821, owned by Robert Morgan of Red Fox Stables), the fabulous show horse Windcrest Benn Beau 13413, and Windcrest Major 12773, all by Upwey Ben Don, and Alezan Victoria 012950, by Pecos.

Belle McLinsley was the dam of Windcrest Fanfair 010592, Windcrest Chief 12772, and Windcrest Yankee 11941, who sired Pondosa Joshua 13190, Eedahow Ballerina 012989 and others in the Pacific Northwest.

Memphis Belle, a full sister to Belle McLinsley, produced Windcrest Sparkle 010590 and Windcrest Flash 12776, both by Upwey Ben Don.

Three other mares bred by E. W. Roberts in southern California went East, too, to make their marks as broodmares of note. Two were by Monterey 7475 (Mansfield x Scotanna), who came to this state in 1944 at age nineteen. Belle Gales 07935 was the dam of Windcrest Belle 010100, Windcrest Gigi 010591, Windcrest Countess 010974, Stockbridge Moonbeam 14783, Stockbridge Susanne 012633, and Stockbridge Susie-Q 011858. Monterey Belle 07120 produced Fairlea Don Juan 13084, Fairlea Troubadour 13912, Windcrest Monterey 11924, and Fairlea Lady Jane 013108. The third mare was Daisy Field 09419, by Bret Allen 9642 (Blackman x Bettina Allen, by Tehachapi Allen 7910), out of Daisy Sonfield 06478 (Sonfield x Daisy D, by Querido). Daisy Field numbered among her offspring three good daughters: Aldot Mademoiselle 012854, Aldot Duchess 012472, and Aldot Princess 011853, all by Windcrest Encore 11940.

The sixty Blackman daughters made an outstanding package, and it's impossible here to talk about them all. Let's just quickly mention a few: La Mesa 06793, Ann Bregman 08451, Cruz 08864, Lady Gay 08216, Lois Morgan 08206, Miss Tayler 08201, Nell Blackman 07931, and Princess Elizabeth 08208.

Blackman and seven of his sons - all stallions - performed an act at Knott's Berry Farm in 1952, known as the "Liberty Drill." The sons were Ambur Oak 10335, Blackman Allen 10147, Canton 10325, Captain Sprat 10326, Idaho B 10324, Texas Sky 9646, and Texas Star 10151. The group was owned by E. W. Roberts at the time and was trained by Mark Smith and Harold Farren. It was a truly unique act, with the eight stallions working well together. Another good son of Blackman was Baacamanto 9980, foaled in 1948 and still alive and well in Oregon. He was the sire of the great roadster Welmore Zorro 15104.

One of the most fortunate crosses on the West Coast was Roland Hill's line-bred program of breeding Querido mares to Sonfield. The Querido daughters were all out of the old Sellman-line mares or out of the first fillies they had in California. There were eighty-six Querido mares and ninety-three Sonfield daughters. Querido 7370 and Mansfield 7255 were full brothers, and Sonfield 7952 was Mansfield's son out of the great mare Quietude 04271, who also was the dam of Upwey Ben Don 8843. Thus, the Sonfield/Querido cross produced mares and stallions of fine quality.

Viking Coronado 20154 (El Dorado King x Blossom's Lass), owned by Viking Ranch. Photo courtesy of LaVonne Houlton.

One of the very good mares from this cross was Alma Sonfield 06713. Her dam, Angel B 05035 was by Querido out of Angel 04209 (Moleskin x Angelina). A grand champion show mare of the 1940s, Alma Sonfield was the dam of Almond Joy 08167 and Hel's Altona 07495. Almond Joy had a show record too, with wins and good placings in halter. Her sire was Sun Down Morgan, mentioned earlier. Almond Joy's sons Poco Aljoy 11485, by Red Gates by Redman, and Orron 11756 both established show records and sired winning get.

Poco Aljoy sired Quiet Son De 13181, whose dam was Analin 07969 (Sonfield x Sallie Ann by Querido), and Orlaine's Breezy 011792. Breezy's dam was Sparkle Lady 07395 by Enowee 8606 (a son of Uhlan 7564) and out of Headlight Lady 05409 (Cuyamo x Geena), all California-bred. Uhlan was William Randolph Hearst's Government-bred stallion, who sired Katrilan 8121, fountainhead of the Muscle Man-Dapper Dan families.

Orron's daughter Oriana 020686 has made an outstanding show record as a western pleasure horse in southern California. Her dam was Belle Romanesque 07704, by Blackman. Another Orron offspring is Orilee 020669, a high-point halter mare and many-time champion. Orilee's dam is Royal Flash 014051, by Muscle Man 10697, out of Addy May Field 07929, who was a Sonfield daughter, out of the good mare Addy C 05279 (Querido x Addy, one of the original Hill mares).

Camille 04097 had nine foals by Querido, six of them fillies. Two of them later were bred to Sonfield: Blossom C 04911 and Blossom E 05159, and her daughter Trixie Blossom 05391 (by Joaquin Morgan) also was bred to Sonfield. However, Blossom C only had one filly by Sonfield and Trixie Blossom had none, so it was left to Blossom E to carry forward this female line with her six foals by Sonfield. (Blossom C did have two good daughters by Sparbeau).

Blossom E's best producing daughters were Bay Blossom 07928 and Anita Blossom 06722. From Bay Blossom came Impala Blossom 011320 and Impala Bay Blossom 013452, and Betty and J. L. McKinley's winning Produce of Dam group at the Golden West Regional Championship shows. Anita Blossom had a number of good offspring, all by Muscle Man. Her last filly, Blossom's Lass 013320, was orphaned at three months of age. This bad start didn't slow the filly down, though, as when her present owner showed her as a young mare in halter she was never out of the ribbons, never below third, and often first and champion. Blossom's Lass has had one son and five daughters to date (Editor's Note: Blossom's Lass ultimately had ten foals; seven fillies and three colts), and two of her offspring have been shown: Viking Coronado 20154 and Viking Quietude 029499. Viking Coronado has had a good show record in both Morgan and open shows, some highlights being "Most Classic Morgan" at Brentwood and N.C.M.H.C. 1973 Reserve High-Point Park Saddle Horse. His daughter, Melodic Princess 025574 was Reserve Junior Champion Mare at the Golden West Regional two years in a row. At this writing, Viking Quietude, a yearling mare, has five ribbons from five shows, plus being Reserve Champion Mare at Elk Grove.

Bonnie Sue 05436 and Miss President Morgan 06917 (b. 1946), by Sun Down Morgan 7388 (Raven Chief x Texsky). Photo courtesy of NMMH.

Mention must be made of a few other mares. One was Bonnie Sue 05436 who came to California in 1942, and two months later foaled a colt by Squire Burger that Merle Little registered as Senor Morgan 8647. Subsequently bred to Sun Down Morgan, mentioned earlier, Bonnie Sue had three fillies, Marlene's Morgan 06111, Duarte Maid 06389, and Miss President Morgan 06917. All four of these Morgans were shown successfully on the southern California circuit and all bred on to some extent. Marlene's Morgan, for example, was the dam of the H. P. Boyd's well-loved old mare, Gertrude Mae 09794. Miss President Morgan was the dam of Poco's Dream Girl 08614.

Betty Joaquin 05632 (Joaquin Morgan x Dan's Betty) was one of the very good mares bred by Roland Hill. Foaled in 1940, she ribboned in halter, and won in a variety of performance classes - stock horse, trail, and child's horse. As a broodmare she gave us several good Morgans, including Poco's Ace of Spades 11912 (sire of Poco's Queen 011118) and the fine mares Senorita Morgan 06390 and Mornaquin 08168.

One cannot stop without at least a brief mention of the fine mares raised by Mr. and Mrs. W. L. Linn of Turlock, or of W. L. Carter's extensive breeding program, which was founded on Sonfield mares. The J. Clark Bromileys fostered Morgans of the Sellman/Hill/Hearst cross. The foundation mares of Frank and Frieda Waer came from out of state, but through breedings to Monte L 8423 and his son Rex's Major Monte 9996, their offspring became part of the Western contingent.

So many mares and mare families have not been mentioned that should be covered - the Gay Mac daughters, Montabell's get, the Uhlan mares, the Spars, and many more. Still, we have pretty much reviewed the mare families in microcosm.

In an article on linebreeding in *The Morgan Horse* magazine, May 1958, Charlene Custer stated: "A pedigree is a blueprint of the characteristics that make up a purebred animal . . . When a pedigree is extended for eight generations, it shows definite patterns of the individuals that influence size, shape, quality, color, temperament, way of going, and disposition of your horse." She expressed what I have always believed very well. Richard Sellman built his band of Morgans from what he considered to be the best of the old time, true type Morgans. These were the kind that came West in the 1920s. Roland Hill and other judicious breeders blended their blood with the best of the Government lines, primarily from Bennington and General Gates. Morgans descended from these well-planned, well-bred, well-proven California mare families are still the modern breeders' best bet for type, quality, and temperament.

Morgans of Yesterday in Nevada and Arizona
1981

Unlike their neighbor, California, where Morgan history can be documented from Gold Rush days, Nevada and Arizona came quite late into the Morgan fold. The beginnings of a breeding program in Nevada didn't happen until the latter part of the 1920s. The Cananea Mining Company at Lochiel, Arizona owned the stallion Jackson's Rolls Golddust 3258 for a time (1870s or 1880s), but if he was used at the stud there it was not on registered Morgan mares. A dozen young Morgans came to Arizona from the Sellman Ranch in Texas in 1925, but a third of them went back to Texas the following February, and only one of the remaining colts sired two registered foals – and those not until 1944 and 1945.

Melville Haskell of Tucson, Arizona, owned two daughters of Sweet Briar 6305 that were bred in New Mexico. They were Sweet Sultana 05816, f. 1920, and Starry Glow 05817, f. 1921. Sweet Briar was a son of Croydon Prince 5325 and Hippolyte 03222 by Borden's Ethan Allen III 3987. Haskell is of particular interest because he was a member of the early American Quarter Horse Association's board of directors, an executive committee member in the early 1950s, and one of the founders of Quarter Horse racing.

The man who bought nine colts and three fillies from Sellman in 1925 was Jack C. Kinney, also of Tucson, one of five honorary vice-presidents of the A.Q.H.A. during 1941-1944. Quite a number of the earlier-registered Quarter Horses in Arizona had Morgan or part-Morgan antecedents, some through the Headlight Morgan son Bobbie Burns 6180. In fact, Quarter Horses with Morgan blood – generally through their dams – were bred at Tucson, Paulden, Tolleson, Prescott, Casa Grande, Marana, Flagstaff, Gilbert, Nogales and Patagonia in the 1940s and early 50s. Six Morgan stallions were sold to Arizona residents between 1927-1937. A dozen stallions and sixteen mares went there between 1938-1950. It is interesting to speculate on how many of these ended up as the anonymous "Morgan Horse" or "Morgan Mare" in the back of some old Quarter Horse pedigrees.

Those six stallions mentioned above were all purchased as yearlings or two-year-olds. The first one to come to Arizona was California Allen 7584 (Querido x Tab), sold by Roland Hill to Cornelius H. Tesky of Mayer, Arizona, in February 1929. In December 1936, the V Bar V Cattle Co., Rimrock, Arizona purchased Ingenuity 7959 (Monterey x Carol), foaled in Montana, and then owned in Wyoming. The mare, Carol 04678, is of special interest. She was by the Government-bred Revere 7422, out of the Sellman-bred mare, Alibirdie 04282, bred by the U.S. Range Livestock Experiment Station in Miles City, Montana. Foaled in 1929, she was sold in 1936 to the Spear-Morgan Livestock Co. in Sheridan, Wyoming, and she produced three A.Q.H.A. registered foals in that state!

In 1938, the Arizona Livestock Company of Phoenix and Seligman bought Sea Cliff 8020 from J. Sheldon Potter of San Francisco, and two Hearst-bred yearlings, Jack London 8041 and The Senator 8042 from the Kings County Land and Cattle Company. Sea Cliff was by Don Juan 7623 x Roverta 04467. Jack London and The Senator were both by Uhlan 7564 out of Hill-bred mares.

None of these six appears as the sire of registered Morgans in Arizona up through the early 1950s. If they weren't all gelded, they were crossed on range mares in their home areas.

Within a few years, A. N. Kay had purchased another stallion, Alonzo Sentney 8441 (Sir Linsley x Baby Dix) and the mares Addy Spar 05629 (Sparbeau x Addy), Fawnette Spar 05626 (Sparbeau x Fawn K.) and Joaquin's Angel 05633 (Joaquin Morgan x Angela A.). Mr. Kay registered four Morgan foals by Alonzo: Don Cossack 8950 (x Fawnette Spar) in 1941, Sun Valley Lu 06274 (x Joaquin's Angel) 1944, Gingerbread Maid 06544 (x Fawnette Spar) and Luana 06543 (x Joaquin's Angel), both in 1945. He sold the stallion to C. L. Harelson, Glendale, Arizona in 1944.

The U.S. Department of the Interior and the San Carlos Apache Tribe purchased five very well-bred young Morgan stallions for the improvement of Reservation stock: Golden Light 8062 and Silver Tip 8036 in 1938 from H. T. Hineman of Kansas, both by Silver Crown 7828 (Spotlight x Gold Floss), and in 1945 Chock L. 8727, Pearl's Allen 8363 and Plainsman 8268. The Agency did not purchase any Morgan mares for their program.

Volume VI of the *Morgan Horse Register* records a number of transfers to Justin Dart, Dart Cattle Co., Rimrock, Arizona, in 1940 and 1941; however, some of these horses went to Massachusetts, some to California, as Dart had interests in all three states. In 1942 he had two colts and a filly, and another colt in 1943, all sired by Squire Burger. All four went to California breeders, two alongside their dams. Merle Little of Monrovia got Bonnie Sue 05436 and her colt, who grew up to be an excellent individual and sire, Senor Morgan 8647. At the same time Little obtained the mare Fontaine 05272 and her colt Rey Del Mundo 8638. W. D. Fulton of Camarillo purchased the filly High Valley Mecca 05938 (x Carmel Snow 05656). Mr. and Mrs. F. J. Munson purchased the mare Zuana X-05441 – part of Dart's California band – and the following spring she produced the fine horse Juzan King 8741.

Several sales of Morgans to residents of Arizona were recorded during those years, but no real breeding programs of any size resulted, although W. L. Graves had made a good beginning, at the Tonto Rim Ranch, Payson, Arizona. Between 1932-1935, four mares and a stallion – all by Raven Chief 7116 (Morgan Chief x Baby Girl) – were purchased from F. A. Fickert of Tehachapi. These were: Tonto's Roamer 8196, Copper of Tonto 05331, Tonto's Queen 05330, Tonto's Traveler 05340 and Wendy Morgan 05332.

Tonto's Queen and Wendy Morgan each produced a foal by the Raven Chief son Eagle 8189 in 1939. In December 1941 Graves sold Tonto's Roamer, Copper of Tonto, Tonto's Queen and Mary Jane Morgan to the Bermans Stock Farm. The following year they all went to John F. Van Leuven, where they became the foundation for the "Morgans of River Way" at Three Rivers, California.

Another pair of Arizonans bred Morgan mares to the good stallion Silver's Dick 8133

Silver Ranger 7813. Photo courtesy of NMMH.

(Silver Ranger x Dan's Baby), purchased by I. E. Muse, Yarnell, Arizona, from W. P. Thornhill, Miami, Texas in 1938.

Silver's Dick was beautifully bred in the lines so admired by Westerners over the years, and it's a pity he didn't have a large court of mares to draw from. His sire, Silver Ranger 7813 was by Querido, out of Angelina, she by Texas Allen (Headlight Morgan and The Admiral breeding). Dan's Baby was doubled up on the blood of Headlight Morgan 4683, with lines through the dam's side back to old Billy Root 9.

Silver Ranger sired a number of Palomino horses in Texas that found their way into old Quarter Horse pedigrees, and Silver's Dick probably did the same in Arizona. In 1945 Charles Williams of Wickenburg, Arizona purchased the stallion. Howard S. Sanford, also of Wickenburg, had the good mare Mary Blossom 05281 (Querido x Camille) who produced Timsbury Rose 07536 (by Gay Mac) in 1948, Timsbury Violet 07850 (by Silver's Dick) in 1949, and the colts Timsbury Johnny Jump Up 10665 and Jack-in-the-Pulpit 10881, both by Silver's Dick, in 1951 and 1952.

Ralph A. Fisher of Phoenix purchased Luana 06543 (mentioned previously) from A. N. Kay as a weanling, and got from her two foals by Silver's Dick: Alazana Duquese 07778 in 1949 and Tobe Jr. 10639 in 1951.

There was a lot more Morgan activity in Nevada between the 1920s and 1950s thanks primarily to one man, Clark Ringling, at Lovelock. He bred eleven foals by Royce 7748 (Winterset x Potena), ten by Black Winter 9540 (Flyhawk x Midnight Beauty), seventeen sired by Revere 7422 (Mansfield x Folly), thirteen by Vanguard 8234 (Romax Light x Kitty Edna), and two by Dewey 6481 (General Gates x Mrs. Culvers).

Black Winter 9540 at 18 months of age, by Flyhawk 7526. Photo courtesy of NMMH.

Interestingly, the foundation for Clark Ringling's Morgan broodmare band was Red Bessie, a mare of old Spanish-California stock, foaled about 1905 at the Clark Ranch, Inlay, Nevada (between Lovelock and Winnemucca). In 1917 Red Bessie produced a chestnut filly, Flora, by the American Saddle Horse, Nevada Chief (A.S.H. 5835), from which Ringling got three daughters important to the story of his band of Morgans. The first was a black mare, Bessie, f. 1923, got by the Thoroughbred stallion, Rifle Shooter, son of imported Star Shoot, by Isinglass. Bessie's first foal was the black mare Falcon, f. 1927, by Dewey 6481.

The second of Flora's trio of daughters was The Lovely One, f. 1926, also by Dewey. The third was another Dewey daughter, Vera, a chestnut, f. 1929. Vera's line lives on through her one daughter, Golden Revere X-05554, by Revere. Bred back to her sire, this mare produced the stallion Sunshine R. 8315, f. 1940. In 1943 Sunshine R. went to Washington, after siring four foals for George P. Rutledge in California. They were Sunshine Revere 8965 and Sunshine Sue 06083 (both out of Dulcet), Eagle Dan 8769 (x Ginger Ale) and Belle Starr 06283 (x Star Dust). Sunshine R. had two owners and a number of offspring in Washington. In April 1963, C. D. Parkinson of Eugene, Oregon purchased him, and the following spring he obtained a son of the old horse, Stormy H. 11753, out of Gay Girl. In 1964 Forrest Jones, Termo, California, purchased Stormy H.

Ringling bred Flora's daughter The Lovely One back to her sire, getting Anneka Van Horn X-05541 in 1930. From this double General Gates line mare Ringling got one colt, Lovelock 8311, which he sold, and four mares: Anneka Revere 05369, Anneka's Red Girl 05542 and Peggy Revere 05368, all sired by Revere 7422, and Dell V. 05306, by Vanguard 8234.

The Dewey daughter Falcon was bred back to her sire, producing the bay mare Fanchon X-05553 in 1931. Fanchon produced one colt, five fillies. One of her daughters was Brown Leaf R. 05366, among whose offspring were Winnemucca 8312 and the mare Van's Lady 06071, dam of Royce's Falcon 06817, one of the best broodmares in the long breeding program of the late W. T. Carter. In all, Ringling raised thirty descendants of Bessie, twenty from The Lovely One, and two from Vera. Not a bad legacy from one old Spanish-California mare!

In 1917 and 1918 the Government was buying cavalry horses throughout the West. At the time, concern was expressed that our army was the poorest mounted of any in World War I. Consequently, the Remount Service was organized. It was quite a long program, with changing goals over the years. Remount-owned Thoroughbred stallions were placed in Elko County, Nevada in 1921-22. Over the years Arabian and Morgan stallions stood for Remount Service as well. The Bureau of Animal Industry loaned studs from the U.S. Government Morgan Horse Farm in Vermont to the Remount Service. Revere 7422 was one of eight Morgan remounts stationed in the Midwest and West. Ringling got seventeen foals by this stallion between 1936-1941. As late as 1945 the Remount Service was still in the market for a considerable number of stallions (including Morgans) in the western Remount area. These studs were then loaned to farmers and stockmen for the improvement of horses being raised in the U.S. Early Remount stallions stood for a fee of no more than $10.00. During the 1949 breeding season, Revere was stationed with Harold E. Bradford at Susanville, California.

Revere 7422. Photo courtesy of NMMH.

It was Ringling's belief that "A horse that hasn't disposition that made the Morgan famous is not a good Morgan regardless of his pedigree or conformation." He had Royce 7748 brought out from Kansas in 1943 to head up his breeding program. Foaled in 1930 in Iowa, Royce was a good-looking black Morgan, just over fifteen hands, weighing around 1075 pounds. He was a well set up horse, muscular, with a well-laid shoulder, strong, short back, good length of croup, nicely crested, and with good width between the eyes. Important to Ringling was the fact that Royce had an excellent disposition, and he passed it on to his get.

In 1946 Ringling purchased the weanling Black Winter 9540 (Flyhawk x Midnight Beauty), whose dam was a full sister to Royce. Ringling raised ten foals by Black Winter between 1948-1953, and eight of them were black.

The other stallion Ringling used to a large extent was Vanguard 8234. Foaled in Nebraska in 1939, his sire was by Romanesque, his dam by Winterset. Vanguard sired three colts and ten fillies during three seasons (1942-1944) at the Ringling Ranch. For length of time in the business and number of Morgans bred and owned, Clark Ringling topped all others in Nevada. As in other parts of the West, there were those in Nevada who had Morgan blood in their Quarter Horses — for example, Shorty Hopkins of Winnemucca had the A.Q.H.A. registered Tony Hopkins (13, 125), f. 1945, dam: Helen by a Morgan horse (it's a good guess her sire was old Revere). Benny Binion at Las Vegas raised a number of Quarter mares by Rocksprings (P-25, 336), whose dam was by Headlight Morgan.

When G. A. Wessich, later of Linden and Stockton, California, lived in Nevada he purchased the stallion Peerless A. 8017 (Querido x Alkali) and the mare Katrina 04262 (Joe Bailey x Lucia) from Roland Hill. He raised three colts from this pair before moving to California.

Cuyamo 7974 (Redwood Morgan x Jocbo Brownie) was sold to Nevada in 1942 at age eleven. Several other people had one or two Morgans at Ely, Austin, Winnemucca and Reno in the early 1940s, and a very few foals were raised.

The only other Morgan breeding program of any size in Nevada during this era was that of the Carson Indian School at Stewart, Nevada. In August 1940, the school obtained the brown stallion Euchre 7769 (Monterey x Bronita) and six mares, all bred by the U.S. Range Livestock Experiment Station, Miles City, Montana. Euchre came from F. C. Ruddy of Billings; the mares all came from the Crow Indian Agency in Montana. Five of the mares, Falita 04775, Glacier 04825, Grand Slam 04827, Grosbeak 04828 and Gyration 04829 were by Monterey, and the dams of the first four were of Sellman breeding. The sixth mare, Dalita 04683, was by Revere, out of a Sellman mare. The school bred sixteen foals from these mares 1942-1945, and transferred nine of them to the Wind River Indian Agency at Fort Washakie, Wyoming, together with Dalita, Falita, Grand Slam and Gyration in 1945 and 1946. It seems likely that Euchre went with them, since his son Buckles 9623, f. 1946, was listed in the Register as having been bred by the U.S. Indian Service at Fort Washakie. Falita and Grosbeak were sold not long after this move.

Considering their late start, and their spread-out, rather sparse populations then, Arizona and Nevada did make important contributions to the Morgan stock of the western region. Descendants of many Morgans mentioned above can be found in breeding programs today. In Susanville, California, Millard Ulch, E. B. Coffin and Emma Randrup intensified the Revere lines. You'll find Revere back in the pedigrees of Joyce Straw's Alamar Morgans in Auburn, California. W. T. Carter drew quite heavily from the Royce lines in his program, and R-J Morgans in Delhi, California has raised many well-known show horses from Mr. America 12938, a descendant of old Winne-

Royce 7748. Photo courtesy of NMMH.

mucca. Jimmy Smith raised a lot of good Morgans by California King 11383 (grandson of Winnemucca) during the years he lived in California, and won consistently with his show string from that line. Sunshine Revere 8965 stood at stud in the Klamath area of California.

Black Bart 12320, out of Royce's Falcon, sired some fine foals and placed fourth in a big stallion class at one of the Golden West National Morgan Horse Shows in Sacramento, shortly before his untimely death. If you've ever watched the tandem pair driven by Evelyn Harrod, you've seen a bit of the legacy of Clark Ringling and his stallion Royce.

And besides all that, there are still those unsung Morgans that didn't hurt a lot of Quarter Horses even a little bit, when it came to breeding a cowman's ideal of a good stock horse!

Morgans in the West: The Development of a Type
1984

Part I

During my teen years in the 1940s, I spent all my summer vacations on my uncle's cattle ranch in Northern California's Siskiyou Mountains. Cold Creek Ranch was a 1,280-acre paradise to a young girl who loved horses, cattle, wild country and coyotes singing in the night. Uncle Ed bought me the perfect horse, a small bay, part-Morgan mare; she and I were both fourteen. I will never know a better horse. What other blood Minnie carried we didn't know, but she had all the attributes that make the Morgan horse special. From her year and place of birth it is probable that she was a granddaughter of one of the Sellman Morgans brought to California by Reginald Parsons in 1920.

Cold Creek Ranch contained a varied terrain, from green, sweeping meadows to lava-pitted, brushy hills; from dry, crumbly ground to fir-covered ridges leading up to a mountaintop fire look-out. It was a land that demanded a sensible, sure-footed horse with lots of stamina.

Together, Minnie and I explored every inch of the ranch and the surrounding countryside. She was a dainty mare who never, never stumbled, never wore out. There was a gaiety about her – she moved with head up, ears perked, never missing a thing, yet with never a balk or a shy. Only once did she refuse what I asked her to do, and perhaps that saved my life. I had opened a wire gate down by the creek and started to lead her through, but she balked. It was so unlike the mare that I turned around to see why. There in the grass near my feet was a large rattlesnake, coiling itself to strike.

During those memorable summers I came to know some fine registered Morgans – the wonderful Redman 8056, a handsome young stallion named North Fork, the sweet and typey mare Balkitty 04437 (maternal half-sister to Mountcrest Sellman), and her two sons Copco Joe and Copco Silva. My uncle had another half-Morgan mare, a big-bodied bay that was a marvelous cow horse. It is more than coincidence that years later, when I began to buy horses of my own, they were Morgans. The first was a great-grandson of North Fork and the second had Redman in her pedigree. All of these horses were from Sellman-bred stock.

California has a heritage of huge, sprawling cattle ranches, dating back to the days of the

North Fork. Photo courtesy of the National Museum of the Morgan Horse.

Spanish Californios. As early as 1849 Morgan stallions were being brought into the state. In time, many of the range horses throughout the state carried a degree of Morgan blood. When the old Spanish land grants were broken up and taken over by Americans, the raising of beef cattle was still a major industry in the West. Much of the land occupied by these ranches ran through the foothills of the Coast Range or the Sierra Nevadas, and even the valley ranches made use of summer grazing in the high country. Many horses were required in the operation of these ranches, and these horses had to have special qualifications to succeed in the work required of them. The basics were intelligence, stamina, tractability and balance.

The horse with "cow savvy" has to be able to use his head. He's alert to what is happening in the herd, ready to turn the cow that tries to break away. He has to be able to go all day, often in rough country. He's easy on his rider, not wearing them both out with high-strung antics. For balance, the cow horse must have good legs, very good feet, a well-laid shoulder, high wither and the ability to get his quarters under him on downhill slopes, stops and quick turns – we call him "handy." He will be rather short-backed and deep-chested, with a natural arch to his neck, clean in the throatlatch, and with nice, big nostrils to ensure a good air intake.

In the 19th century Morgan blood helped improve the quality of utility and stock horses on huge ranches of California's central and upper Sacramento valleys, for such men as General John Bidwell, Jesse D. Carr and James Ben Ali Haggin.

Bidwell, a leader of the first overland party to California in 1841, purchased the 26,000-acre Rancho Arroyo Chico in Butte County. By 1855 the ranch carried 12,000 cattle and 1,588 horses, plus other livestock. Bidwell's John Morgan reportedly sired the best of stock. The general bred and raised Black Prince 179, whose sire was a black Morgan stallion that caught Bidwell's eye on a trip across the plains around 1855.

Jesse Carr bought the fine trotting stallion and sire Redfield's Vermont 121, and Morgan blood was mixed with the local stock for many years on the vast Carr & Haggin ranch.

Wine Creek Black Hawk 1323 was brought in 1861 to the Union Ranch near Folsom, California, where he was offered at stud. Many more examples could be cited, and it is interesting to note that more than two-thirds of these early Morgan imports were sons or descendants of Black Hawk 20. However, by the turn of the century, there was nothing left of the old pure Morgan stock on the West Coast.

By 1920 several western cattlemen again realized that Morgan horses had all the qualities they required, when bred in certain strains. The first place these Californians went for their foundation stock was to the Sellman ranch in Texas. Their second source was the U.S. Government Morgan Horse Farm in Vermont.

It is important to remember that the so-called "Western" Morgan had the same ancestry as his Eastern counterparts. For example, the "Western" stallion Sonfield 7935 and the "Eastern" stallion Upwey Ben Don 8843 were out of the same mare, Quietude 04271 (Troubadour of Willowmoor x Ruth). It is also necessary to explore the composition and development of the Sellman Morgans, as they relate to today's Morgans in the West.

In the history of any light horse breed the names of a few breeders stand out in bold type. Occasionally, fortune smiles on a particular horseman just by chance. But more often than not, a man's program succeeds because he has spent years of careful study, not only on bloodlines but also on results. He selects the best of stallions for his mares, and concentrates always on breeding up. If he has been as wise as he had hoped to be, breeders generations later will proudly say their horses trace to his stock. Such is the case with Richard Sellman.

Sellman, a Marylander, moved to Rochelle, Texas, in the late 1800s, and founded the 40,000-acre Mountain Vale Ranch. The number of Morgans identified as Sellman's in the III, IV and V volumes of *The American Morgan Horse Register* is an astounding one – 689. He also had more than twenty broodmares designated by color only, sired by Major Gordon 4924, and apparently foaled between 1886 and 1899. One of his first mares was sired by an English Coach Horse. From 1905 through 1925 Sellman-bred foals were produced by 273 mares. The peak year was 1921, when fifty-four colts and fillies were born. The average over the first eighteen years was thirty-five foals. In 1924 only four colts were registered.

When Sellman began his breeding program there was much cross-breeding going on – a practice he deplored. In a limited sense, the infusion of blood from other stocks was necessary, but in some areas this was carried to such a degree that the true Morgan pattern was being lost. Sellman wanted to save the old-time, distinctively typey Morgan for posterity. For this purpose he selected six of the most representative stallions to be found, trying to stay within eight generations from the foundation sire, Justin Morgan 1.

The stallions chosen by Sellman descended in tail-male lines from two of Justin Morgan's best sons, Sherman Morgan 5 and Woodbury Morgan 7. Major Antoine 4776, Gold Medal 4847, The Admiral 4871 and Red Oak 5249 traced, through two sons of Black Hawk 20, to Sherman Morgan. Major Gordon 4924 and Headlight Morgan 4683 sprang from descendants of two of Woodbury Morgan's sons.

Many mares used in the early stages of the breeding program at Mountain Vale Ranch were daughters of Major Gordon, a stylish black stallion with a star on his forehead. He was foaled about 1880 and lived to be nineteen years old. Sellman purchased him in 1886. Major Gordon stood sixteen hands high, weighed 1,260 pounds and had very fine action. His sire, Young Octoroon, won many races in his day.

The legendary Headlight Morgan was Sellman's foremost sire. By Ethan Allen 2nd and out of Lady Stratton, and a runt as a weanling and yearling, Headlight Morgan was selected by the Morgan Horse Club of America as the best living representative of original Morgan type in 1900.
Photo courtesy of the National Museum of the Morgan Horse.

Headlight Morgan was one of the breed's outstanding sires. He was a deep red-chestnut, with a wide stripe and one white foot. He was beautifully bred, being one of the best-known sons of Ethan Allen 2nd 406, and out of the famous mare, Lady Stratton by Vermont Morgan 462. A third son of Justin Morgan, Bulrush Morgan 6, is also found in Headlight Morgan's pedigree. Bulrush was renowned for his soundness, powers of endurance, muscular development and longevity; traits that he passed on to his progeny.

Headlight Morgan was the kind of horse that inspires legends. Foaled in 1893, he was already twenty-one years old when Richard Sellman bought him, and he lived almost twelve more years. He was bred in Illinois, foaled in Kansas, and orphaned when just a few weeks old. He ran with the range horses all summer and was brought in with the weanlings that fall. From this bad start he was a runty yearling, with a thick, shaggy coat that didn't shed off until he was two. Broke to both saddle and harness, he was used as a cow horse for several years – his owner even roped coyotes off him.

Headlight Morgan's first registered foal arrived in 1899. The next year he was selected by the Morgan Horse Club of America as the best living representative of the original Morgan type, and awarded a silver trophy. The stunted orphan colt, who weighed only 850 pounds as a young horse, developed into a powerful, heavily muscled, 1,200-pound stallion, beautiful enough to capture the silver medal as the best of his breed. He was swift and agile, with a reputed 22-foot stride from a flat-footed start. He was a sure sire, with 174 registered sons and daughters of fine quality, and fully deserved the name he was often given – "King of the Morgans." Richard Sellman must have purchased him in late 1913, as his first crop of Texas foals didn't arrive until 1915. From then through 1921 he sired 112 foals for Sellman.

Another of the Sellman stallions was Major Antoine. Through the second dam of his grandsire, Meteor, Major Antoine carried the blood of Revenge 8, another son of Justin Morgan. Major Antoine was foaled in 1901 in Amboy, Illinois. His sire, Meteor Jr., won six firsts at state and county fairs from 1897 through 1899. Sellman purchased the black colt from his breeder, Mrs. C. Antoine, and had forty-seven fillies and sixteen colts sired by him. Probably his best son was The Jew 6274, who sired fillies almost exclusively. Major Antoine disappeared from the pages of the registry volumes after his 1908 foals were recorded.

Major Antoine and Gold Medal had almost identical breeding, both being by Meteor Jr., out of daughters of General Lee, sire of six race-winning Morgan trotters. Gold Medal's career at the stud was short, too – he had twenty-eight foals between 1906 and 1910, then was sold, and evidently not used at stud again.

The only stallion in the Sellman group to produce more purebred foals than Headlight Morgan was The Admiral, with 187. Foaled in 1903, this chestnut son of Jubilee de Jarnette would have stood out in any group of stallions. He came from a line famous for its beauty and accomplishments. Reading backward up the tail-male line we find Justin Morgan, Sherman Morgan, Black Hawk, Ethan Allen, Daniel Lambert, Jubilee Lambert and Jubilee de Jarnette – all outstanding in appearance and trotting speed. Daniel Lambert sired more than one hundred race winners, nine of which won fifty races or more. He was the source of fine trotting stock for generations. His son, Jubilee Lambert, also won on the trotting track and was good enough to be chosen as the mate for the incomparable Lady de Jarnette, probably the greatest show mare of all time. Their son, Jubilee de Jarnette, was exceptionally attractive and a show-ring star in his own right.

On his dam's side, The Admiral traced to Morrill 55, descendant of Bulrush. This combined the very best in Morgan bloodlines, giving The Admiral a full measure of beauty and speed from Sherman Morgan, plus the extra soundness and development from the Bulrush strain. It is no wonder, then, that he sired many of the best-quality Morgans of his era. His band of daughters was outstanding; they were uniform in appearance and disposition, and they in turn produced foals of excellence.

The last of the stallions purchased by Sellman was Red Oak, a powerful, handsome bay horse, who stood fifteen hands and weighed nearly 1,100 pounds. Foaled in 1906 in Middlebury, Vermont, Red Oak was also deep in old-time Morgan blood. His sire was General Gates 666, great-grandson of Ethan Allen 50. His dam was Marguerite, whose pedigree contained the names of Sherman Morgan, Black Hawk and Hale's Green Mountain Morgan 42. The latter also had won the silver cup for being a near-replica of old Justin Morgan. General Gates, senior sire at the U.S. Government Morgan Horse Farm, was said to closely resemble Black Hawk 20, and his colts were beautiful, sound and strong. His progeny gained notice in the old 300-mile endurance rides (1918 through 1925), and he was named the outstanding sire in the rigorous Cavalry tests. As a result of competition in the Vermont trail rides (1937 through 1948) it was noted that the first sire lines of breeding came from Mansfield through Bennington to General Gates.

As a yearling, Red Oak was first in a class of twenty colts. He then was purchased by the U.S. Government, and was one of the most popular stallions bred at Middlebury, Vermont. Red Oak stood at stud for several years at the State Agricultural College in Amherst, Massachusetts. Sellman probably purchased him in 1918. Between 1919 and 1925 Red Oak sired 84 foals for Sellman and four for Texas A & M College.

According to many authorities, it is of little value to breeders to check beyond the third generation in a horse's pedigree. They say that the blood of any one ancestor beyond that point can have little bearing on the product of the present mating. There are sixteen horses in the immediate pedigree of a registered animal. Behind the sixteen stand hundreds of horses within the extended pedigree. The possibilities for gene combinations are staggering. The chance of one animal seven generations back having great influence over the makeup of a new foal appear very slight.

Yet, in the long view, these early progenitors do have great value to the breed today – especially in the case of volume breeders with the foresight of a Richard Sellman. The progeny of the six Sellman stallions were responsible for whole families of Morgans in many areas of the West. Because their owners liked the original stock, they stuck pretty close to the family system, frequently keeping within the same strain rather than infusing the blood of outside stallions to any great degree.

To illustrate, the authors' mare, Gimma 010133, now twenty-six years old, was the foundation mare at Viking Morgan Ranch in Modesto, California. In this mare's extended pedigree the six Sellman stallions appear sixty-four times. She has eighteen crosses to Headlight Morgan alone. In all, fifty-seven Sellman mares and stallions are named 125 times in her extended pedigree. It has been said that Richard Sellman could spot horses of his breeding in any band of Morgans. I like to think that if Sellman could have seen Gimma in her "young days" he would have recognized her. Often, when outside blood was desired, these early breeders turned to another distinctive family group – the sons and grandsons of General Gates. This in time resulted in the Sellman/Hill/Hearst strain of Morgans that has proved to be so popular and successful in California.

Richard Sellman used many sons of his six major stallions and later in his breeding program did purchase a few other studs. He grouped his mares into family units and bred them accordingly. In the first half of the program, daughters of Major Gordon were bred to Major Antoine, The Admiral, and Gold Medal. The Admiral was used on the Major Antoine mares. Some of The Admiral's daughters were bred back to their own sire, or to one of his sons, but most of them were bred to Headlight Morgan. Still later, Sellman bred mares by Headlight Morgan to Red Oak and his sons, and so on. Sellman didn't want his breeding program to end at his front gate. He often sold mares by the boxcar load, with a carefully selected stallion to accompany them. In this manner, many units of Sellman-bred stock moved to other areas of the west.

Reginald O. Parsons re-introduced the purebred Morgan into California in 1920, when he purchased a carload of broodmares and fillies, and the stallion Baldie's Boy 7117 (Headlight Morgan x Baldie Antoine) from Mountain Vail Ranch. Parsons owned a beautiful spread, Mountcrest Ranch, near Hilt, California, a hamlet between the Klamath River and the Oregon border. Seven of the Sellman mares were in foal. The next spring one of them, Kitty E., produced the first Morgan "native son" of the present century, Mountcrest Sellman 7289, by Joe Bailey 7119, a son of Headlight Morgan. Four other mares had Joe Bailey foals that year, and two were by Dot, a son of Morgan Chief. Baldie's Boy sired one colt in 1922 and four fillies in 1923, out of the Sellman mares. Between 1924 and 1927 Parsons sold most of his Morgans to Northern California and Southern Oregon people, but he kept Mountcrest Sellman until 1932, when William Randolph Hearst purchased the stallion. No transfers are recorded on the last eight of Parsons' horses.

The Sellman Morgans, both mares and stallions, made a sizable contribution in the formative stages of development of the Texas Quarter Horse in the first quarter of this century. The most shining example of this is the AQHA stallion Two Eyed Jack (178,246), who today is the number one world champion Quarter Horse sire. His offspring have amassed more than 11,000 halter points and almost 8,000 working points. They have earned 149 register of merits and sixty-seven

AQHA championships. No other stallion's get have come even close to this record. A close look at the pedigree of Two Eyed Jack shows that his dam, Triangle Tookie (70,166), is a maternal descendant of the Morgan stallion Redolent 7295.

Redolent, foaled in 1920, was bred by Richard Sellman, sired by Red Oak, out of Minnie K. by Headlight Morgan. Fellow Texan Tom Burnett purchased him from Sellman about 1925. Redolent was bred to one of Burnett's "riding type" mares, which produced the registered Quarter Horse mare, Triangle Lady 10 (P-445) in 1930. This mare was the dam of the palomino Lady Hancock (3637), whose daughter was Triangle Tookie. Tom Burnett founded the big Triangle Ranch near Wichita Falls, Texas, and there produced outstanding cutting and roping horses. He became one of the "big" breeders of Quarter Horses, and Redolent is to be found close up in many of the early Triangle pedigrees, through several of his daughters. It should be noted also that Jubilee King stood at the Triangle Ranch from 1934 through 1941, and many of the Triangle mares were by him. Redolent spent the rest of his life at Burnett's, and died when he was about twenty-five years old. Redolent's full brother, Romance 7306, Headlight Morgan and his son Bobbie Burns, and a number of others, all Sellman-owned, are also in the foundation of many Texas Quarter Horses, primarily through their daughters. Another Headlight Morgan son, Rondeau 7214, found his way into AQHA pedigrees (though generally not by name) after being sold by the Sellman estate. He was successively owned by Robert Dean, The Matador Land and Cattle Company, and the Adair's big J A Ranch at Paloduro, Texas. The Swenson Brothers' big SMS spread near Stamford, Texas, obtained a group of Sellman mares in 1914, together with the young stallions Red Bird 6775 and Gotch 5979. The colts were both by The Admiral, and were to head up the SMS stud. Eventually Arabian blood was added to the stock, and fine cutting and stock horses resulted from this cross. One example was the bay gelding Rey Boy (15, 810), foaled at SMS in 1943, and owned by "Wild Bill" Elliott of Hollywood. Rey Boy's sire was the Quarter Horse Billy, by King (P-234). His dam was by Niwad (Arabian), out of a daughter of an SMS Morgan stallion.

This little glimpse into the Quarter Horse world indicates that the California ranchers of the 1920s and 30s were catching on to what the Texans had known for some time: Sellman Morgans were ideal for a rancher's needs, and also greatly improved the crossbred native stock.

Part II

During the first half of the twentieth century there was a great need for good stock horses among large ranchers and cattlemen in both the Mid-West and the Far West. Fortunately for breeders today, these men recognized the value of the Headlight Morgan offspring – both from his early Kansas foal crops and his later Texas sons and daughters. Eventually, descendants of both Headlight Morgan families found their way into California and Pacific Northwest breeding programs.

Headlight Morgan's first crop of thirty-five Texas foals in 1915 was exactly half as many as the seventy he had sired during all the years he stood in Kansas. It would seem that an impeccably bred, grand champion stallion should have had a bigger mid-west court, but distance and a sparsely populated area were against him at the turn of the century.

Forty different persons bred mares to Headlight Morgan while he was in Kansas, and 60 percent of them were one-time breeders. Margaret C. Parks bred five of his earliest offspring, and Dick and Fred Skinner between them only got nine. The Kansas foals, with two exceptions, were all born within a radius of about fifty miles in a little chain of villages near the Oklahoma border in southwestern Kansas, from Fowler to Arkalon, along what is now Highway 54. The Parks quintet was born at Englewood, southeast of Fowler.

Headlight Morgan averaged less than five foals a year – his biggest Kansas season was 1909 when eight foals were born. Between 1899 and 1914 he sired twenty-five colts and forty-five fillies that we know of. Fourteen of his daughters were unregistered but produced registered offspring, and nine of these mares were bred back to their sire, as were a number of his registered daughters. At least nine of his Kansas sons (two of them unregistered) sired registered Morgans. From this first Kansas Headlight Morgan family descended an enormous number of Morgans spread all across the country. Three important early sons were Dr. Casto 5795, Easter Allen Morgan 6597, and Justin Headlight 7008.

Dr. Casto was bred by Fred Skinner, foaled in 1908 at Meade, Kansas. His dam, Diamond, was by Young Telescope, son of Telescope Ethan, by Holabird's Ethan Allen 63. Dr. Casto is known to us primarily through his son Spotlight and daughter Mirtle. Spotlight gave us the stallions Silver Crown and Jack Sprat, and the mares Kanza and Edomala. H. T. Hineman of Dighton, Kansas bred Jack Sprat. His sire Spotlight was out of Gold June, granddaughter of Ben Franklin 1508. Jack Sprat's dam, Gold Floss, was a half-sister to Gold June. Charles F. Ayer of Meeker, Colorado purchased Jack Sprat in 1933, and from him descended a whole family of "Ayr" surnamed horses, many of which were eventually purchased by E. W. Roberts of Hi Pass, California. Silver Crown, a full brother to Jack Sprat, was bred to Kanza, Mirtle and Edomala, doubling the Headlight Morgan strain. Kanza also produced the mares Sun Spot and South Spot by another closely-related stallion, Chocolate.

Dee Dee Chocolate, a champion stock horse of the 1960s, also had a heavy concentration of Headlight Morgan blood. Her sire was Double Chocolate, whose sire Chocolate and dam Joice traced to Headlight Morgan through both their sires and dams. Additionally, "Dee Dee's" dam was a Major R. M. granddaughter, giving one more line back to the old horse through Mariah K., dam of Major R. M.'s sire, Romanesque.

Jolly Roger 8479. Chestnut, foaled May 9, 1941. Joe L. Young, owner and up. Photo courtesy of the National Museum of the Morgan Horse.

John F. Parks of Morrill, Nebraska bred the second son of importance, Easter Allen Morgan, foaled in 1909. He was very well bred on both sides of his pedigree. His dam Bessie Morgan 0241 was by Flying Morrill, son of Vermont Ranger by Morrill 55. His second dam, Sunrise, was by the Hanchett Horse, son of Hale's Green Mountain Morgan 42, and third dam by Sherman Black Hawk 51. The best horse Easter Allen Morgan gave us was the stallion Texas Allen 6650, whose producing daughters became part of California's foundation stock.

One daughter, Addy, was dam of a whole line of "Addy" mares. Texsky was the dam of the handsome sire Sun Down Morgan. From Angelina descended the fine "Angel" family of mares. Areadne was one of the first of the Sellman mares in California. Tab produced Tehachapi Allan, Tejon Chief, plus some fine mares for Roland Hill. Another of the Texas Allen daughters in California was Texanita, another of Hill's purchases, and dam of the good mare Jinglebells and others.

114

The third important early son of Headlight Morgan was Justin Headlight, foaled in 1912, and bred by E. O. Palmer of Meade, Kansas. His dam Dollie was said to be a Standardbred pacing mare of good road qualities. Among his offspring were the mares Pretty Lizzie, Fashion and Mandy Light, and the stallion Easter Light whose dam was the registered Saddlebred mare Queen Dexter. Easter Light was bred almost exclusively to his half-sisters Fashion and Pretty Lizzie. From Easter Light and Fashion came six full brothers and sisters, all bred by C. G. Wells at Aetna, Kansas. From one of the daughters, May West, came the well-known sire Easter Parade.

Many of Headlight Morgan's early daughters were good producers, but the top three were Sunflower Maid 02401, Hazel S. 01000, and Lady Skinner 01424. Sunflower Maid was foaled in Kansas in 1910. Her dam was Fanny P by Julian Morgan, son of Winnebago Chief, a Morrill 55 grandson. This mare went to the U. S. Government Morgan Horse Farm in Vermont where she produced five colts and five fillies. One of her sons was the great sire Linsley 7233, sired by General Gates. Sunflower Maid's daughter Quenelda by Troubadour of Willowmoor was the dam of the New England sire Peter Mansfield. Virgil (Bennington x Quenelda) sired Vixen, dam of the famous versatility winner Manito.

Silver Rockwood 8617.
Photo courtesy of the National Museum of the Morgan Horse.

The Hiebert Brothers at Hillsboro, Kansas used a cross of Romanesque on Linsley mares very successfully. One of their colts was Plains King. Another was Hiebert's Challenge (bred by Elmer Brown), whose name was changed when he came to California to El Cortez, a fine Western sire. Elmer Brown of Halstead, Kansas based much of his breeding program on Linsley blood. O. E. Sutter of Wichita also preferred Linsley and other Headlight Morgan lines. The full brothers Hawk Jim, Rosco Morgan, Chocolate, and Major Linsley (Linsley x Lady Spar) had Headlight Morgan on both sides of their pedigrees.

Hawk Jim became the sire of a good many of Merle Evan's Devan Morgans in Ohio. Devan Hawk by Hawk Jim went to Alabama as a yearling and proved Morgan versatility by participation in 100-mile trail rides, dressage, hunt, barrel racing, and cutting. Many of Sutter's Bar S Morgans carried double lines to Headlight Morgan. R. S. "Pop" Sentney was another who combined several of the lines to Headlight Morgan.

Jolly Roger, foaled in California in 1941, became the foundation sire for Joe L. Young's Pineland Morgans at LaGrange, Georgia. Jolly Roger was by Rosco Morgan, out of the Brunk-bred mare Herodona.

One of the good performers a few years back was Ran-Bunctious. Both his sire's dam and dam's dam had lines leading back to Headlight Morgan. His sire Black Ran-Bo was out of Black Ranger, whose dam was a Chocolate daughter. His granddam, Locket, was by Hawk Jim.

The stallion Chocolate came from the family of another top Headlight Morgan daughter, Hazel S., foaled in Kansas in 1906. Her dam was Diamond, by Telescope Ethan, the second dam said to be trotting bred. Hazel S. was an excellent producer, and her offspring were equally good. Daughter May Hudson was the dam of Maggy Linsley, Lady Spar, and May Rockwood. Sons of May Rockwood include Allen Hudson, Chief Wabaunsee, Roubidoux and Silver Rockwood, all worthy sires.

Silver Rockwood was a great roping, cutting and pick-up horse in the Montana and Dakota region in his young days, greatly sought by rodeo cowboys as the mount to win on. He also excelled as a parade horse. At Shawalla Morgan Farm in Washington, he was bred to many mares of Hill and Sellman breeding. Some of his sons were Kilgoran Rockwood, Mills Pride and Captain Gates, in Canada, Rockfield (second and third dams of Headlight Morgan blood) and Shawalla Prince, sire of California's super stock horse Bourbon Prince. Shawalla Prince was out of Helen Field (Sonfield x Helen Mala, second dam Hemala by Headlight Morgan). Other Hazel S. offspring included the stallion Line Allen (by Linsley) and mares Hazel Dude and Hazel L., whose daughter Rocky Hazel was another fine producer.

The third of Headlight Morgan's great early daughters was Lady Skinner, foaled in Kansas, probably around 1906. She was out of Daisy, a fine road mare said to be Morgan. From her daughter, Nellie Skinner, descends a huge family, including Dan's Baby, who was the third dam of Silgal's Improver (he was by Charlie Sentney, a double Linsley), sire of many Theis Ranch Morgans; the stallion Dixie and his daughter Baby Dix, dam of Alonzo Sentney; Cavey, whose daughter Zona Skinner was the dam of Mabel Owen's early sire Bright Star, and Orcland Farm's mare Paleface – dam of Orcland Silver Don, Orcland Queen Bess and Orcland Youlenda. Then there were Dan's Bess – granddam of Chilocco Star – and Skinner, dam of Raymond S. Sentney and Skinners' Cocoa, whose offspring mostly carried the "Tejas" prefix.

This last family was bred by W. P. Thornhill of Texas, later of Arkansas, and was very much an inbred family, crossed on Silver Ranger, by Querido, out of Angelina by Texas Allen. Part of this large group of Morgans became foundation stock in California, part became Sentney stock, and a good deal of it went into the breeding program of the Theis Brothers in Kansas. This put together a high concentration of Headlight Morgan blood. For example, the mare Especially had ten of the sixteen lines in her fifth generation going to Headlight Morgan. When the Theis Company offered 75 head of Morgans for dispersal in March 1953, the bulk of the mares went to J. Cecil Ferguson's Broadwall Farm in Rhode Island where they produced many winners, including Broadwall Drum Major.

A 1947 article stated, "Linsley-bred stallions and mares are as prominent or more so than any other line of Morgan breeding in the mid-west range area and are used by many in the far west." Russell I. Phipps owned a large Hereford ranch near Whitman, Nebraska where he had the Morgan sire Rocky R. M. (Romanesque x Rocky Hazel). R. S. Sentney spent years putting together his working Morgan band at Table Top Stables in Kansas. All were sold at public auction April 4, 1951, and featured a mixture of the bloodlines of Headlight Morgan, Jubilee King, Linsley and Querido.

In the pre-WWII era cattlemen worked toward producing a "suitable stock horse of about 15 hands, with substance, heart, and body capacity for carrying a good load," the article continues. T. W. Daniels, who had been riding Morgan and Morgan-bred horses for open range cutting for forty-five years said in a 1961 *Western Horseman* article, "The bone structure of these Morgans from the feet up is put together for rough mountain work. They hold their heads up and are eager and happy when working. They never seem to tire – even in old age…the Morgan Horse is built to take the roughest mountain terrain possible, and do it with ease."

O. E. Sutter, the Hieberts, "Pop" Sentney, Robert Tynan, Jr., Locke Theis, and George Hineman produced Morgans mostly for their own use with cattle. Roland Hill had the same goal. So did J. S. Potter, Mrs. Sid Spencer, Dr. C. C. Reed, "Jiggs" Kuck, Warren Halliday, Vail & Vickers, who ran over ten thousand head of cattle on their Santa Rosa Island Ranch, and other Californians. Morgans had the brains, stamina, and attitude for stock work, and they could look pretty doing it besides.

Following his move to Rochelle, Texas, Headlight Morgan sired 112 more foals of high quality and uniformity from 1915 through 1921. He bred his last mares at age twenty-seven. From 1920 on, Roland Hill, Reginald Parsons, F. A. Fickert, and a few other Californians thus found a good source of stock at the Sellman Ranch. Mares were brought out in large numbers, proven stock combining the blood of Red Oak, Headlight Morgan, and the old Major Antoine-Major Gordon-The Admiral and Gold Medal lines. Carefully chosen stallions were also brought out. The daughters from these breedings were crossed to General Gates line sires, Uhlan, Sonfield, Querido and Gay Mac, or to the Headlight Morgan grandson, Mountcrest Sellman and his sons.

E. W. Roberts bred mares of Linsley blood to the Mountcrest Sellman son Redman, and Querido mares to Redman's son Blackman. In 1946 he purchased the entire stud of C. F. Ayer, adding the "Ayr" line to his program. Dr. C. C. Reed from San Juan Capistrano was a breeder of Hereford cattle, and he used Morgans as cow horses. They were mostly mares of Hill (old Sellman) breeding, with the Government-bred Gay Mac as his main sire.

Querido was bred to the Sellman-line mares, and their daughters in turn bred to Sonfield, producing excellent stock. Mary Smith of Camarillo, California founded her band of black Morgans with Hedlite 7977 who was line-bred to Headlight Morgan.

William Randolph Hearst bred mares from the Hill/Sellman lines to the Headlight Morgan grandson Mountcrest Sellman, and to the Bennington son Uhlan. These carried the prefixes "Sunical" and "Piedmont" to a large extent. From this Sellman/Hill/Hearst family descended California's outstanding sires Muscle Man and Dapper Dan, and their offspring can still do it all.

Montabell (Mountcrest Sellman x Jinglebells) was another good California sire. Bred to his half-sister Serenata, he got Senator Gift, a 15.2 hand, 1200-pound stallion packed with Headlight Morgan genes. In 1966 and 1967 Senator Gift, ridden by Lali Brunson, won the grueling Feather River Endurance Ride. This is a race requiring the utmost in speed, nerve, agility and stamina. In 1967 Senator Gift set a record for speed, finishing with a good fifteen lengths' lead.

These days jeeps, planes, and feedlots have supplanted the old working cow horse in many areas, and the focus on breeding has changed. Still, those same old Morgan families that were so at home on the range have moved as easily into the show ring to become stars in the pleasure and specialty divisions. A couple such come quickly to mind. The first of two to come to mind is the great mare Keystone's Rome Beauty (Keystone x Etna). Keystone's dam, Redlass, was by Redman, out of the Brunk-bred Easter Lass. Etna was also by Redman, out of a Brunk mare, Tarna. In 1941 Dr. Ina Richter purchased Tarna and Easter Lass as yearlings from J. C. Brunk of Illinois and brought them to California. Warren Halliday bought both mares in March 1944 and bred them to Redman. Redlass and Etna were foaled the following spring.

Keystone was a top halter and performance horse in the Pacific Northwest, whose offspring inherited his willingness to work. His daughter Keystone's Rome Beauty was certainly no exception, and double granddaddy Redman had a good deal to do with her abilities, too. Marjorie Hambly (now Marjorie McCrorey) purchased "Rome" in the fall of 1962 after a four-state search for a mare to replace Belle Heather in the show ring. Rome had a good one to follow as Belle Heather was a consistent winner in both hackamore and bitted stock horse classes in open competition.

Belle Heather, incidentally, came from the Davis Breeding Farm, an operation noted for producing good working horses. Belle Heather's sire was the Jubilee King son Red Vermont. Her dam Heather Angel Field combined the blood of Sonfield and Querido with the old Sellman lines through Moleskin and Easter Allen Morgan, grandson and son of Headlight Morgan. This breeding followed Sellman's own idea of crossing particular types of families.

After a good month of schooling, Marjorie began riding Rome through the rugged mountains of southern California on pleasure rides and cross-country competition events, and also in parades.

The mare placed third in the parade division of the Morgan Horse Breeders and Exhibitors Association 1963 high point system. In 1964 Rome participated in six North American Trail Riding Conference competitive rides, winning the Morgan division. She was Reserve Champion Heavy-weight Competitive Trail Ride Horse and was second in over-all points in all divisions. In 1965 Marjorie turned the mare over to Sam Cisneros to ready her for the show ring. Sam was a young trainer with marvelous hands and seat. There was a great unity between the pair in the ring where everything flowed together, and soon many stock horse classes were being won in both open and Morgan competition. That year Keystone's Rome Beauty stood third in the Southern California Morgan Horse Club's high point system, and the next two years she was high point horse.

In 1966 Rome was entered in stock horse, western riding, western pleasure, reining and English pleasure classes, and also in parades. Tom Miles of San Bernardino rode her in the junior division, placing in hunt seat, pleasure, equitation, and in stock horse, juniors to ride. That year, Rome won four of the eight Morgan Horse Breeders and Exhibitors Association high point trophies. The following year she added working cow horse to her list of wins, and more high point trophies. Throughout their show ring years, Marjorie and Rome continued their trail ride activities and parade participation. In 1968, Keystone's Rome Beauty retired the all-around high point trophy presented by the Morgan Horse Club of Southern California. She also won the M.H.B.E.A. High Point English and Western Pleasure awards, and a place in the hearts of many as one of the best.

The other example is the nationally famous black gelding El Mejor. Of the fourteen animals in El Mejor's fifth generation, only one does not trace back to General Gates or the Sellman stock. That one is the Brunk-bred Pat Allen (Allen King x Patrona, by Senator Reade).

In a long show career, El Mejor won about everything that could be done in the pleasure and specialty divisions and garnered an unequalled number of high point horse awards at the Golden West shows year after year after year. At the 1973 Grand National in Oklahoma City, El Mejor took two grand championships (open jumper and working hunter) and three top ten awards. He competed in western pleasure, trail, trotting race, open jumper, hunter hack, advanced western pleasure, English pleasure, Morgan versatility, family class, and stock horse open at the 1975 Golden West Regional Champi-

Sonfield 7952. Picture taken in February of 1947.
Photo courtesy of the National Museum of the Morgan Horse.

onship Morgan Horse Show, winning sixteen ribbons, including nine firsts and seconds. That fall he garnered two more Grand National championships (western trail and stock horse) and four more top tens.

It has not been the intent of the author to slight or devalue the other sire lines of any of the Morgans mentioned in this article – Jubilee King, Flyhawk, Agazizz, the Brunk mares, and others all played their part in the development of these horses. However, the focus here has been on the importance of one outstanding sire, Headlight Morgan, in the development, spread, and worth of the "Western" Morgan. And it is interesting to note that these same old families from the Sellman band – the Major Gordon foundation mares, bred to Major Antoine and The Admiral, then with subsequent crosses to Headlight Morgan, Red Oak, Gay Mac, Sonfield, and Querido – are the same lines that are being sought by today's Morgan sport horse enthusiasts. The capabilities needed by the "new" sport horse and the "old" western using horse are the same, and it's hard to improve on an old family recipe.

The Redman/Blackman Story
1992

This is really the story of three horses: a stallion, his son, and his grandson - a family affair that was to have a lasting and far-reaching effect on the Morgan breed. For me, it began when a teenager fell in love with a gorgeous, red chestnut stallion named Redman – the "son" of this story. While growing up, I spent every summer at Cold Creek Ranch, my uncle's 1,280-acre Hereford ranch in northern California's Siskiyou Mountains. Our good "cow horse" was a part-Morgan, as was my own mare. Two of our near-neighbors had Morgans, and to the south was the Kuck Ranch, where 'Jiggs' Kuck and the Schultzes were breeding Morgans with the Siskiyou prefix. Off to the northeast was beautiful Mountcrest Ranch, where California's Morgan history was reborn in this century. However, the Morgans were long gone from there by then. But, on with the story.

Redman (Mountcrest Sellman x Red Dot), sired just 62 offspring, but left a lasting impression on the Morgan breed. He is shown here with Warren Halliday, his owner from 1942 to 1958. Photo courtesy of the National Museum of the Morgan Horse.

It was 1945, and Warren Halliday had just moved his horses and household up from the Owens Valley to the tiny hamlet of Etna, in Siskiyou County. To the north, the county borders Oregon. It is a region of high mountains and rugged terrain, yet it contains some more rolling country and a number of beautiful valleys. Here, Halliday established his Blue Heaven Ranch, on the flat south of Etna – almost a half-section of meadow and hay land. Yet, it was just a short ride to the Marble Mountain Wilderness, or going farther north, into Klamath National Forest land.

Redman was in his prime in 1945, a strong, well-muscled, compact horse who looked like he could take you over the toughest trails, and he had traveled many of them, as Warren loved the wilderness. To me, Redman was just beautiful, with his rich color, proud stance, and friendly attitude.

Actually, it was very fitting that Redman had come to Siskiyou County. His sire had been foaled at Hilt, some forty miles north of Etna "as the crow flies." No story of Redman and his descendants would be complete without looking first at his sire, Mountcrest Sellman, and a man responsible for more Morgan history than he ever knew: Reginald H. Parsons.

The property known for many years as the Mountcrest Ranch was first settled about 1852 by Rufus Cole. It was a stagecoach stopping place for many years until a railroad was completed to Ashland, Oregon in 1887. The region had value for stock raising, farming, and timber cutting, and the pretty valley encouraged settlement. The town of Hilt sprang up about a mile south of the Cole Ranch. Over the years, Hilt was owned by two different lumber companies and was probably the last of the company-owned towns in northern California. Around 1975 the Fruit Growers Supply

Company completely dismantled the site and graded it to plant alfalfa and grass, "so that it can be utilized by our Mountcrest Ranch lessee."

Sadly, in the words of Warren C. Bayliss, son of Parsons' former ranch manager, "Except for the land, there is really little left of what was once a show-place of ranches in the West, little left at Mountcrest Ranch that would tell a visitor of the glorious days of its existence. The buildings, fences, and immaculate developments are all gone. The land has been sold – Hilt is gone, too. There will always remain, however, the memory of a beautiful ranch, Mountcrest, and the wonderful lands surrounding it, in the eyes of hundreds of people who visited Hilt and Mountcrest." I remember that the fence posts were painted white with red "caps."

In 1911, Parsons purchased two ranches from the Cole family, and later acquired a third, where he had a hunting lodge. One of the ranches was the Circle P, the other became Mountcrest. Parsons had homes in Seattle and in Medford, Oregon, where he had extensive apple and pear orchards. Originally, he used Mountcrest as a wintering area for the horses and mules used to farm his orchard lands over the Siskiyous. He also owned properties in the Methow Valley, near Chelan, Washington, where Shorthorn cattle were raised and land along the Snoqualmie River near Seattle. Parsons was a very wealthy man. He was Mountcrest's owner in absentia, and a resident manager supervised the work at the ranch.

Parsons was from a Massachusetts family that had made its fortune in the whaling days. He married Maude Bemis, a descendant of the family who founded the Bemis Bag Company, the "premium burlap sack producer in the United States." Parsons attended the Colorado School of Mines and the University of California. He became an eminent philanthropist and a respected national figure in the world of business and agriculture.

Parsons' every enterprise began with the best that could be obtained. When he switched from Shorthorns to Herefords in 1925 he selected prime "Domino" stock and established an outstanding herd of beef cattle. The seed stock for his select flock of Southdown sheep were owned by the Queen of England, and these won many prizes at livestock shows. Mountcrest initiated a strain of white Leghorn chickens into the West. These were select stock, hens mated to the best of imported roosters, and their egg production was closely monitored. Some 5,000 laying hens provided premium hatching eggs, which sold for $1.50 a dozen when ordinary market eggs brought 25 cents a dozen.

All this is to show that Parsons did not stumble accidentally across the Morgan horse. Again, he went to the best source of stock at that time – Richard Sellman of Rochelle, Texas. From Sellman, Parsons obtained twelve mares and a stallion in 1920. Six of the mares were in foal. The mares were a typical Sellman blend of the bloodlines of Headlight Morgan, The Admiral, Major Antoine, and Major Gordon. The stallion was Baldie's Boy by Headlight Morgan, and out of Baldie Antoine by Major Antoine. He sired five Mountcrest foals in 1922-1923, and was sold to D. E. Alexander of Klamath Falls, Oregon in 1924. There is no further history of this horse.

Kitty E (The Admiral x Puss by Gold Medal) came in foal to Joe Bailey (Headlight Morgan x Polly B. by The Admiral). The resulting 1921 foal was the chestnut colt Mountcrest Sellman. Parsons kept him the longest, and sold him to William Randolph Hearst in April 1932. I've never seen a picture or description of Mountcrest Sellman, but I remember his half-sister, Balkitty, well. She was sired by Baldie's Boy and owned by Joe and Hattie Silva who lived north of Cold Creek Ranch. Balkitty was a pretty, chunky chestnut mare with a sweet disposition and an especially nice head. She had a daughter who looked very much like her, but the younger mare was apparently never registered. Balkitty's only two registered foals were Copco Joe and Copco Silva, both owned by the late Byron White of Montague, California.

For whatever reason, Parsons' venture into Morgans was quite brief, spanning less than a decade. He registered fourteen foals between 1921 and 1926. There were a few individual sales and nine head sold at a dispersal on October 16, 1926 to persons in the area and in southern Oregon. Oddly, with few exceptions, all of the Mountcrest-owned Morgans slipped into oblivion after they left the ranch. Some of the Morgans were probably retained at the ranch for saddle use, but the last foal was born at the ranch in 1926. Apart from Balkitty and Mountcrest Nan, who eventually went to Dr. Ina M. Richter, there is no further history for most of these horses. Of the original stock, only two mares left a line to carry on: Frisky A, through her daughter Georgette, who was owned by Schultz, Kuck, and Shultz of Yreka, California, and Kitty E, through her son Mountcrest Sellman (who incidentally was Georgette's sire). Georgette had several foals at the Kuck Ranch, all sired by their fine stallion North Fork – these formed part of the "Siskiyou" line of Morgans.

It is quite likely that the Parsons stock was responsible for a number of part-Morgan horses that existed in upper Siskiyou County before World War II, since his was the only known source of pure Morgan blood in the region in the 1920s and 1930s. The cross was usually to Thoroughbred or to Quarter-type stock.

The Morgan in the West in the period up to the early 1950s was definitely a western and stock horse breed. True, they served other functions, but their greatest popularity stemmed from the ability to successfully compete against other breeds by working cattle better than most on the large cattle ranches that still dotted the high country. After the big market drop in the early 1950s that led to the dispersal of many large registered Hereford herds along the western tier of states, the focus, of course, had to change. But, in the era of the stallions of which I write, much emphasis was still on the type of Morgan who could get his hindquarters under him and move off his front end to turn a cow. He had to be strong and sensible and smart, sure-footed in the toughest terrain, and still retain that special beauty and appeal that marked him as a Morgan. The descendants of these Morgans easily made the transition from cattle ranch to show ring.

Mountcrest Sellman sired forty foals between 1926 and 1943. Hearst bred the majority of them and many carried the "Piedmont" prefix. His career at stud was quite sporadic. Between 1926 (two foals) and 1932 (one foal), there is a blank. His largest foal crops came between 1933 and 1937. After that he only had three foals, one each in 1939, 1942 and 1943. The pity of it is that Mountcrest Sellman was such a good sire. His daughters were excellent producers, and several of his sons became fine sires, notably Redman, Antman, Cloverman, Kenelm Morgan and Montabell – the most

prolific of the quintet, whose offspring often carried the suffix "Gift." Two of Montabell's daughters became foundation mares for Mary H. Smith's black Morgan band, the "Hedlite's." These two were Piedmont Cresta (dam of Hedlite's Bob E A and others) and Piedmont Rosemarie (dam of Hedlite's Rudy T and others).

Much could be written about all the fine descendants of Mountcrest Sellman's sons and daughters, but it is time to move on to just one of them, the stallion Redman. If Redman had had just one foal, and that one Blackman, he would still have earned the admiration of us all.

Redman was foaled April 26, 1936. He was bred by Hearst, but foaled the property of Clarence J. Ferrari of San Francisco, who sold him as a two-

Blackman and seven of his black sons comprised a drill team which performed daily in 1953 at Knott's Berry Farm n southern California. The horses' trainer was Mike Smith. Photo courtesy of the National Museum of the Morgan Horse.

122

year-old to R. L. Welborn of Campo, California. Contrary to a common belief, E. W. Roberts never owned him and only used him at stud for two seasons. Welborn bred Redman twice to the Brunk-bred mare Gojea (Go Hawk x Jeanne by Knox Reade). Her 1941 foal was a filly, Red Ann. Welborn rebred the mare and sold her the following spring to E. W. Roberts. In late June she foaled, and Roberts must have liked the looks of the black colt that he named Blackman, because he bred two mares to Redman in 1943 and eight mares in 1944. Redman's only other foal for Welborn was Red Leaf, who foaled in 1940 and was out of a mare registered by the American Trotting Register, Calumet de Long.

In April of 1942, Redman was sold to Warren Halliday, then of Bishop, California. The beautiful photograph of Warren and Redman in the mountains, with Bishop Pass in the background, is a favorite of mine – that is the horse I remember. Between 1940 and 1959, Redman sired just sixty-two foals, almost equally colts and fillies. In a way, it is too bad that he went up to Etna where there was little chance of getting any outside breedings – in fact, he only bred two outside Morgan mares during his years at Blue Heaven Ranch.

Halliday brought with him to his new ranch eight mares and two fillies, and from these he raised twenty-nine foals. Two of his mares, Easter Lass and Tarna were Brunk-bred, four were daughters of Sonfield, one was a daughter of Gojea, and the others were a combination of California breeding tracing to Querido, Sonfield, and the old Sellman stock. They were a very nice group of mares – chestnuts, bays and browns.

While Blackman was his sire's most famous son, Redman did have others who bred on, especially Red Gates in southern California, and Redman's Bay Boy and Billy Rebel in Oregon. Several of the mares bred by Halliday went on to make a name for themselves. For example, there was Redlass, who was sold as a yearling to Karen Brauns of Wenatchee, Washington. Bred there to Pomulus, she produced one of the Pacific Northwest's premier show stallions and sire, Keystone, and the fine mare Pommelass (dam of Keystone's Sage Dust). Two other Redman daughters went from Blue Heaven Ranch to Washington. These were Red Bess (out of Bessie Sonfield) and Etna (out of Tarna). Red Bess was owned by the Brauns family, and Etna by Susan Eskil of Entiat, Washington. Both mares were bred to Keystone, and produced a number of fine offspring. Bred to Pomulus, Etna produced the well-known mare Pomula. Another daughter was Keystone's Rome Beauty, who was Marjorie (Hambly) McCrory's well-known show mare. Keystone was the sire of Leo Beckley's fine show stallion Montey Vermont.

This small group of Redman offspring did much to enhance the Morgan breed in the Pacific Northwest, and his descendants could be seen among the top contenders in a wide variety of classes.

Halliday pretty much went out of business in 1951. He sold Redman that spring, and the horse was sold again in 1952 to Dr. Ina M. Richter of Kedron Farm in Solvang, California. Halliday sold his last two Redman daughters in 1953. Dr. Richter got eight foals from Redman between 1953 and 1956, among them the good broodmares Kedron Cutty Hunk and Kedron Cutty Sark. Dr. Richter took the latter mare with her to Missouri, to carry on her Morgan breeding program there. A Cutty Sark son, Kedron Champagne, also went to Missouri where his son Kedron Cointreau sired a good number of foals.

Redman was transferred on October 15, 1958 to Gene and Shirley Mathews in Santa Ynez, California. Among his last foals were the above-mentioned Billy Rebel, Hank and Louise Boyd's good mare Gertrude Mae, and Ida Red, of whom more later. But now it's time to switch the scene to Southern California and the Morgans of E. W. Roberts.

Ed Roberts was one of a kind. The bare bones of the story are that he owned a manufacturing company in Los Angeles, that he became one of the largest breeders of Morgans in the country, that he sent Morgans to China, Hawaii, and New England, and that he owned Blackman. As a human being, he seems to have been larger than life. Sumner Kean, former editor of *The Morgan Horse*, called him "a regular powerhouse of a man." He said, "Roberts has so much bounce that he leaves you on the ground; so much grasp and vision that you flounder behind him. So much brass that he could tickle Queen Elizabeth under the chin – and get away with it." That's quite a description.

Roberts owned Hi-Pass Ranch in San Diego County, near the Mexican border, which he had purchased in 1939. He also owned a forty-acre field in the Imperial Valley where 40-50 mares from one to four years of age were pastured. As they matured, they were moved to Hi-Pass to be bred.

Roberts purchased his prospective broodmares from several sources; consequently they came with different breeding and characteristics. Through judicious breeding and selection among his stock, he planned, over time, to establish an individual and distinctive strain of Morgans. One might argue that Roberts really wasn't in business long enough to accomplish this ambitious goal, but he built his own stock on a foundation of established families that brought with them their own kind of uniformity. It was basically the same foundation used by Roland Hill, William R. Hearst, and other early California breeders. There was much Sellman stock in the background, including a good deal of Headlight Morgan blood. Two other favored lines were those established by J. C. Brunk in Illinois and Elmer Brown in Kansas. Consequently, Roberts' Morgans had the blood of General Gates through Red Oak, Linsley, Mansfield, Querido, and Sonfield, as well as some Allen King, Knox Morgan, Penrod and Jubilee King in the background.

These were the lines that built the prized "California" Morgans of an earlier day – well-muscled horses with good, dense bone, sensible dispositions, and worlds of heart and endurance. They weren't just pretty; they were built to last.

In 1942, Roberts purchased his first two mares, Dorothy Abbey and Gojea, from R. L. Welborn. Both mares had come from Illinois. That year he also purchased three Hearst mares (the dam of one was also the dam of Redman) and

The Brunk-bred Jubilee King 7570 (Penrod [Allen Franklin x Black Bess A] x Daisette [Senator Knox x Daisy de Jarnette]). Photo courtesy of the National Museum of the Morgan Horse.

two mares Otto McClure had obtained from the Elmer Brown estate. Roberts continued to build up his mare band over the next few years, and, in 1946, he purchased twenty-five mares from Charles F. Ayer of Meeker, Colorado. This group formed the backbone of his breeding program for several years.

The Ayers mares carried a lot of Linsley and Red Oak blood. This was an interesting purchase, in that Roberts selected several families of mares. He must have especially liked Angela K, because he got not only that mare but also five of her daughters and four of her granddaughters. Several other mares were purchased together with one or two of their daughters. Six of the mares foaled in 1946 (three had fillies, which were given names ending in "ayr"). Ayer had originally purchased three of the mares Roberts bought in California. These were Angela K (Querido x Angelina),

Queensen (Winchester x Queen Allen), and Sallysen (Winchester x Sallie Bee). Winchester was by Mansfield and out of Narissa. A fourth mare, Myra L, was by Romanesque and out of Maggie Linsley. The rest were bred by Ayer, and were sired by Homerayr, Jack Sprat, or James R M. Two of the 1946 fillies were by Homerayr, who was a son of James R M and Poppit – one of the mares Roberts bought with two of her daughters; James R M (Romanesque x Lemax) was bred by Elmer Brown; Jack Sprat (Spotlight x Gold Floss) was bred by H. T. Hineman in Dighton, Kansas. Much of the old Ayers stock had come from Elmer Brown. Fourteen of the mares had been bred for 1947 foals, all by Easter Parade, whose sire was by Juban. In the period 1947-1951, the Ayers mares alone accounted for seventy-one of the foals born at Hi-Pass.

In 1947, three high officials of the Chinese government toured the United States in search of quality horses to upgrade the native stock in China. The plan was to place these imports with the National Horse Administration Bureau and with various military stallion stations. The Chinese selected a good number of Morgan mares and stallions, including nine head from Roberts. Their plan was to breed Morgan stallions to Mongolian mares, and to breed the Morgan mares to Morgan stallions for more purebred sires for later on. Several of the mares were in foal when sold. While the Chinese dignitaries were in California, Roberts took them on a tour through the California desert, the Imperial Valley and into Mexico. They were houseguests of the Roberts' the night before they left.

The horses were loaded on the Philippine Transport in San Francisco, housed in specially made stalls on deck. Among the Roberts group were two Redman sons and four Ayer mares. The ship docked in Shanghai on October 22. Red Lancer (Redman x Hacienda Salome) was assigned to the Military Sung-Ming Stud in Yunnan Province. The only casualty of the trip was Red Rex (Redman x Meta Knox), who cut himself through the chest jumping an iron fence and had to be destroyed.

There was much excitement about this program, and it would have been fun to follow the progress of the Morgan group. The Communist take-over of China made this impossible, however, and one can only guess at the probable fate of the horses.

In 1951, Roberts sold three stallions and fifteen mares to Lester and Aylmer Robinson of Kauai, Hawaii. Most of these were intended for the Niihau Ranch on Kauai; a few went to the Kekoha Sugar Company and the McBryde Sugar Company, and two were owned by Sinclair Robinson. Quite a breeding program ensued on Kauai. Four of the mares were in foal when sold. Among the mares were four from the Ayer group. Stallions used were Earl Warren (by Blackman), his son Redlands, two Blackman grandsons, and a son of Monte L, bred by Roberts but foaled on Kauai. In 1957, Roberts sold the stallions Otto McClure (by Red Gates) and Memphis Beau Brummell (out of Memphis Belle by Blackman) to the huge Parker Ranch in Kamuela, Hawaii.

In 1952, Roberts advertised that eighty-five registered Morgans would be offered at sale on Sunday, December 14, at W. L. Linn's Sales Yard in Turlock, California. The blood of Blackman was to be featured, and stallions, mares, foals, and show and pleasure horses were to be offered. Imagine the logistics and the cost of shipping so many head over half the length of the state. Whether that number actually went through the sale is unclear, but the results must have been disappointing. Only twenty-seven transfers were recorded from the sale – two geldings and twenty-five mares – fifteen of them precious Blackman daughters.

In the early 1950s, a daily horse show was put on at Knott's Berry Farm (one of southern California's top tourist attractions) by trainer Mark Smith, his two sons, and their wives. It was a combination circus and "Wild West" show, and one of the popular acts was a Liberty Drill, performed by eight black Morgan stallions – Blackman and seven of his sons. It seems that Roberts had sent these horses to Smith for training in 1951. Roberts gave Mark's son, Harold, Tom Dewey (Blackman x Neta Knox), which Harold trained as a roping horse and later sold to Grosse Pointe

Farms in Michigan. At this time Roberts had a good friend, the late J. Glenn Francis, who shared his love of horses. The two men worked closely together – so much so that Mrs. Sophie Francis says it was sometimes hard to tell who owned which horses. The equipment used in the Liberty Drill has been kept, well oiled and cared for, in the Francis' tack room all these years.

By 1956, Roberts was looking toward retirement and cutting back heavily. By then he could say, "I believe I have developed a nice strain of typical Morgans." Following a visit to the ranch by F. O. 'Ted' Davis, then president of the Morgan Horse Club, a group of mares were readied for shipment to Windsor, Vermont. To "add bone" to the Windcrest line, the two men had selected what Roberts considered to be the best of the young stock. Six of the mares were of the Redman/ Blackman family. One of them was Liz Taylor (Bikini x Lizzyayr), who later became dam of Windcrest Playboy, Windcrest Playgirl, Windcrest Harmony, Windcrest Major and Windcrest Benn Beau, all bred by Davis and sired by Upwey Ben Don. 'Liz' was also the dam of several "Alezan" Morgans.

Another of the mares was Belle McLinsley (Blackman x Belle McClure), from whom Davis got Windcrest Yankee, Windcrest Fanfair, and Windcrest Chief, before selling her to a party in Connecticut. A third mare was Memphis Belle, full sister to Belle McLinsley. Bred twice to Upwey Ben Don, she produced Windcrest Sparkle and Windcrest Flash, before she, too, went to Connecticut.

Davis sold the other mares of this line, Lizzie McClure (Otto McClure x Liz Taylor), Daisy Field (Bret Allen x Daisy Sonfield), and Justina Morgan (Blackman x Dorothy Abbey). These six Redman/Blackman mares left many descendants in the East, and more than a few established fine show and breeding records. (For a detailed history of the eleven Roberts mares, see Moises Roizen's article, "F. O. 'Ted' Davis and The California Connection," November and December 1987 issues of *The Morgan Horse*).

Glenn Francis had made the boxcar trip to Vermont with these mares. Over the years, he had acquired a number of Blackman sons and descendants, and, in 1964, he got the old stallion. The Morgans selected by Francis were true to the original Morgan type – relatively small, stocky and short-backed with lots of muscle, good sense and tractability. Francis gave small clinics at his place near Campo, California, where he taught amateurs the basics of horse care and training. Participants were impressed when he used a stallion to demonstrate the various techniques and suggestions. Several people got their start with Francis' Morgans, and swear by their sensible and willing dispositions and true "old" type.

It is impossible to do justice to this whole line of Morgans in just one article. Each family within the line is worthy of elaboration, and everyone who has owned, or presently has, descendants of the Mountcrest Sellman, Redman and Blackman families could tell us much about them. Many of these Morgans dominated the breed and open horse shows of their day. A good number made their mark in competitive trail rides. Their solid temperament made them excellent mounts for junior riders. They were loved family horses. You can find them not only in the West, but spread across the county. The Morgan world is richer today because there was once a horse named Mountcrest Sellman.

One interesting facet of this family of Morgans is that line breeding so often led to even better individuals. That brings us to the example of Ida Red, Redman's last foal.

Ida Red was born August 1, 1959. She was out of Princess Elizabeth who was by Blackman. Orval and Elaine Smith owned four of Ida Red's twelve foals, including Orlaine's Fantasia, by Ro Mac. Tom and Teri Brisco bought Fantasia, who became Tomeri Morgans' first show horse. The Briscos leased Ida Red in 1967 and bought her in 1970. Her first foal for them was Tomeri Lisa, who won quite a bit in-hand, was a fun roadster show horse, and a great trail horse. Among Ida Red's other notable offspring were Tomeri Glory Bound, who had quite a successful career in roadster, and Tomeri Mr. Big Stuff, who garnered more than thirty championships – including six regional championships – over an eight-year show career. Ida Red's last foal was Tomeri Country Rose, who began her show career at age seven and has to her credit ten in-hand championships and several championships in both pleasure driving and park harness.

What's interesting is that, with the exception of three early ones, all of Ida Red's foals were sired by stallions tracing in some degree to Mountcrest Sellman, Redman or Blackman. The mare lived to be just three weeks short of her twenty-seventh birthday. Teri Brisco has this to say of 'Liz', as they called her. "Outside of producing our wonderful babies and putting the name Tomeri on the books, Liz was a great and valued friend to me. She showed me what this great breed is all about, from begin tough and gutsy to being soft and motherly. We had many wonderful hours together. As long as we are breeding, Ida Red lives on in her children and grandchildren here at Tomeri."

I come to the end of this article feeling I've only scratched the surface. So much more could be told. About Florence Coffey, who began with Blackman Allen, Orphan Annie, and Jeanne Allen - all by Blackman - and walked off with armloads of ribbons and trophies for them and their offspring in California and Oregon. About the grand junior mount, Sheriff Morgan (dam by Montabell), on whom Danny Weinberger rode to fame at the age of nine. About the trotter Jim Dandy Gift and the roadster par excellence Welmore Zorro. About the "Ramona" horses, the "Impala" Morgans, the "Gifts," the "Hedlites," the "Keystones," and the "Big Bends," and of the wonderful Blackman daughters, like Lady Gay and Margaret Collins – so much left unsaid.

Perhaps another day....

The Legacy of Linsley and His Sons
1995

On May 5, 1910, a bay filly was foaled on the property of James M. Wood of Meade, Kansas. Named Sunflower Maid, she was one of Headlight Morgan's earliest foals. Her dam, Fanny P., was very well bred, carrying the blood of old Morrill 55 through both sire and dam. Handsome, intelligent, and gentle, Morrill was a pure trotter, fast for his day. Given her pedigree, Sunflower Maid was well endowed to become a first-class broodmare.

In 1911 Sunflower Maid and her dam were sold to the U.S. Morgan Horse Farm in Middlebury, Vermont. There she was bred to General Gates, Scotland, Donlyn, Troubadour Of Willowmoor, Bennington, and Mansfield, producing ten foals from 1915 to 1927. It was her 1918 foal who ensured Sunflower Maid a place among the breed's great mares. This foal was Linsley by General Gates, founder of a remarkable Morgan dynasty. Linsley was chestnut, with a strip and three white pasterns and ankles.

He apparently remained Government property throughout his lifetime, as no transfers are recorded. Still, his history as a Morgan sire is completely tied to the breeding program of Elmer Brown of Halstead, Kansas. It is thus well to explain a bit about that program before proceeding further.

Edgar Brown had a bay mare named Daisy, a good roadster said to be Morgan. She must have been foaled about the turn of the century or earlier. From their fine road mare the Brown brothers got three fillies:

The stallion Linsley, whose offspring and descendents have had a huge impact on the Morgan breed. Photo courtesy of the National Museum of the Morgan Horse.

Sallie and Bess by Rowdy Blue, and Lady Skinner by Headlight Morgan, bred by Dick Skinner of Meade, Kansas, foaled in 1909, and registered by the Browns. Elmer Brown registered colts by Dude Hudson from Sallie and Bess in 1912.

The Brown brothers also acquired Helen S (f. 1906) and Hazel S. (f. 1906), both by Headlight Morgan. From Helen S came Bird Hudson (f. 1910) and from Hazel S. the mare May Hudson (f. 1911), both by Dude Hudson (Fred Hudson x Velma by Dude). In 1913 the Browns acquired the weanling colt Sparhawk (Dart x Lucy Hale by St L) and in 1915 Elmer got a two-year-old mare, Donbelle (Donald x Belle C Graves by Billy Roberts), from C. C. Stillman of Cornwall, New York. From 1917 to 1938 Donbelle produced fifteen foals for Elmer Brown, eight of them by Linsley.

Donbelle's first foal was Sparbelle (by Sparhawk), who became the dam of fourteen Brown-bred foals, ten of them by Linsley. Donbelle will be remembered best as the dam of five outstanding Linsley daughters, and as the second dam (through Sparbelle) of Linspar and Sparbeau, and (through Sparta) of Sir Linsley.

May Hudson produced Lady Spar, dam of Chocolate, Rosco Morgan, Hawk Jim, and four other foals by Linsley.

Hazel S. had two foals by Linsley, a filly, and in 1924, Line Allen, who was primarily a broodmare sire. Lady Skinner produced three foals: Pennie (by Linsley), sire of three registered offspring; Jannace (by Sparhawk), dam of Jane L by Linsley; and Hazel (by Dude Hudson), foaled in 1919, whose story is unique.

Hazel's only registered foal was the Linsley son Pal (f. 1926). Pal was bred by Elmer Brown and owned by Vernon Hoff of Spearville, Kansas. Registry transfers disclose a succession of seven owners of this horse through 1947. What all these people did with Pal is not known, but it was not until 1949 that he shows up as the sire of two registered foals – a filly, of whom nothing more is known, and a colt, R P Linsley – the only son of an only son. But that's enough to gain Pal a place in Morgan annals, for R P Linsley's second offspring was the fine show horse and sire Rex Linsley. He also sired, among others, the good mares Black Chip, Elain L, and Linela.

The Linsley son Pal had seven owners during his lifetime. It later was discovered he was the sire of two registered foals, one of them R P Linsley. Photo courtesy of the National Museum of the Morgan Horse.

Elmer Brown's breeding program falls clearly into three phases: before, during, and after Linsley. Foals born through 1921 were either by Sparhawk or Dude Hudson. From 1922 to 1933 all mares had Linsley foals with two exceptions – foals by Rockwood in 1930. There were fifty-one Brown-bred Linsley foals during those years, and five more the result of outside breedings. The number of unregistered foals sired by Linsley during these years for the Remount Service and for area farmers is not known.

It is interesting to note that from 1921 through the 1930s Elmer Brown bred his mares exclusively to Morgan stallions in the United States Army Remount Service. Linsley and Rockwood both stood as Remount stallions, and from 1934 on Brown used Romanesque and Tehachapi Allan, both of whom had been transferred into the Government service. These two were bred in large part to daughters and granddaughters of Linsley, the rest being older mares who had earlier been bred to Linsley himself.

The Remount Service was a branch of the U.S. Army Quartermaster Corps. In 1913 a horse-breeding program was started, encouraging farmers to improve the quality of their stock and to produce a type of horse suitable for cavalry use. Several breeds were used in the program, including Morgans. The Bureau of Animal Husbandry leased stallions from the U.S. Morgan Horse Farm to the Remount Service, and the War Department purchased several others. Any stallion accepted into the program had to be approved by the War Department and owned by the Government. Army Purchasing Boards selected stallions on the basis of overall quality with emphasis on disposition, conformation, soundness, and hardiness – qualities essential in a good cavalry mount of light artillery horse. Some stallions were kept at Remount Stations; others were placed with farmers who had facilities and knowledge suitable for the breeding of mares. Elmer Brown was such a man. He loved Morgans, and was an early promoter of the breed.

Under the Remount Horse Breeding Program, mares could be bred for a stud fee of $10 (later $25). Mare owners kept the fillies, and the Government held an option to purchase colts as three-year-olds for $150. If the mare owner wished, he could keep a colt by paying the regular stud fee. Colts absorbed into the Remount Program were not breed-registered; hence many good ones were lost to their particular breed.

Despite this, thirty Linsley sons were registered, of whom eighteen sired at least one foal, adding 238 colts and fillies to the Morgan gene pool. Sons having the most offspring were Chocolate (49), Hawk Jim (36), Sparbeau (34), Linspar (34), and Rosco Morgan (25). Also, there were twenty-three registered Linsley daughters, many of whom became outstanding broodmares, and three unregistered daughters who figured in early pedigrees.

In 1946 Earl B. Krantz visited some fifty-nine Morgan breeders across the country at the direction of the Morgan Horse Club. As he traveled from New England to the Midwest and on through the range section to California, Krantz noted that one of the top bloodlines being used everywhere was that which sprang from Linsley. Concerning Elmer Brown (who died in 1941), he commented that, "Mr. Brown believed in his horses, talked of them to other ranchers and Remount officials during Depression years. He scattered the blood of Linsley, possibly his best sire, far and wide."

With each generation the Linsley line recedes farther into the distance and other bloodlines are added in. Still, his offspring and descendants had a massive influence on the breed in their time, and they were the foundation of many important breeding programs for which we can be thankful today.

For example, if Beamington is in your horse's pedigree, you can claim a bit of the Linsley legacy. His second dam, Elberty Linsley, was by Linsley, and his sire's dam was the lovely Jenney Lake, whose second dam's sire was Linspar.

The Linsley son Linspar had an enormous impact on the L.U. Sheep Company's breeding program. Today Linspar's descendents can be found across the country. Photo courtesy of the National Museum of the Morgan Horse.

Linsley won the Morgan class at the 1921 Kansas State Fair and his family has continued its winning way in a broad range of disciplines up to today. Bearing in mind that many other horses enter into an individual pedigree, and with no intent to slight those animals in the discussion to follow, let us trace just the threads that lead back to Linsley through some of his sons.

Linspar

Linspar was foaled April 17, 1925, property of Elmer Brown, who sold him in April 1928 to the L. U. Sheep Company in Dickie, Wyoming. He shared a boxcar on the trip west with the Brunk-bred Flyhawk. For years the two shared paddocks and pastures and were bred to each other's daughters, so they often are found close together in the same pedigrees.

At the time of their arrival, L. U. Sheep Company had a group of grade mares sired by an unspecified son of the great Dan Patch, and a ten-year-old half-Thoroughbred mare named Lady. From 1929 through 1934 these Dan Patch granddaughters and Lady produced twenty-three mares, eight by Linspar, fifteen by Flyhawk. These unregistered mares formed the nucleus from which the company's extensive breeding program grew.

At the next stage, Flyhawk daughters were bred to Linspar and vice versa. Fillies from this cross were carefully evaluated, registered, and joined the broodmare band. Colts were usually gelded and trained to become part of the large remuda needed for the vast ranch's sheep and cattle operations. These were not registered. Of Linspar's thirty-four identified offspring, only one colt was registered and he had limited use at stud.

The Brunk-bred Flyhawk (Go Hawk x Florette).
Photo courtesy of NMMH.

Of the thirty-three Linspar daughters foaled between 1929 and 1940, eleven were unregistered and sixteen were X-registered. From this rather modest start, descendants of Linspar can be found across the country, from Washington to Louisiana, from California to Massachusetts, and points in between.

Linspar's daughters gave us seventy-nine fillies and thirty colts. Among their descendants were a lot of good horses and quite a few great ones.

One thinks of mares like Carmel Show, foundation dam for Joe Young's Pineland Morgans in Georgia; and Jenney Lake, a champion herself and dam of Mr. Breezy Cobra, Hurricane Lake, Precious Stone, and Nighty Night. From this same family – descendants of the unregistered Duchess – came Max High Fidelity Kid, Arana Field, and Panorama, to name just a few.

From Valentine, whose sire was Linspar, we got Big Bill B, Captain McCutchen, and Nugget's Val Hawk. Descendants of Mallow included Senatefield, Kane's High Society, Dickie's Pride, The Gay Cadet, Mac Della, King Bob, and Morgana La Fee.

Varga Girl, Keystone's Gorgeous (and others of the Keystone prefix), California sire Midnite Sun, and Leo Beckley's fine stallion Montey Vermont, descend from Linspar's daughter Ishawooa.

Other Linspar offspring mares like pretty Osogay (dam of Green Trim's Topmiss), Vivian La Sorciere, Sage Queen (dam of Big Bend Top Joy), and Quaker Maid enhanced the breed. To the male side can be added Morgans like L U Colonel (grandsire of Topside Eager Beaver), Bonfire, Chico's Flame, Escalanta, Kenney's King Cotton, and Ern Pedler's Little Fry.

Among Linspar's descendants we find everything from cow horses to fine harness champions, from roadsters to parade horses, from halter winners to notable sires and dams – and speedy Escalanta, who beat Utah's AAA champion Quarter Horse in five straight races.

Chocolate

Elmer Brown sold Chocolate at three years old to R. V. Mills, who had him eight years but registered no foals. A May 15, 1946, *Western Livestock Journal* advertisement read: "FOR SALE: Good registered jacks, some range broke; registered Morgan, Palomino, and Quarter Horses. Hineman's Jack Farms, Dighton, Kansas." George E. Hineman owned Chocolate twice, getting 12 foals the first time (1937-1940) and 18 the last (1944-1949). Hineman sold Chocolate in 1940 to W. P. Thornhill of Miami, Texas, who began raising Morgans in the Texas Panhandle in 1927 from two Headlight Morgan sons, Dan and Dixie Dan, and Nellie Skinner (dam by Headlight Morgan). Nellie's offspring were later bred to Silver Ranger, as were mares Thornhill obtained from Sentney. Thornhill's mares produced 13 foals by Chocolate (1941-1942).

Thornhill sold Chocolate to R. S. "Pop" Sentney of Hutchinson, Kansas, in 1942. Sentney was a staunch Morgan booster who had studied the early *Morgan Registers* thoroughly before selecting his initial stock in 1939. He began with Sir Linsley, two Linsley daughters, a granddaughter, and three mares from Thornhill. Sentney bred, bought, and sold a great number of Morgans, often hauling truckloads of horses to out-of-state buyers. In 1943 he got three Chocolate foals, then sold Chocolate to Hineman.

Chocolate is the Linsley son with the most offspring, 49 registered. Sixteen of Chocolate's daughters and 12 sons bred on. Four other sons went to El Salvador. Photo courtesy of the National Museum of the Morgan Horse.

From 1939 through his April 1951 dispersal, the Registers disclose sixty-one Morgans transferred to Sentney and 142 transferred from him. Sometimes he owned the same horse twice. Of sixty-nine head sold between 1948 and 1951, more than two-thirds traced to Linsley through his sons or daughters, and more than half that group were of Chocolate's line.

Sixteen Chocolate daughters and twelve sons bred on. Four other sons went to El Salvador. Chief among his sons were Powerful, Model, and Raymond S Sentney.

Powerful was successively owned by Hineman, Pine Ridge and Rosebud Indian Agencies, Sentney, and O. E. Sutter. Most Rosebud stock carried the prefix "R. B." One of Powerful's daughters there was Carolyn S Sentney, dam of Suzay, a wonderful mare who produced five champion daughters – Foxy Ann, Foxfire's Suzay, Foxy Sentora, Foxy-Rose Marie, and Foxy Juanita – before her untimely death in 1960. For Sutter, Powerful sired many good "Dot S" Morgans, including Dot S Dolly, second dam of Stuart Hazard's Funquest Falcon. Powerful was one of the Sutter Ranch's best cow horses. He was gelded in 1950.

Model, bred in Kansas by Willis Grumbein, proved to be a good sire for the Buchholz family in South Dakota, and often was bred to his own daughters and granddaughters.

Other Chocolate sons worth mentioning include Red Rockwood in Iowa (his daughter, Red Sparkle, was dam of the mare Broadmoor's Bonnie), and Double Chocolate, sire of the fabulous mare Dee Dee Chocolate, tops in the stock and cutting horse fields.

Best - or luckiest - of Chocolate's sons was Raymond S Sentney, bred by Thornhill, owned by Sentney, and sold to Locke Theis of Dodge City, Kansas. The Theis Company owned three ranches where good using horses were needed. Theis purchased mares of Thornhill and Brown breeding, and Charlie Sentney by Sir Linsley. From Charlie he got a great broodmare sire, Silgal's Improver. Raymond's daughter, Brown Mae, was the dam of Wawayanda Bay Maebel. Brown Mae's dam, Silver Mae, traced twice to Linsley.

Theis mares combined the blood of Linsley, Querido, Headlight Morgan, and Old Sellman stock – a uniform band of great quality. Many colts were gelded for ranch use. The breeding program was discontinued in 1953, with seventy-five head of Morgans, including several three-way packages, offered for sale. J. Cecil Ferguson bought twenty-four head for shipment to Rhode Island. He sold nine, keeping fifteen outstanding mares and their offspring. From them descended numerous, well-known "Broadwall" Morgans, Broadwall Drum Major among them.

Chocolate's daughters include Mae, South Spot, Chocolate Ann, Tejas Nell (dam of Black Ranger, who is dam of Black Ran-Bo), Tejas Ina Maeleta (whose daughter, Black Annie S Sentney, produced good "Topside" Morgans in Colorado), Suzan Sentney (granddam of UC High Life), and Orange Blossom (dam of thirteen good ones for J. C. Jackson in Montana). Other traces of Chocolate's line live on through Morgans with prefixes like Shawalla, Funquest, Tapnor, Tejas, Stockbridge, Amarillo, Colbrook, Broadway, Wales Farm, Larigo, Eedahow, and the suffix Vona.

Hawk Jim

It's easy to tell of this Linsley son. In a word: DEVAN. Bred by Elmer Brown, Hawk Jim was foaled in 1929 and sold at his dam's side to O. E. Sutter of Wichita, Kansas. Sutter's four Hawk Jim foals left little history. Bar S Don sold to Lionel Quick in Louisiana, who did use him at stud.

No transfers of Hawk Jim appear in the *Register*. Sometime around 1934 he entered the Remount Service, and was placed in Ohio with Merle D. Evans about 1937. He was one of eight Morgan stallions still in the dwindling Remount Program in 1949.

In 1934 Evans purchased the Mansfield son Captor and his full sister, Dimity, from the Morgan Horse Farm in Middlebury. In 1937 he got three yearling fillies there, Gleneida, Gorgeous, and Gracious Lady; and Ceres, who had a filly (Roz) at her side by Delmont and was bred back to him, producing Tippy Tin in 1938.

All of Evans' purchased Morgans traced, like Hawk Jim, to General Gates, tail male. Nothing more is heard of Gracious Lady, but the others formed the base on which all "Devan" Morgans were founded.

Evans considered Mansfield "the greatest Morgan that ever lived, outside of Justin Morgan." In more than four decades of breeding Morgans he didn't deviate from his original line-bred plan. His stock was steeped in Mansfield and Linsley blood. In 1946 Evans added Captain Fillmore, whose sire, Fillmore, was a full brother to Captor and Dimity. To further strengthen the line, he purchased 19-year-old Payday (Mansfield x Glady) in 1964, getting seventeen foals by him in 1965, and one each in 1966 and 1968. Twelve of them were from mares of Hawk Jim's family.

Hawk Jim sired seventeen colts and fifteen fillies for Evans. First came Star Hawk, maternal half-brother to the immortal Fleetwing. He left a multitude of descendants. Besides "Devan" other prefixes continuing his line were "Serenity," "Twin Brooks," "Mr. R's," "HLM," "Kennebec," and "Amber's."

Hawk Jim's offspring Tippy-Dee is best remembered for the show horse Chico's Flame and the mare Replevin, from which some Blackacre and Casland Morgans descend. The mare Glenhawk, another Hawk Jim offspring, gave the breed White Cap, Devan Val, Devan Troubadour, Devan Deb, Devan Glendevere, and others. Again we find "Serenity," "Mr. R's," as well as "Gra-Vand", "Casland," "Tamhattah," "Springmont," "Kinglow's," and "Troutbrook" Morgans in that family.

Lady Hawk's first foal was the versatile champion Devan Chief ("Millsboro"), sire, among others, of The Gay Contessa. Many more were added through her grandson, Devan Gremar's Shawn; sons, Devan De Vere and Devan Paradise; and others.

Large families sprang from Hawk - Prince, Silverhawk, and Devan Hawk ("Sunset," "Kennebec," "Overlook," "Pineland"), and daughters Hollyhawk, Dimhawk, Lady Tess, Fancy Free, Star Shine, Devan Flake, Devan Dot, and Devan Pam. Son Wilmot Prince sired Downer's Debutante (dam Linet by R P Linsley) and others.

A nice example of the Devan influence is Sunforest Commando, a National Champion Stallion and 1994 Reserve Grand National Western Pleasure Stallions Champion. His dam, Devan Fortuna, traces five times to Hawk Jim through Silverhawk, Lady Hawk, Star Shine, and Tippy-Dee.

Rosco Morgan

Elmer Brown sold Rosco Morgan as a weanling in 1927. By 1951 he'd had seven more owners. He sired twenty-five foals in Kansas, Iowa and Illinois. From there, Rosco Morgan's descendants found their way into thirty-two states, including Hawaii.

His first foal was an unregistered mare, Dixie, in 1933. Dixie's daughter Amorita's five offspring included Myrita (dam of Wales Farm Major Bet) and Arribonita (second dam of the stallions Jona and Wales Farm Captor, and dam of the mare Arribella). Rosco's other foals came from twelve mares of predominantly Jubilee King, Allen King, and General Gates breeding – three of the latter through Linsley.

Notice must be taken of Rosco Morgan's daughters Bonnie Sue and Rosco's Romance, and sons Anthony Eden, Illini and Jolly Roger.

That May 15, 1946 *Western Livestock Journal* also carried this announcement: "Carmel Snow, Morgan Mare by Night Tide, was recently sold by Merle Little, Monrovia, Ca., to Major Joe Young, Pittsburg, Ca. She was bred by the L. U. Sheep Co., Dickie, Wyo." There was more to this statement than they knew. Carmel Snow was owned by Helen Greenwalt, sold to Justin Dart, and then to Little. Her dam, Kaycee, was a Linspar granddaughter.

Major Young, ending his Army career, was about to return to Pineland, Georgia. He bought the mare, some Jersey cows, two Sonfield daughters, and a young stallion he described as "broke to the max, with a fabulous disposition and horse sense, and handsome besides" – Jolly Roger. Young went with them all in a boxcar to Georgia in November 1946. "Pineland Morgans" was about to be born. Hundreds of fine individuals sprang from the forty-four colts and fillies Young got from Jolly Roger, beginning with the breedings to Carmel Snow and the Sonfield mares.

Bonnie Sue and Anthony Eden went to California. Anthony Eden sired a number of "Hel's" Morgans for Hugh Logan of Glendale, California. Justin Dart sold Bonnie Sue, in foal to Squire Burger, to Merle Little. From her Little got Senor Morgan, Marlene's Morgan (dam of Hank and Louise Boyd's Gertrude Mae), Duarte Maid, and Miss President Morgan, dam of Poco's Dream Girl and others.

Rosco's Romance was the dam of Mary Lasater's stallion Royal Hobo, whose sire was Royal Major by Illini. Illini (f. 1941) is best remembered for three fine siring sons: Royal Major and Tony Boy in Iowa, and "Debacon's" handsome show horse and sire, King Benn, in Minnesota.

Sparbeau

Sparbeau (f. 1930) went to Nebraska in 1943, and then had six owners in California. Roland Hill had him from 1937 to 1940, getting twenty-seven foals, mainly from Querido daughters.

Sparbeau had terrific influence on Morgan stock in the far West. Many daughters were excellent broodmares, and two sons were especially important. These were Stanley Hunewill's Dude Spar and Sparbeau's last foal, Memphis Beau Brummell, bred by E. W. Roberts of Hi Pass, California.

Memphis Beau Brummell sired few foals, but one was Shawalla Buck, whose many sons and daughters pretty well blanketed the Pacific Northwest. Offspring of Diamond Duke, Shawalla Silver, Shawalla Ringo, and a host of others bred by C. E. Shaw of Walla Walla, Washington, and other breeders trace to Shawalla Buck.

Offspring of Dude Spar's daughters formed a valued part of breeding programs at "Sky Ridge" in California, "West's" in Missouri, and "Pfeiffer" in the Pacific Northwest, to name a few. A good representative was Sparfield, bred by Leo Beckley. His sire and dam were both by Dude Spar. Sparfield and his sons and daughters appear on many pedigrees of the A. G. Baughmans' "Desiderata" Morgans in Philomath, Oregon.

Bred by Roland Hill, Dude Spar was foaled on the property of S. H. Hunewill and Co. of Bridgeport, Connecticut. A great many "Circle H" Morgans descended from him, his sons and daughters.

Prominent among Sparbeau's daughters was Princess Tonya. Her daughter, Princess Elizabeth, was the dam of Princess Victoria, whose son, Triton El Capitan, sired many Morgans at Point Reyes National Seashore Park's Morgan Horse Farm. Another daughter of Princess Elizabeth was Ida Red, beloved foundation mare for Tomeri Morgans in Southern California.

Starlight Lu by Sparbeau was the dam of Eco Lujo, whose son, Eco Jubilo, was well known on the California show circuit some years ago. That line lives through the Morgans at La Serena Farm in New York.

Beau Belle went to Vermont in 1956, where she had fifteen foals – thirteen carried the "Toplands" prefix. Betty Spar, on the other hand, had two good daughters who went to Beckridge Morgans in Washington. They were Rosalee Of Lone Pine and Lone Pine Boogie.

Sparbeau with Miss Jean Hill up at the Bakersfield Frontier Days in 1937. Jean won this $250 saddle and bridle for best working cow horse at the show. Photo courtesy of the National Museum of the Morgan Horse.

Other Sons

A brief note should be made of important Linsley lines from lesser-known sons. Major Linsley's daughter, Bar S Lady (dam by Silver Tip Morgan), left many fine descendants. Ranger L sired the stallion Ormandy and the mare Maurcena L – from whom many excellent "Sunflower" Morgans descend. Sir Linsley's son, Dakota Thunder Cloud, sired an important family, and Sir Linsley's daughter, Dakota Nellie, and his descendant, Honor, were the foundation of many "Oak Acres" Morgans. Three other good Sir Linsley offspring were Charlie Sentney, Sir Jonathan, and Lady Ester. Harris Linsley sired Rapinier, Linsley's Lynella, and Josephine H Linsley, who bred on. Max Linsley's one son was Camanche, sire of Jane Wood, Broodmoor's Bonnie and others.

Linsley Captain had four foals, one being Bette Linsley, dam of the Texas stallion Tehachapi Rock (f. 1947). Silver Tip Morgan had two daughters, Trixie (f. 1930), unregistered, out of Chestnut by Linsley, and Silver Sparta out of Sparta. Silver Sparta was dam to Bar S Lady (f. 1934), mentioned earlier.

An unregistered chestnut mare by Line Allen was the third dam of Van's Pride, a Kansas stallion by Linsley's Allen. Van's Pride was the sire of several good ones, including Casland Masterpiece. H. H. Herst of Kansas bred seven of Line Allen's dozen offspring, and all of them bred on to some extent.

At the end, we have only scratched the surface in our attempt to follow all the golden threads that stretched back in time to the outstanding Morgan stallion Linsley. In researching this article, I filled a three-ring binder with just the descendants of his sons. Far too many to list, but a rich legacy, indeed.

Morgan Families: The Working Western Family
Printed as one of a four-part series on the recognized "families" of Morgans:
Lippitt, Government, Brunk and Working Western
1996

"The fact is, a well-reined Western horse is so well in hand at all times and at any speed that he can be stopped and turned in his tracks, no matter how fast he is running with scarcely any pull on the bit. A good rope horse is so well in hand and knows his work so well the rider hardly uses the reins at all. Horse and rider work as one . . .It takes three years or more of very careful training and lots of work to make a real well-reined cow horse even by the best reinsman, and then to make a top animal, he must have a horse with lots of cow sense to start with."
Roland G. Hill (*The Morgan Horse*, December 1942)

Roland Hill and his family owned, during his lifetime, more registered Morgans than anyone before or since, with the exception of Richard Sellman. In the late 1940s he had 80-100 registered Morgan geldings at the Horseshoe Cattle Company ranch near Elko, Nevada, alone. We'll return to him a bit later.

Morgan horses came to California with the early gold seekers. First known of the emigrant Morgans was St. Clair 48, who arrived in 1849. He sired 600-700 foals in the Sacramento area, including fine stallions, outstanding broodmares, and record-setting trotters and pacers. His untimely death in an 1864 stable fire warranted a lengthy eulogy in the *Sacramento Union*.

Many excellent Morgan stallions were brought to California during the next few decades. One man drove a herd of horses purchased in Vermont across the plains to California in 1859. Losses were small, and 122 head came safely through the long journey. More than two-thirds of the early arrivals were sons, grandsons, and great-grandget of Black Hawk 20. Some were splendid carriage horses; others were used in

Hedlite. Photo courtesy of NMMH.

Standardbred breeding programs, while still others became the first of the Working Western Morgans on vast ranchos of the period. Men of great wealth and prominence - William Chapman Ralston, Ansel Ives Easton, James Ben Ali Haggin, John Bidwell, and others - owned many.

The first organized overland party reached California on November 4, 1841. One of its leaders was 22-year-old John Bidwell, an exceptionally able and determined young man. Within a few years he'd discovered gold and acquired the huge Arroyo Chico Rancho in Butte County, the original grant containing "5 leagues of land." An 1855 agricultural census shows that Bidwell had 4,265 acres planted to grains, 13,326 head of American and Spanish cattle, 3,636 sheep, 7,550 hogs, and 1,588 horses. Bidwell founded the city of Chico on a portion of his land, plans for which included a broad avenue for exercising and racing horses. Morgan stallions he owned were Black Prince, John Morgan, Smith's Morgan, and Bidwell's Rattler.

The fabled Ben Ali Haggin arrived in 1849, seeking and finding a fortune. In 1850 he and his brother-in-law, Lloyd Tevis, founded "Haggin & Tevis," trading in horses and buying stock from newly arrived emigrants. The two owned 400,000 acres in Kern County where they raised alfalfa, cattle, and a variety of horses. Haggin was also in partnership there with Jesse D. Carr. Their interest was in developing Standardbred racing stock. The broodmare band included several descendants of St. Clair and two Black Hawk-line mares. Haggin owned Bismarck, a double Black Hawk descendant. Carr had Redfield's Vermont, a great-grandson of Black Hawk.

James G. McCracken also favored the Black Hawk family. He brought several stallions to the state, and bred some excellent stock. Many won first premiums at early state fairs, some as "Horses of All Work."

Wine Creek Black Hawk, Prince Morgan, Vick's Ethan Allen Jr., Keokuk, McCracken's Black Hawk, and David Hill 2nd are just a few of the Morgans who stood at area ranches for the improvement of stock. By the time the old stallions and their offspring had died, the number of California horses with some degree of Morgan blood was enormous. A chestnut mare with four white stockings, bred by Haggin in Kern County, has many descendants today through her granddaughters, Dulcet and Laydee. This mare is the only known link between two centuries. Registered Morgans did not reappear in California until 1920.

In May of 1920 Reginald Parsons, a wealthy gentleman rancher, purchased Baldie's Boy (Headlight Morgan x Baldie Antoine) from Richard Sellman. That winter twelve Sellman mares arrived by boxcar and were taken to Parsons' beautiful Mountcrest Ranch in Hilt, California. Seven of the mares were in foal – five to Joe Bailey (Headlight Morgan x Polly B. by The Admiral) and two to Dot (Morgan Chief x Dot N. by The Admiral). Among the seven foals in 1921 was Mountcrest Sellman (Joe Bailey x Kitty E [by The Admiral]), founder of a great family of his own.

Baldie's Boy sired five foals, 1922-23, and Mountcrest Sellman two (1926), for Parsons. By 1927 Parsons had sold Baldie's Boy, nine Sellman mares, and seven young Morgans, all of them lost to the breed. Nine head are unaccounted for. Parsons may have kept them for ranch use, or perhaps sold them without transfers. He bred no registered Morgans after 1926. Balkitty (Baldie's Boy x Kitty E.) had two registered foals. I remember a daughter who looked just like her, but who wasn't registered. Mountcrest Nan (Baldie's Boy x Berta) eventually went to Dr. Ina Richter of Kedron Morgans. And there was Georgette (Mountcrest Sellman x Frisky A).

Fast-forward two decades and a few miles southeast of Hilt, to a chestnut Morgan stallion named North Fork. He could pose – head high, ears perked, eyes dreamy – as if listening for far-distant hoofbeats. But, if cattle were around, you'd better be alert when you put your foot in the stirrup. By the time your leg swung over the cantle you were on the move. North Fork's business was working cattle.

Because of my fond memories of him, I was pleased to note that Painters Pine Ridge and Renwood Evening Star – World and Reserve World Reining Champions at the 1995 Grand National – were both descendants of North Fork through their dams. Sharzana, who was top ten in open reining, also traces to him, through both sire and dam.

North Fork sired twenty registered foals (1941-1950), nineteen of them from just three mares. Of these, one son and seven daughters had registered offspring. From this small group, North Fork's descendants spread through California and the Pacific Northwest, and even to Quebec.

Sellman, Parsons, and Hill all figure in the story of this horse, typical of so many of that time, making his a tale worth telling.

J. Sheldon Potter had purchased Don Juan 7623 (Querido x Addy [by Texas Allen]), Daisyann, and Roverta from Roland Hill in 1930. The mares were by Pat Allen and out of Red Oak daughters. This proved to be a great investment; Roverta had sixteen foals and Daisyann had seventeen.

Roverta's 1937 foal by Don Juan was North Fork, sold in 1939 to the ranching partnership of Charles A. Schultz, Julius Kuck, and Robert J. Schultz of Yreka, California. He was taken to the Kuck Ranch, northeast of Montague, in charge of Julius "Jiggs" Kuck (pronounced "Cook"). The ranch, founded in 1877 by Jiggs' grandfather, consisted of five thousand acres under fence and one thousand leased acres on Willow Creek Mountain. The ranch carried some five hundred head of registered and commercial cattle on land full of timber, rimrock, and lava.

Curly Brown, an area old-timer, said that "rocks toughen hooves, hilly pastures build muscles, (and) deadfalls teach a colt to pay attention to where he puts his feet." He was right. The part-Morgan mare I had up there in my teens was the most nimble and sure-footed horse I've ever ridden, no matter what the terrain. We were the same age when I got her, so her Morgan blood could only have come from Reginald Parsons' stock. There were no other Morgans in the Siskiyou Mountains when she was foaled.

Jiggs Kuck believed registered Morgans could work cattle up there as well as "cold stuff" could. The partners purchased three mares: Parsons' Georgette, previously mentioned, and Oretia A (Silver Ranger x Oretia) and Tabette (Querido x Tab) from Roland Hill. In the background of them all we find Sellman stock.

In 1941 the partners purchased the noted sire King Shenandoah from F. R. Dzengolewski in Illinois to cross on North Fork's daughters. Sadly, King sired only one foal here. Jiggs was riding him in the mountains and the stallion dropped dead after jumping a log. Ryder (Sonfield x Angel A) was purchased from Roland Hill to replace him. Ryder sired eleven foals (1945-1949), ten from North Fork daughters. Ten carried the ranch prefix "Siskiyou."

Kuck Ranch Morgans were fine but strong boned and heavily muscled. Raised among lava, they worked cattle over the roughest ground, clearing obstacles without hesitation. Neighboring ranchers bred their grade mares to North Fork and bought his sons, daughters, and grandget, quite a few were thus lost to the breed.

In 1949 the Morgans were dispersed. Foals were sold with their dams at auction. Jiggs kept two saddle horses, Foothill and Siskiyou Dude; and Robert Schultz took North Fork and Ryder. Both went to Scott Valley, where they later died, Ryder after running into a rake. Betty Kuck (Jiggs' widow) says, "Dude and Foothill were excellent horses, and we had them into the 1970s. All business, not kids' horses."

Among the many descendants of North Fork were the mares Re-Wind Of Sundown, Siskiyou Cricket, Skyfield Gemini, Bonnie Rebel, and Ranchita Queen; and stallions Char-El Dodi, Domino Major, Norsisk, Siskiyou Stan, Siskiyou Red, and Juan Bravo.

Two cattlemen brought Sellman Mor-

Squire Spar, Morgan Cutting Horse Champion.
Photo courtesy of the National Museum of the Morgan Horse.

gans into California in 1922. Frederick A. Fickert had a large spread in Bear Valley, near Tehachapi. He went to Texas after seeing the Morgans Roland Hill had gotten there. Fickert bought fourteen mares of predominantly Headlight Morgan blood, and Raven Chief (Morgan Chief x Baby Girl [by

138

The Admiral]). Raven Chief's California foals included the good sires Colorado, Chestnut Chief, Sun Down Morgan, Eagle, and Tonto's Roamer.

Roland Hill's extensive cattle operation at Tehachapi called for good using horses, and he wanted to improve on the stock he had. He sent a cowboy to Texas in February of 1922 to buy a Morgan stallion. The man chose Redwood Morgan (Headlight Morgan x Bonne A [by Major Antoine]), whose arrival prompted Mr. Hill to go to Mountain Vale in April for more Morgans. He bought three geldings and sixteen mares, all but two of them by Headlight Morgan, his sons, or a grandson. Two mares had foals at side, and six were bred for 1923.

Redwood Morgan sired four foals in 1923, then was sold to the Cebrian Brothers' Cuyamo Ranch at Maricopa. He is best remembered for his sons Blackhaux and Cuyamo, bred by Duval Williams; and Hacienda Chief, bred by Roland's brother, Russell Hill. Williams had the old chestnut Haggin mare mentioned earlier whose unregistered dam, Lady (by Bender), was the dam of Dulcet and Laydee, by Cuyamo. Mr. Williams also bred Cuyamo's maternal half brother, Hedlite, purchased by Mary H. Smith in 1936.

Sun Down Morgan excelled in in-hand classes and was a proven sire of quality colts. Photo courtesy of NMMH.

In 1924 Hill purchased a dozen young mares from Sellman, one by Headlight Morgan; one by his son, Sooner; and the rest by Red Oak. Two more Red Oak daughters came from the Sellman Estate in 1925.

Hill's land in the Tehachapi Mountains was "all up and down" country that required sure-footed, well-muscled horses. The Morgans were used for cattle work — roping, branding, cutting, and hard range riding. His cutting horses were lightning quick. Hill said, "We have no use for a horse that is not a good handler, or one that cannot do a hard day's work whenever asked to, no matter how fine a pedigree he has or how stylish and fine looking he is." (*The Morgan Horse*, December 1942)

These early Sellman-bred Morgans were the foundation on which countless California breeding programs were based. Through sheer force of numbers, Roland Hill's Morgans dominated the market. This was good; it ensured continuation of well-proven bloodlines for years to come. Richard Sellman had shown that, given enough time and enough stock, a man could develop a uniform family of horses with an aptitude for the work he needed done — horses with "cow sense," if you will. Roland Hill became Sellman's California counterpart. The family registered more than 550 Morgans between 1923 and 1954, and continues to raise Morgans today. Stallions had to prove themselves as using horses before being put to stud. Scores of colts were gelded for use on the range. Mares who didn't produce quality using horses were culled.

Hill used eleven purchased stallions throughout the years, some more successfully than others. Brunk-bred Pat Allen was the sole sire of California Morgan foals in 1924 and 1925. Big, powerful, and energetic, Pat Allen sired forty-nine foals in three seasons for Hill.

Querido was purchased as a yearling from the U.S. Morgan Horse Farm in Vermont. This full brother of Mansfield laid a grand foundation for the generations that followed. His offspring were smart, easy to train, and quick to learn. They made excellent all-purpose horses. Querido sired one hundred fifty foals for Hill (1927-1938), and then went to Hawaii. His daughters were excellent broodmares, crossing especially well with Sonfield. Querido's most famous sons went out of state in 1935 – Silver Ranger to W. P. Thornhill in Texas, and Tehachapi Allan to Elmer Brown in Kansas. Brunk-bred Pongee Morgan sired thirty-two foals between 1927 and 1929, twenty-two of them fillies. William Randolph Hearst bought twelve of them and ten Querido daughters to form his broodmare band in San Simeon, California.

Short-lived Winchester (Mansfield x Narissa) was purchased as a yearling from the U. S. Morgan Horse Farm. His eight foals included Sallysen and Queensen, foaled on the property of C. F. Ayer in Colorado. Their dams, Sallie Bee and Queene Allan, were Querido daughters out of Sellman-bred, Hill-owned mares. Their "ayr" offspring are found in the pedigrees of some Working Western Morgans in Utah. E. W. Roberts of Hi Pass, California, purchased Sallysen and Queensen in 1946, and sold the latter to China's Ministry of National Defense in 1947.

Joaquin Morgan (Romanesque x Margett L [by Linsley]) came as a foal from Elmer Brown in 1935. Trained to work cattle, he sired thirty-four foals, including some excellent daughters, before being sold. He didn't really suit Mr. Hill, being very strong-willed and independent, and sometimes mean.

Sparbeau (Linsley x Sparbelle), bred by Elmer Brown, had five owners before Hill got him in 1937. A good cow horse, he sired twenty-eight foals before being sold in 1940. Hill-bred sons included Silver Dan, Danspar, and Dude Spar, the latter foaled property of S. H. Hunewill & Co. in Bridgeport, California. The Hunewills had several Sonfield daughters, developing from them and Dude Spar many fine "Circle H" Morgans. They later leased then purchased the great sire Condo to cross on their mares. Lee Spar (Dude Spar x Iva Lee Field) sired Sparfield, a fine reining and cutting horse at the Wagon Wheel Ranch in Halsey, Oregon; and Squire Spar, most successful in reining and cutting competition for Joseph Olsen in Utah, and later for Dick Nelson in Ohio. Sparfield Heidi (Sparfield x Beaver State Gem), owned by Desiderata Morgans in Philomath, Oregon, was Champion Cutting Horse at the 1995 Columbia Morgan Classic.

Linsley's dam, Sunflower Maid 02401 (Headlight Morgan x Fanny P.) Photo courtesy of NMMH.

Sparfield appears three times in her pedigree. In 1942 J. Sheldon Potter got the Sparbeau son Francisco from Roland Hill. He bred Morgans primarily for his own ranch use.

Roland Hill got El Cortez (Romanesque x Viola Linsley) as a weanling. He was sold in 1941, as were his six daughters and two of his sons. Four colts were probably gelded.

In December 1939 Mr. Hill bought Sonfield (Mansfield x Quietude). Sonfield was a wonderful addition to the gene pool of California's Working Western Morgans. He was an outstanding sire, and one of the best stock horses of his day. He appeared on the May 1940 cover of *The Western Horseman*, and was *Western Livestock Journal's* "Horse of the Month" in September 1947. Sonfield sired more than 180 Morgans for the Hill family. The cross with Querido mares was especially fine. His progeny included top stock horses, show ring stars, and fine sires and dams.

In December of 1940 J. S. Potter sold the weanling colt Don Felipe, a full brother to North Fork, to Dean Witter, who later purchased four mares from Potter – one from Roverta and three from Daisyann. These formed the foundation of Witter's "Lone Pine" Morgans at Covelo, California. Witter purchased the stallion Rosefield (Sonfield x Rose Mala) from Hill in 1942, and traded him in 1958 to the J. C. Jackson Ranch in Montana for Revenue M (Fleetfield x Katelette). Still later, Witter got Sonfield's Sammy from Leo Beckley in Washington.

Beckley had purchased Sonfield when he was twenty-two, and gave the "aging" stallion a whole new career. Sonfield was still a working horse, and Leo said, "It was a real thrill to ride him over the hills – and especially behind cattle, as he was always alert for a dodging cow or calf. He could turn and be away so fast that all the rider had to do was sit tight." Sonfield lived into his thirties, siring more than 225 registered foals in all. In 1950 the Horseshoe Cattle Company registered four Quarter Horse mares out of Helen Field, Katrina Field, Emily G Field, and Tabie Field – all registered Morgans by Sonfield.

The Remount stallion Tehachapi Allan.
Photo courtesy of the National Museum of the Morgan Horse.

For a time Roland Hill owned Brown Knox (by Senator Knox), who sired ten foals from 1942 to 1945. Four were fillies, all sold. The Hamel Brothers of Davis, California, purchased Black Knox (x Angel D) and had several mares and two stallions from Hill as well. Lester Hamel said the stallions were fine working cow horses who really enjoyed their work.

In 1947 Hill had Lippitt Morman brought all the way from Quebec, got two fillies from him, and sold him to Merle Little, who made good use of the stallion.

Many ranchers got Morgan stallions from Hill to cross with their grade mares. Vail & Vickers, for example, ran 10,000 cattle on their Santa Rosa Island Ranch, and had many three-quarter Thoroughbred mares. In 1947 they bought Mahan Field (Sonfield x Helen Mala [by Querido]) to breed to these mares to produce cow horses for the ranch.

Clarence C. Reed, physician and cattle rancher, bought Gay Mac (Mansfield x Dewdrop) in April of 1942, and got fifty-six foals from him out of eighteen mares who came to him directly or indirectly from Roland Hill. All the mares traced to Sellman stock through their dams; more than half were Querido daughters. Outstanding among them was Bessie Ro. Bred to Gay Mac, she produced Ro Mac, Bess Gates, and Flika.

Ro Mac was a proven cow horse, and many of his offspring exhibited a natural ability to work cattle. His daughter, Sissey, was the dam of Californio, sire of the reiner World's Edge Goldhawk, Juan Bravo, and others. Ro Mac's son, Vaquero Mac, was the grandsire of renowned Primavera Valdez, owned by Bob and Carol Simpson of Yuba City, California. Californio's sire, Tio Lalo, was by Mahan Field.

From Bess Gates came Dapper Dan, a fine stallion with a wonderful disposition. His daughter Dapper Dolly's stock horse career was cut short by an accident. Another daughter, Kellys Pretty Pixie, was the dam of Francis and Edith Kellstrom's Waytobe, the 1993 World Reining Champion and sire of Marklyn Hill Destiny, Reining Champion at the 1995 Columbia Morgan Classic. Dapper Dan is found tail-male in the pedigree of Butch Martin's champion cutting horse, Blacksaddle Sunkist. This Wyoming horse also has two crosses to Muscle Man through his dam.

Flika was the dam of Muscle Man, another California great, whose offspring excelled in many fields. One was El Mejor, a black gelding out of Cresta's Kitty Clover. He was the 1975 Grand National Champion Stock Horse, Champion Trail Horse, and top ten in four Western Pleasure categories. He was the 1975 Nor-Cal Champion Specialty Horse, and was the Golden West Regional Morgan Horse Show's High Point Horse for ten consecutive years. Shown by Larry Mayfield for the Phil Piazza family of Morgan Hill, El Mejor was a perennial crowd pleaser.

Minuet Spar (Muscle Man x Sister Spar [by Dude Spar]) was the dam of Doug and Diana Christie's mare, Mantic Minuet. She was the 1980 National Champion Stock Horse, went reserve in 1981, and was National Champion Stock Horse and Working Cow Horse in 1982.

Gay Berta (Gay Mac x Roberta Ro) produced Tia Margarita (by Tio Lalo), dam of Primavera Valdez, Montana Harvest, and 1992 World Open Reining Champion Brass Buckle. Valdez has four crosses to Gay Mac, six to Querido, one each to Mountcrest Sellman and Sonfield, and a lot of old Sellman mares in his background.

It is time to bring William Randolph Hearst's contribution into focus in what I have long called the Sellman/Hill/Hearst family of Morgans. As indicated earlier, Hearst started with Mountcrest Sellman and twenty-two mares from Roland Hill – the Sellman/Hill part of the equation.

Mountcrest Sellman sired sixteen colts and nineteen fillies at San Simeon (1933-1937). One son, Allancrest, was owned in Hawaii. Outstanding sons of Mountcrest Sellman were Warren Halliday's Redman, O. C. Foster's Montabell, and Mary "Sid" Spencer's Antman. Among his daughters were three bay "Piedmont" mares, upon which Mary H. Smith founded her Hedlite Morgans. Mrs. Spencer and Mary Smith both raised Morgans for their own cattle ranches.

Mary Smith purchased Hedlite (Blackhaux x Jocbo Brownie) to breed to the three Hearst mares: Piedmont Cresta, Piedmont Rosemarie, and Piedmont Eudora.

From left to right: Piedmont Rosemarie and her 1944 filly, Piedmont Cresta, and Piedmont Eudora. Photo courtesy of NMMH.

Their dams were by Querido and out of Sellman-bred mares Hill had brought from Texas. Mary had found a magic key here. With two chestnut exceptions, all her foals from 1939 to 1952 were black. Hedlite's Kitty Clover (Hedlite's Bob E A x Piedmont Cresta) was the dam of the great sire, Hedlite's Micky Waer.

Mary "Sid" Spencer raised one hundred fine Morgans throughout a 47-year period, good mountain-raised horses, many of whom sold to local ranchers. It all began when her father gave her Antman (foaled in 1936) and they bought some mares at a Hearst dispersal. In 1959 Mrs. Spencer bought 18-year-old Rusty (Eprus x Pongata). His dam was one of the Pongee Morgan daughters Hill sold to Hearst in 1929. Trained at three as a stock horse by his breeder, Ray Welbanks, Rusty had spent his life working in rough mountain country and siring "some of the finest cow horses area men had ever ridden," mostly from grade mares.

Mr. Hearst purchased Uhlan (Bennington x Poinsetta) from the U.S. Morgan Horse Farm in 1930. Uhlan sired seven foals (1932-1933), then went with other horses to Hearst's million-acre ranch in Chihuahua, Mexico, for three seasons, it seems. He sired six more foals (1937-1938) at San Simeon. Sold in 1937, he went to Nevada in 1941 and was heard of no more. Three of his sons went to livestock companies in Arizona – Jack London, The Senator, and Pico Chief.

Uhlan's son, Piedmont Apache (x Pongata), was the sire of Phil Morrison's beloved stallion, Sonoma, who spent most of his life doing all kinds of work on the range in Oregon. Apparently some of Uhlan's and Mountcrest Sellman's offspring went to the Hearst ranch in Mexico. Uhlan's last two Hearst-bred sons were Katrilan and Uhlan Ro.

Katrilan was the sire of Katrilan Prince, whose son, Trilson, was the sire of Dapper Dan and Muscle Man, both bred by Clark and Effie Bromiley, who bred so many fine Morgans.

In 1940 Mr. Hearst purchased Hacienda Chief (Redwood Morgan x Kitty Jay [by Querido]) from Russell Hill. Gelded in 1947, Hacienda Chief sired twice as many fillies as colts. Daughter Hacienda Dot was the dam of Chuckanut Hacienda by Katrilan, whose son, Classy's Pride, sired the good mare T-Bone Buttons, foaled in Nebraska in 1966. This mare was a double grand champion in cutting (futurity and novice) and was Reserve Champion Stock Horse at the first Grand National in 1972, then owned by Dick Nelsen of Mohican Farms in Ohio. One of Button's foals is Kirsten (Nelson) Farabee's Cool Cajun Cat, a "comer" in reining.

Because he raised Arabians, Mr. Hearst experimented on crossing them with Morgans, developing what he called "Morabs." Seventeen mares and one stallion were accepted in the Morgan Register with X-numbers under the old Rule II, which was rescinded in 1948. The stallion, Antman, was out of a daughter by Antez, a famous racing stallion and outstanding sire who went to Poland. Gulastra, one of the prominent Arabian sires of his day; his son, Rahas; and five others were bred to Hearst's Morgan mares. The stallion, Sheik F (by Sonfield), was out of the "Morab" Princess Sabab X-05076, which brings yet another sire line into the Sellman/Hill/Hearst family of Morgans.

Early on I mentioned Painters Pine Ridge. His dam is Primavera Ramona. In her background you will find many Working Western Morgan sire lines such as El Cortez, Querido, Sonfield, Raven Chief, Pat Allen, Headlight Morgan, and Gay Mac; and familiar names like Linsley and Red Oak. The last three also crop up in the background of his sire, Blackwood Correll. It made a happy combination!

William Randolph Hearst and His Morgan Horses
2001

He loved to ride the golden hills of the Santa Lucia Mountains, following oak-fringed trails, along shaded creeks and through brushy hollows. Or he might urge his horse to a high place where he could watch the tide dash foamy waves against the rocky shore or catch a glimpse of the sun, drowning in the glittering sea.

He loved this land, these far flung acres that he owned. And long before his fabled "castle" was even a dream on paper, he told his mother that a month of riding, swimming, and camping here was a happier time by far than a month at Europe's poshest spas.

After five years of construction, the "castle" was ready for occupancy in 1927, although building continued on the site for two more decades. In 1929, William Randolph Hearst began to put together a Morgan horse breeding program by purchasing fourteen young mares from Roland Hill. There were five yearlings and nine two-year-olds. Twelve of them were daughters of the Brunk-bred Pongee Morgan (Allen King x Galva). Three lines of this stallion's heritage traced to Daniel Lambert 62. The other two young mares were by Querido (Bennington x Artemisia). The dams of all of them were bred by Richard Sellman and sold to Roland Hill. On June 1, 1931, Mr. Hearst purchased eight more Querido daughters, and again the dams of them all were Sellman-bred, Hill-owned. Here we have the foundation of what came to be called the Sellman/Hill/Hearst family of Morgans.

A band of Morgan mares owned by Roland Hill.
Photo courtesy of the National Museum of the Morgan Horse.

To breed to his mares, Hearst purchased two fine stallions, Uhlan (Bennington x Poinsetta [by Troubadour Of Willowmoor]) and Mountcrest Sellman (Joe Bailey [by Headlight Morgan] x Kitty E [by The Admiral]).

* * * * *

William Randolph Hearst was born in 1863, and grew up in a milieu where fine horses were the norm. So much has been written about the unimaginable wealth amassed by George Hearst and passed on to his only son that, suffice is to say, the horses "Willy" grew up with were among the best to be had in their day. George Hearst loved horses, and like his friends and business partners, he kept well bred trotting horses and handsome pairs and teams for his wife's carriages. Horses were used in the cattle operation and late in life George Hearst began breeding Thoroughbreds for the Eastern racetracks. Among his friends, James Ben Ali Haggin, Jesse D. Carr, William Chapman Ralston, Leland Stanford, and others had raised some of the finest Morgan horses on the West Coast in the early days. It seems likely that W. R. Hearst had seen some of them in his youth.

The younger Hearst owned several breeds of horses through the years. He was especially fond of Palominos, which were highly popular in the 1930s and 1940s. He had a stallion named Don Pedro and also had one registered as Wonderman (PHBA 7223). At one time The Harvester, one of the most popular Palomino stallions of the time, stood at stud at San Simeon. Another colorful breed to be found at the ranch was the Appaloosa and there were also some "just horse," for riding and general ranch work. But it is the Morgan breed that concerns us here, and to some extent also the Arabian horses Mr. Hearst owned and bred.

One of the properties owned by Hearst was the Babicora Ranch at Temosachic, Chihuahua, Mexico. Here, waterfowl, wild turkeys, and deer abounded, and Hearst raised cattle and horses on a 900,000-acre ranch. It is a sad fact that no breeding records were kept on the horses, and we have only tiny glimpses of the program that must have had some depth.

What we do know is that Hearst had both Arabians and Morgans on the Mexico ranch. One clue comes from the first Quarter Horse Register, where the dam of a bay mare Supreso (AQHA 6762) is called a "Hearst mare, by Uhlan [Morgan]." The year of birth for Supreso is given as 1932, but this date must be off a few years, as Uhlan's first foals were born at San Simeon in 1932.

It is assumed that Uhlan was taken to Mexico in 1932 after breeding a few mares in California. He had no registered foals here in 1934, 1935, or 1936. Another piece of the puzzle is found in the pedigree of Monita Gift X-0606, bred by O. C. Foster and sired by Montabell. Her dam was Neita, described (*AMHA Register*, Volume VI, p. 182) as an "unregistered mare, bay, foaled 1935 or 1936, bred by Hearst Sunical Land and Packing Corporation at their ranch

When Mr. Hearst began putting together his Morgan breeding program, he purchased 14 mares from Roland Hill, 12 of whom were by Pongee Morgan, pictured here. Photo courtesy of the National Museum of the Morgan Horse.

in Mexico where breeding records are not kept. There were both Morgans and Arabs on their ranch at that time and this filly is known to be at least half registered Morgan blood. The sire is probably Morgan and the dam Arab and Morgan cross."

Between 1933 and 1941, Hearst registered eighteen mares and one stallion who were half-Morgan/half-Arabian, under the old Rule 2 in the Morgan Registry. Hearst called these cross-bred horses "Morab," and an "X" preceded their registration numbers. Hearst used seven Pongee Morgan daughters and six Querido daughters in his Morab experiment, breeding the mares to fine Arabians. Antman X-8318 was the only stallion in the group. Sired by Mountcrest Sellman, he was out of the unregistered Pontez, a daughter of Antez (ASB 448), a famous racing stallion and an outstanding sire who was sold to the Arab Horse Breeding Society in Poland in 1934. Antman's second dam was Pondette, by Pongee Morgan.

Hearst's Morabs were an attractive lot and when bred back to purebred Morgan stock they produced many excellent individuals. Antman, for one, had many fine offspring. Oscar Burroughs of Windswept Ranch in Knightsen, California, had three Antman daughters in his broodmare band:

Shasta Daisy, Bo Peep, and Little Sweetheart (who was as lovely as her name implied). Mr. Burroughs had a strict evaluation program in effect whereby foals had to pass repeated and rigidly consistent evaluation of both disposition traits and physical conformation before they were registered. Sometimes this meant that a foal's registration might be delayed into its second year. Only when individuals came up to the standard that was set for their own replacement stock would they carry the prefix "Windswept" in their names. Offspring of the three mares named above carried the coveted prefix.

"Rule 2" admission to the Register covered "any meritorious stallion, mare, or gelding, having 1/32 or more of the blood of Justin Morgan: provided the sire and dam were bred in approved speed or roadster lines." This rule was rescinded as of January 1, 1948, and well it was, because there was such disparity of what the non-Morgan part of the pedigree might consist. Crosses were made with Saddlebreds, Standardbreds, some Thoroughbreds, some unregistered horses "said to be of Morgan blood," and some Arab blood too, prior to the Hearst project.

The gamut could run from a horse like Tim Finigan X-7212, "foaled 1919, bred by Richard Sellman; sire-Woodrow Wilson 6290, dam-Nita C., pedigree unknown," to "X" Morgans with generations of pureblooded excellence on both sides of their pedigrees, as was the case with Hearst's "Morabs." Gulastra (ASB 521), foaled in 1914, was a very prominent Arabian sire in this country. He sired three of the Hearst Morabs, and his son Rahas (ASB 651) sired four more. Ghazi (ASB 560), bred by William R. Brown's famed Maynesboro Arabian Stud in Berlin, New Hampshire, became one of the senior stallions at San Simeon. He sired four of Hearst's Morabs. Kasar (ASB 707), bred by W. K. Kellogg, was the grandson of desert-bred Arabians imported to the United States by Homer Davenport. Kasar sired three of the mares in the program - Sunical Bud, Sunical Dot, and Fawn K - and his son Ansarlah (ASB 1281) was the sire of Antellah, later owned by E. R. Roberts of Los Angeles.

Sabab (ASB 710) was a descendant on both sides of his pedigree of *Deyr, a desert-bred stallion of note, imported by Homer Davenport. Princess Sabab X-05076 and Sunup X-05216 were his daughters. Joon (ASB 439), the seventh Arabian stallion used on Morgan mares by Hearst, was the son of another of Davenport's desert-bred stallions. We have spoken here of the horses going back to the foundation stock of the Arabian Horse of America. These animals were selected for their excellence in conformation, endurance, and disposition, and were possessed of lovely heads and finely arched necks.

Fawn K X-05077 (Kasar x Red Tawn [by Querido]), foaled in 1933, was the first-born of the Morab experiment. She was the dam of Fawnette, whose daughter, Clovernette, was the dam of California King, a well-known central California sire some years back. Clovernette was a granddaughter of Mountcrest Sellman and the Querido mare Clover Bud. Jimmy Smith of Turlock, California, bred and raised several full siblings by California King out of Lady Gay (Blackman x Gay Jipsey), and when he showed them in Get of Sire and Produce of Dam classes, they were hard to beat. California King was a full brother to Bevi, dam of Condevi by Condo, owned by the Mosher Brothers in Utah. Fawn K was bred by Hearst and owned by Jean (Hill) Borelli. She was sold in 1942 to the Jeppesens, who later moved to Oregon, where they bred her several times to Abbott. Her California offspring included the mares Fawnette, Fawnette Spar, Fawnette A, and Fawnita Peerless. Fawn K produced a dozen foals between 1935-1950.

Princess Sabab X-05076 (Sabab x Princess Allan) was another of the top Morab producers. She was bred by Hearst and owned by Roland Hill. Between 1938-1949, she produced nine fillies and three colts. One of the colts was Sheik F, who sired some nice foals including Hank and Louise Boyd's good gelding, Sheik F's Capitan, out of the Querido mare, Katrina Q. Mr. and Mrs. E. W. Roberts purchased Antellah X-05751 at the Hearst reduction sale in August 1942. One of her foals for them was Gayler K, foaled in 1945, by Redman. Two daughters of Gayler K, Miss Tayler and Rose Eastman, were foundation mares for W. A. Lorenzen & Sons of Turlock, who gave the breed many fine individuals under the "Impala" prefix.

Seven other Morab mares had from one to five foals each, and one other Mr. Hearst sold in 1939. We have no history on her, and there were seven of these half-Arab mares, foaled between 1937 and 1940 for whom there is no record at all. It is possible that these joined earlier part-blooded stock on the cattle ranch in Mexico, but no one knows for sure.

Hearst's Morabs were an attractive lot and when bred back to purebred Morgan stock they produced many excellent individuals. Antman, pictured above, had many fine offspring. Photo courtesy of the National Museum of the Morgan Horse.

On the other hand, the history and progeny of the sole "Morab" stallion, the previously mentioned Antman, is well documented. He was one of the fine sons of Mountcrest Sellman who bred on. The story is told that Sid Forsyth's father bought the colt for her at the September 1937 Morgan sale held at San Simeon. The Forsyths, and later Sid and her husband, Dr. H. F. Spencer, continued to breed fine Morgans, especially for ranch work, for many years. Before she married, Mary "Sid" Forsyth had purchased the mares Red Tawn and Sunshine Maid from Hearst in 1940. In 1945, she added Hacienda Buttercup to her band. The mare, Fawn K, mentioned earlier, was out of the mare Red Tawn, one of three offspring born at San Simeon. Sunshine Maid produced four foals for Hearst before she was sold. Hacienda Buttercup was by Hacienda Chief, out of Buttercup A by Pongee Morgan.

Mr. Hearst purchased Hacienda Chief in March 1940 from Russell Hill. His sire was Redwood Morgan, and his dam was Kitty Jay by Querido. Hacienda Chief sired twenty-two foals from 1941-1947 at San Simeon. He was gelded in 1947, and then sold in January 1948. Among his offspring were the stallion War Chief, seven mares with the Hacienda prefix, Golden Query, and Serena, to name just a few.

Going back to the beginning, Hearst purchased Uhlan from the U. S. Morgan Horse Farm in Weybridge, Vermont, in 1930. Seven of his thirteen foals at San Simeon carried the Piedmont prefix. Uhlan's sons were Pico-Chief, Piedmont Apache, Enowee, The Senator, Jack London, Uhlan-Ro, and most importantly, Katrilan.

Jack London and The Senator were sold as yearlings to the Arizona Livestock Company in Phoenix. Uhlan-Ro was sold in utero with his dam, Reba Ro at the September 1937 reduction sale, to the Jones Hereford Ranch in Hollister, California, and he became their herd sire. Pico-Chief and Piedmont Apache were also sold, but Hearst kept Katrilan (foaled 1938).

Between 1942 and 1949, Katrilan sired twenty-four registered foals, slightly more colts than fillies. But we can't possibly leave Piedmont Apache without mentioning that he was the sire of Sonoma. Foaled in 1938, Sonoma already had had three owners when Phil Morrison purchased him in October 1941 and took him to Oregon, where he sired many fine offspring through the years, including foundation stock for the Morrison family's Aranaway Morgans of Grants Pass, and others in the Pacific Northwest.

There is no transfer recorded on Katrilan, and he had no registered foals after the end of the Morgan program at San Simeon in 1949. His first foal was Katrilan Prince, who founded a dynasty of his own through grandsons Muscle Man and Dapper Dan. Morgan breeder Cecil G. Evans of San Luis Obispo, California, purchased nine mares from Hearst during 1948. One was Piedmont Salome (Mountcrest Sellman x Sunbeam Maid), who came with a filly at her side by Katrilan, and bred back to him for 1949. The latter turned out to be a stud colt named Clifford Pride. The Katrilan daughter, Chuckanut Hacienda, produced several foals for the Mosher Brothers in Utah, the first was Red Mesa by Skagit Alki, others were by Condo.

Uhlan was one of the horses sold at Hearst's first sale in 1937. Another of his good siring sons, Enowee, was foaled in 1940 at R. G. Stewart's Rancho Dos Vientos in Camarillo, California. Stewart had purchased Uhlan and three mares at that sale.

Having saved the best for last, we come to Mountcrest Sellman. He sired forty foals, nineteen of whom were colts. Quite possibly a number of his early colts went to the Mexico ranch. They were registered, but we have no history of them. Antman already has been discussed. Other good sons who bred on included Cloverman, Kenelm Morgan, and the two very best: Montabell and Redman.

Redman, foaled in 1936, was out of Red Dot, by Pongee Morgan. He was bred by Hearst, owned first by Clarence Ferrari, then by R. L. Welborn, and finally by Warren Halliday, who kept him for life. In 1941, Mr. Welborn bred the Brunk mare Gojea (Go Hawk x Jeanne) to Redman, and then sold her to Mr. and Mrs. E. W. Roberts, and the foal she dropped two months later was the great Blackman. He had some good sons, Bikini was one, but it was as a broodmare sire that Blackman came to be prized. Two Blackman daughters, Belle McLinsley and Memphis Belle, and a granddaughter, Liz Taylor, joined the mare band at F. O. Davis's Windcrest Morgans in Windsor, Vermont. The author remembers a time when it seemed every breeder in California wished to have a Blackman daughter, but they were getting to be very scarce!

Redman's son, Billy Rebel, did very well in both southern California and later in Oregon. The Redman daughters Etna and Red Bess went to Barklay Braun's Keystone Ranch, where they crossed beautifully with the stallion Keystone. Redman's best years were spent at Halliday's fine ranch near Etna, California, where his offspring bore the prefix "Heaven's."

Montabell was another fine son of Mountcrest Sellman. Owned by O. C. Foster of Los Angeles, many of his offspring had the suffix "Gift."

So many people benefited from the comparatively short-lived breeding program of William Randolph Hearst - the J. Clarke Bromileys, and all who bought Morgans from them; W. L. Linn of Turlock; W. T. Carter of Fresno, and many, many more. It is doubtful whether Mr. Hearst and his guests gave much thought to this, as they enjoyed long days in the saddle in the Santa Lucia Mountains, with a picnic along the way. Maybe some rode Morgans, maybe they didn't.

But, by continuing to use the bloodlines so carefully developed by Richard Sellman and taken over and nurtured by Roland Hill in his own well thought-out breeding program, William Randolph Hearst, in essence, passed along the golden package of genes for uniformly handsome, well-conformed, good tempered, and intelligent Morgans to the next generation of breeders and beyond.

POETRY
Cowboy Poetry

Ern Pedler and Flying Jubilee.
Photo courtesy of the National Museum of the Morgan Horse.

Cold Creek Remembered
1958

One summer day, in my sixteenth year,
I called my horse and gathered my gear,
And stood by the pasture gate to see
The little bay gallop up to me.
Her tail flowed out like a silken banner,
And her head flung up in a carefree manner,
While her friendly whicker let me know
That she, like I, was eager to go.

That little mare that I loved so well
Had Morgan blood, as you could tell.
Her lines were typical of the breed;
Her action was very smooth, indeed.
The gentle, large eyes, spaced wide apart,
Bespoke of courage, and plenty of heart.
I thought her the best little horse on earth,
And I kissed her neck as I fixed the girth.

I paused for a moment, and looked about
At the beautiful land, to plan my route.
We stood in a country of scenic views;
About us towered the Siskiyous,
And off to the south, Mount Shasta gleamed -
A land made like Heaven, or so it seemed.
The ranch was my kingdom, that day long gone,
For I had two sections to ride upon.

Away to the east the long meadow lay,
With its waving grass that would soon be hay,
And through it wandered the Cold Creek stream,
Well-stocked with trout, a fisherman's dream.
Beyond the valley were tree-clad hills,
Where the stream fell down in sparkling rills,
Tumbling wildly down its rocky course,
From the heights, and the hidden spring, its source.

But then, if instead I looked to the west,
The journey was different from the rest,
For across the road, beyond the corral,
Were dry, yellow hills and chaparral;
And beyond them waved vast fields of grain
That led back up to the hills again.
Beyond the last hill was a sudden drop -
That hill had a lookout post on the top.

But we chose the meadow of grass and flowers,
And we rode content through the sunlit hours.
The grass by the creek was as soft as lawn,
And there, in the brush, we startled a fawn.
For a moment its soft brown eyes held me,
Then it tottered away, behind a tree.
And later, a coyote, with shaggy locks,
Slunk out of sight in the tumbled rocks.

We mounted the crest, where the burn had been,
And I tethered my horse and surveyed the scene.
I thought of the bountiful hand of Him,
Who formed this valley, these hills, that rim.
And when I looked up the sun had gone,
And the cumulonimbus were rolling on,
As the wind came on with a sudden gust,
Raising the leaves and swirling the dust.

Then the rain beat down and the thunder crashed,
While all about us the lightning flashed;
And I held up my arms to the pelting spray,
For I loved the sky to behave that way.
The black thunderheads kept rolling on,
And, quick as it came, the storm was gone!
The humped-up Herefords came out of their daze,
Fanned out in the field, and began to graze.

With my heart high up as a heart can go
I leaped in the saddle and headed below.
My sure-footed horse picked her way with care,
While I sent a song on the new-born air.
Then, out on the flat she danced with glee,
And leaped o'er the creek and a fallen tree;
She flew 'cross the meadow on fleet, sure feet,
And cleared the fence in a bound so neat.

The years have sped by, since that glorious day,
And Minnie now feeds on celestial hay;
But my heart comes back to it, o'er and o'er,
That magical, mystical day of yore,
When my life was unfettered, and free and grand,
And my heart was touched by a Heavenly Hand.
And my hope for Heaven includes a day
When I ride once again on my beautiful bay!

Joseph
1959

He was tired, and worn and worried;
They had come such a very long way.
And his eyes filled with weary frustration
At the close of this troublous day.

He had searched through the town for a lodging,
For somewhere to shelter his spouse;
But the doors of them all closed against him,
Every hostel, and hovel and house.

Then he came at last to a stable
And carried his Mary within.
So the Christ Child was born in a manger,
Since there had been no room at the inn.

And this Babe was the Lord of the lowly,
The gentle, the meek and the mild;
But Joseph, that moment, thought only
That this little mite was his child.

And he smiled at the Infant before him,
Lying sweetly asleep on the hay,
While the star in the east had already
Marked the spot for the world, with its ray.

While the shepherds came down from the hillsides,
And the Magi drew near through the night,
Gentle Joseph watched silently over
His son, with a father's delight.

And he dreamed on a bit, of the future,
In his mind saw the boy growing tall,
Then his weariness gathered about him,
And he rested his head on the stall.

Sweet sleep, gentle Joseph, befall you,
With your plans for your child all unfurled;
You will find soon enough that this Infant
Belongs for all time to the world.

No Sale
1960s

Well! I got so mad this mornin'
That it almost spoilt my day!
I rode down to see my neighbor
About buyin' up his hay;
But when I got to his corral
I saw an ugly sight:
He was "breakin' in" a bronco,
And he had him snubbed down tight.

The hard, hemp rope was bitin' deep,
And cuttin' off his air.
The poor cayuse was dark with sweat,
And blood-drops flecked his hair.
His knees were skinned, his eyes were wild,
With terror and with pain,
And my neighbor grabbed a twist of ear,
And mounted him again.

I turned away, and tried to spit;
My mouth was dry as dust.
I heard the horse's whistlin' breath,
As though his lungs would bust.
And soon he stood as still as death,
His head a-hangin' low,
With no more spirit than a cow,
And no more pride to show.

My neighbor dusted off his pants,
And lit a cigarette.
"The hoss that I can't handle,"
He said, "Ain't been born yet."

What do you think I told him,
Before I rode away?
"I just came by to tell you
That I sure don't want your hay!"

A Sheltie Will Do
1960s

There are small dogs and big dogs,
And middle-sized too,
But for dogs of just-right size
A Sheltie will do.

There are sweet dogs, and mean dogs,
And placid ones too,
But for just the right nature
A Sheltie will do.

There are smart dogs and dumb dogs,
And so-so dogs too,
But if you want the best dog
A Sheltie will do.

They are bright, they are jaunty,
And beautiful too;
They are faithful and loving,
With hearts that are true.

For a romp in the meadow,
A friend when I'm blue,
For love in all seasons
MY Sheltie will do!

A Journey into Yesterday
1962

I felt it when I reached the hill -
The tug of bygone days -
Forsooth, my heart remembers still
Its long-lost childhood ways.
My eyes rejoice to see once more
This earth of rich, red hue;
I know it as I did before -
'Twas worth returning to.

The manzanita bushes stand;
Their brick-red trunks I know;
I thought them gaunt against the land,
But pretty in the snow.
These rocks I do remember well -
They crumble at the touch.
See, as before, the pieces fell;
Oh, I remember much!

Now, down the hill and into town!
That well-remembered street,
Where time on time, and up and down,
I skipped on dancing feet.
Here was the store my Father had;
- I 'most can see his face!
I do recall, when snows were bad
They banked and hid the place.

Now up the street, and to the left,
My music teacher's place;
Dear, sweet old house, long since bereft
Of her most gentle grace.
This maiden lady I loved so
Was old when I was small;
Her copper hair was turning snow,
Her life was at the Fall.

To teach me scales, she had the means
To make me practice well -
Each perfect try brought jelly beans.
(I hesitate to tell
How I thought more of granted sweets
In those days than I should);
But still I'm sure those precious treats
Came more than I was good.

When this dear lady touched the keys,
And played a certain song,
A grip of sadness all would seize
And tears would fall ere long.
She played about a Perfect Day,
When it was at its end;
Her heart in all her music lay,
And music was her friend.

If I have spoken long and much
Of this one person's ways
'Tis only that her gentle touch
Has colored all my days.
Because of her, I feel the swell
Of music in my soul -
I feel the Heaven and the Hell
In the melodic whole.

Now here's the church, where once I went
Each week to Sunday School;
In these old walls my mind was bent
To live the Golden Rule.
It does not seem to me, somehow,
This place has aged at all.
I almost hear (let me dream now)
My Mother's footstep fall.

My Mother - she is everywhere
In this antique old town;
I hear her lovely laughter here,
And there I saw her frown -
Just down the street, the day she heard
I'd walked the ancient flume;
(She banished me without a word,
To ponder in my room).

Here stands the Church of Saint Canice,
A block away from home.
The Father, in his priestly peace,
Spoke often of 'dear Rome'.
He sometimes let me ring the bell -
I loved its somber sound.
And in his garden - strange to tell -
Bright colored birds were found.

And here I spy the old stone wall
We used to play upon.
I still can hear the owner call
"Please do stay off the lawn!"
'Twas here we played our cowboy dreams
Of 'Bob Steele' and 'Tom Mix' -
How many, many years it seems,
Since I was only six!

Now, turn the corner, 'round we go,
And up the steepest slope,
And at the top should be, I know,
- It's standing still, I hope -
A white house and a gardened hill.
Yes, there it still does stand!
Hello, Dear House! I'll look my fill -
I thought you once so grand!

The ivy grows along the ground
The way it used to lay.
Has time stood still, or have I found
The gate to yesterday?
If I could peek inside your door,
Dear House, would I still find
My skate marks on your hardwood floor -
The clock I used to wind?

And on my walls would I still see
Red roses all in bloom -
Those roses chosen just for me,
To decorate my room?
I do recall a lilac bush,
And snowball trees as well,
And purple flags and evening hush,
And rose petals that fell.

And here were our bonfires lit,
To roast things in the Fall;
Like chestnuts - let me think a bit -
Now well do I recall
Marshmallows soft, and apples red,
We pushed into the blaze.
Such simple, carefree lives we led -
Such pleasures filled our days.

In winter they closed off the street,
And children owned this hill
To sled upon - Oh, what a treat!
And what a lovely thrill
It was to whiz down from the top
And be the first to mark
The fresh new snow, from start to stop!
Alas, for childhood's lark.

So many things about this place
Do I recall full well.
My years spent here were years of grace,
Lived in the gentle spell
Of home and family, friends and those
Who taught life's truest ways;
And in my mem'ry I suppose,
They've gained a golden haze.

And they do say that we may not
Go back from whence we came -
That never can it be our lot
To find the past the same
As when we lived it in our youth.
But I am not so sure;
Our past contains our present truth,
And mem'ry holds it pure.

Written at Nevada City, California, February 23, 1962, when I was snow-bound there.

From the summer of 1932 to the summer of 1934 we lived in Nevada City, California, one of the earliest of the California Gold Rush towns, full of wonderful old houses and with history oozing out everywhere you looked. When I went back in 1962, got snowbound and wrote this poem, Nevada City had hardly changed at all, except that many of the old stores now held antique shops. Today, it still looks much the same, but it's not the safe, leisurely little town that occupied a golden part of my childhood, alas.

Spring Love
1962

"In Spring a young man's fancy turns
To thoughts of love," they say,
But I'm a little different,
'Cause my mind don't work that way.

In Spring I think of new-born lambs,
And foals on wobbly legs,
And settin' hens, all ruffled up,
When someone takes their eggs.

In Spring, I think of fresh green grass,
A-growin' in the sun,
And meltin' snow-chunks tumblin' down
Across the old mill run.

In Spring, I think of buddin' flowers,
And fawns tucked in the shade;
I think of rich, clean-smellin' earth,
Just turned up by a spade.

I think of brand-new things on earth,
And sparklin' skies above.....
I guess the sayin's right at that,
For all those things are love!

What Grandma Told Me
1964

"There's a big old pine on yonder hill,
That stands out black when the moon is yeller,
And there, long ago, when nights was still,
I'd go for to meet my blue-eyed feller.
Me, ridin' up on my small bay mare,
Feelin' the pine-breeze blow through my hair,
Countin' the stars that was twinklin' bright,
…Just like a queen ridin' through the night.

More like than not I would get there first;
Happy inside, 'cause my heart was dancin',
Bangin' away like it shore would burst . . .
Til 'long came my love, with his white horse prancin'.
Lord, what a horse! Though he'd travelled far,
Bearin' my man and his big guitar,
Snortin' and prancin' he'd top the hill.
Nothin' on earth ever held him still.

They was alike in a lot of ways . . .
Big and bold, and proud of bearin',
Nothin' beat them in all their days.
The horse was wild, and the man was darin';
But gentle too, when it came to love,
That I know, sure as God's above!
The horse loved Keith, that we all could see,
And Keith, he loved someone . . . and that was me!

We heard lots of sounds in the quiet air,
With, down below us, the cattle bawlin',
And Keith's stud whickerin' to my mare,
And off on the ridge some coyotes callin',
And the soft wind-whisper in the pine . . .
Well, you have your mem'ries, and I have mine,
And mine are a pine and a darkened hill,
A starry sky, and a world all still.

Sometimes he'd strum on his ole guitar,
And I'd be listenin' and sort of dreamin',
Or maybe I'd wish on the evenin' star,
For the marryin' thoughts that my mind was schemin',
And he'd hold my hand, or he'd sing a song
While we sat on the hill 'neath this pine so strong,
And we'd plan ahead how our life would be
When we'd be together, just him and me.

Now, maybe you think 'cause we met alone
That there was some secret we two was hidin',
But the reason's simple, and not high-blown
That led to all this here evenin' ridin',
'Cause down at the ranch there was always noise,
With the gigglin' girls and the teasin' boys,
And Ma always told him to "set a spell."
And Pa always had one more tale to tell.

Well, that's how it was in them early days,
It was awful hard when a man came courtin' -
The whole dang family was there always;
Each one must say what he thought importan',
And if ever they wanted just each other,
Without Pa and Granny, the kids and Mother,
They'd head for a hill and an old pine tree . . .
'Least that's how it was with my love and me . . .

My land, when I think how the years have passed!
With its fun and laughter and sometimes sorrow,
And I'm here on the hill with the stars at last,
And our Golden Weddin' due tomorrow.
I can still hear coyotes and cattle call,
And time doesn't seem to have passed at all.
...Now you run along, an' be very still,
"Cause your Gran'pa's near to the top of the hill. . ."

Town and Country
1965

Oh, a man gets mighty tired
When he's workin' on the range,
And sometimes he'd like to settle
Down in comfort for a change,
With an eight-to-five position
And a cozy little home,
With a car and boat and workshop,
And no call to ever roam.

For it's wearyin' to ride all day
In rough and rocky ground,
Just searchin' for some strayin' calf
That's bound it won't be found!
In bone deep cold or summer dust
The work goes on the same,
With steers to catch or move or brand,
And colts to feed and tame.

And by the time he hits the sack
With muscles stiff and sore,
He'd like to find a feather bed
And sleep a week or more!
But, oh, so very early,
Before the night can end,
He's up again and out again -
Two miles of fence to mend.

And after that there's stalls to clean,
And then there's feed to haul;
By half-past-noon he's gettin' mad -
He'd like to chuck it all
In favor of a place in town
Without a cow in sight,
Where a man can work a reg'lar day,
And get his sleep at night!

But even while he's thinkin' this
And longin' for a change
He's saddlin' up his horse again,
To check the summer range.
He'll take some salt up for the stock;
He'll have to stay the night,
So, bedroll - coffee - bacon - beans -
And lash that mule pack tight.

Still dreamin' of a city life,
He takes off up the hill,
And his horse is walkin' quiet,
And the air is very still.
For awhile he doesn't notice
That his soul has settled down --
That his eyes are on the pines ahead
And not turned back to town!

"Town and Country" has always had a special place in my heart. I was pleased with the way it turned out when I wrote it; then it became the first poem for which I received payment (from *Western Horseman*) and it was also the first of my poems to appear in a poetry anthology (*The Clover Collection of Verse*, Vol. VI, 1973).

I think there comes a day in the life of every person who takes care of land, livestock and horses when he or she feels just like the fellow in the poem - so much to do; so many things can go wrong; when do I get a vacation around here? and so on. Then something happens - like a new foal born in the dark of night that you can wipe down and help to stand - and you know exactly why you do what you do. And there's nothing in the world so conducive to settlin' down your soul as a quiet ride through the hills on a good horse!

No Home on the Range
1967

Well, I spent the whole day Sunday
Out a-lookin' for the range,
But I couldn't seem to find it,
For there's been a lot of change.

Where we used to pen the cattle
There's a string of new motels,
And just a bit beyond them
Stands a forest of oil wells.

Where I used to ride through sagebrush
From lunch time up to dark,
Now there's fenced-off land with signposts
Saying 'Recreation Park'.

There's a freeway near the river
Where the cattle used to graze,
And the blue sky of the prairie
Has been dimmed by smog and haze.

And I couldn't help but marvel
At this thing we call "progress",
That can change a land of beauty
To a populated mess!

Ace
1968

He was just a skinny stud colt,
All leggy, scared and black,
And I won him in a card game,
On aces, back to back.

All the fellers sorta chuckled
When I brought him home that night,
And I felt a bit embarrassed,
For he surely was a sight.

Why, his tail was full of stickers,
And his mane was half rubbed out;
His coat was dull and dusty,
And his ribs was stickin' out.

He didn't show no promise,
So the bunkhouse boys all said,
And they laughed and poked so much fun
That I started seein' red!

Though he wasn't much to look at,
He was all the horse I had,
And if I was any judge of colts,
He wasn't all that bad!

He had bone beneath that rough coat,
And a real determined eye,
And a breedy look about him,
That would make him worth a try.

So I started in to braggin',
And my tongue began to race,
And I said he'd make a fortune,
And I said I'd name him Ace.

Oh, I told the boys at supper,
And at noon and breakfast too
About the many wondrous things
That black was gonna do!

He would be the greatest stud horse
That the west had ever seen;
He would be the fastest horse on earth,
And sweep the racetracks clean!

He'd have the most cow-savvy,
And the biggest bag of tricks;
He'd be well-known in the cities,
And as well-known in the sticks.

Yep, I did a lot of boastin',
And I had a lot of brass;
I had staked my reputation
On the hope that colt had class!

So, I fed him oats all winter,
And the finest kind of hay;
He got groomed and had his exercise,
And looked better every day.

Then I turned him out on green grass,
With lots of runnin' room,
And he started buildin' muscle,
And he started showin' bloom.

In the fall I brought him up again,
To the old bunkhouse corral.
Soon the way he took to saddle work
Was the talk of Chaparral.

Why, he never did go buckin',
And he never knew to balk;
He moved square and bold and easy,
And he had a good flat walk.

Yep, he took right off to reinin',
And his figure-eights were neat;
He was catty, quick and willin',
And to ride him was a treat.

All through the snowy winter,
I worked him in the barn;
And at night beside the fire
I'd spin my boastful yarn.

Of all the many great things
That Ace was gonna do;
How he'd earn for me my own spread.
And my own remuda, too.

Well, the boys got kind of tired,
Of all that talk from me,
But Ace was sure a lot of horse;
On that they did agree.

Come spring, he won the stallion class
Down at the county fair.
Then I took my winter's savings
And I bought a nice brown mare.

On that I sure drew lucky --
Them horses nicked just right.
You should have seen the filly
That came one April night!

She was black as ink and fawn-legged.
With the biggest pair of eyes;
She was fresh as paint, and sweet as sin,
And I named her Ace's Prize.

I took the stud and filly
On the horse show rounds next spring,
And they seemed to come out wearin' blue
Every time they hit the ring.

I'd been keepin' something secret,
About my stallion Ace;
But the folks found out that autumn
That my horse could win a race.

I took all of Ace's winnings,
And his stud fees from the spring,
And I bought a half-a-dozen mares --
I was buildin' quite a string!

In fact, my boss was gettin' mad,
At all the space they took.
He said he'd have to charge me rent!
That got me kind of shook.

It was gonna take me longer,
To realize my dream;
But old Ace kept right on winning,
And our milk turned into cream!

Now it's fifteen long years later,
And the brag has all come true.
This here eighty lonesome acres
All belong to you know who.

And that handsome band of horses
You see roamin' on the place
Are mostly the descendants
Of my old black stallion Ace.

And that's him, standin' on the hill,
Still strong and proud and grand,
With the "look of eagles" showin',
Like a king on his own land.

Well, it's been a long old story,
But I've one more thing to say,
That comes from deep down in my heart,
As I look at him today.

You can know a lot of horses,
And be proud of many too,
But the one who's just part of your life,
That kind is mighty few.

He's one horse in a lifetime,
And there's none can take his place.
And I wouldn't trade the world right now
For my old black stallion Ace.

"Ace" began with a phrase that just popped into my mind, that I had to write down and follow to see myself how it would end. For me, writing that kind of narrative poem, that just seems to spring to life all by itself, is the fun of being a poet. I like my poems to have a cadence that just flows along when read aloud. I like to create a character who is understandably human -- probably that's why my Western poems are written in the first person. I don't think it's possible to say just how or why a poem was written, at least not for me. With "Ace," once the first couple of lines popped into my head, it was just a natural progression of what I would do if I'd become the unlikely winner of such a colt. I had no idea how it would end until I got there . . . and that's exactly why I love to write poetry!

A Brighter Day
1969

She fell asleep one quiet dawn,
And awoke to a brighter day,
In The Land of Fresh Beginnings,
With the pain all swept away.

And her eyes went wide with wonder
As her understanding grew,
For she stood in God's own meadow,
Green and fresh, and wet with dew.

And her ears pricked quickly forward,
As a voice spoke soft and low,
Saying "Welcome to my stable.
I have called you here, you know."

"For I saw that you were weary,
And I sought to end your fear,
So I brought you to my meadow.
There is nothing frightening here."

"You may roam across my pastures,
You may run, or you may rest,
And old friends wait here to greet you,
Down the meadow to the west."

Then the mare's head went up gaily,
And she nickered eagerly,
as though calling someone to her,
And she pranced excitedly.

And the golden sun's reflection
Gave her coat a copper hue,
As she paused for just a moment
By a pool so clear and blue.

Then the mare who used to tremble
Felt a calmness fill her soul,
As she started down the meadow;
- And beside her walked a foal.

Written in memory of Kane's Miss Universe 09790 (1957-1969) and her unborn foal by Viking Justin.

The Wreck of Buckboard Number Nine
1969

I was making a hand at the old T-Bar-C
In the autumn of nineteen-o-nine,
Just a kid from the city, and one mighty green,
But so sure I could make it just fine.

I had milked me a cow, and I'd rode me a horse,
And I thought I was learning the score,
But I didn't know nothin', as I soon found out,
When the boss sent me off to the store.

Now, the store was in town, and the town was due West,
Just about twenty miles either way -
A real long, dusty ride on a broken-down road,
But a trip you could make in a day.

"Jed, we're out of supplies," said the foreman to me,
"We need grub and we need kerosene.
With the men up at line camp, I've got to send you,
Even though you're so gosh-awful green."

Well! I drew myself up to a scrawny six feet,
And I looked the boss straight in the eye -
Just the picture of insult - "There's nothing to that!
I can do it without half a try!"

Then the boss got a mighty odd gleam in his eye,
But he only said "Well, that's just fine.
You take Muley and Bawly, the new blue-roan team,
And the buckboard we call Number Nine."

Well, my heart kinda sank when I heard him say that,
For that buckboard was battered and old;
Nearly heavy as iron, but nowhere as strong,
And the thought of that team turned me cold.

The new roans were a beautiful matched pair of blues,
With small stars and white socks and black tails,
But that Muley was stubborn, and Bawly was mean,
And together they both could spit nails.

Well, it took us an hour to get them hitched up,
And already I felt pretty sore
From a bite on the shoulder, a kick in the shin,
And my temper was starting to soar.

171

I was half in the seat, and just gath'ring my lines
When the team started off with a bolt,
And we rattled and clanged down the pockety road
While old Number Nine groaned with each jolt.

But I clung to my seat, and I clung to my reins,
Til the team started working just fine,
As the miles sped away to the tune of their hooves
And the creakings of old Number Nine.

Long before you'd imagine, we wheeled into town,
By which time I was feeling real proud,
We had come without mishap - I surely could drive!
And I strutted a bit for the crowd.

But pride comes just before a sad fall, so they say,
And I found that to be all too true.
We'd gone only a mile out of town when my team
Just became an explosion of blue.

Bawly pulled to the left, and then Muley jerked right,
And next Bawly proceeded to buck.
And that was the minute (you might as well know)
When this greenhorn ran clear out of luck.

Muley now was determined she just had to run,
While old Bawly tried hard to sit down.
But that Muley kept dragging the buckboard and her
Til we got two more miles out from town.

Such a kicking and squealing and rearing around
I still hate to recall to this day!
That old buckboard was bouncing and jouncing along
And then landing just any old way.

Now the roans took their bits, and I lost both my lines,
Trying just to hang onto the seat ...
I'm a passenger now, not a driver at all ...
And I had to admit I was beat.

Then old Number Nine started to spit out the grub;
Beans, sacks and cans flew left and right
As the spring seat collapsed and I hit the rough floor,
Leaving only my feet up in sight.

And a flour sack split when I landed so hard -
I was covered with white, head to waist.
Then the team hit the creek and went splashing on through,
While this passenger turned into paste.

About then I was thinking I ought to bail out,
But I came to the thought a bit late;
One front wheel hit a boulder and flew on alone,
While I clung there and pondered my fate.

So we plowed on along for a dozen yards more,
Then old Number Nine gave up the game.
She flopped on her side and then threw up her wheels,
And me -- I was doing the same.

Then old Bawly and Muley they hoofed on alone,
While I picked up as much as I could.
Poor old Nine looked like kindling, and I left her there,
A sad carcass of straps and split wood.

The boss was out feeding those miserable roans
Just as I staggered in late that night;
And the one thing he said to this paste-covered fool
Was "Don't brag til you know you are right."

Doby
1970

I braided a strip of his soft, white mane,
Then tenderly put it away;
And I found, as many have done before,
That "Goodbye" is so hard to say.

His body was weak, and his eyes were dim,
But I didn't picture him so;
For awhile last evening I saw him as
He had looked, once long, long ago.

I saw him again on a warm, spring day --
We'd loped a good mile just for fun --
He was twenty then, but you'd never know
By the all-out way he had run.

I looked farther back, and I saw him now
With two little girls on his back,
Looking strong, yet gentle, and handsome too,
In his coat of white and of black.

I saw in my mind a kaleidoscope
Of happy and wonderful years --
Those two girls and me, and a Pinto horse --
Then I saw no more for my tears.

For so many years he had given us
The best that a horse has to share,
All the trust and friendship and gentleness,
And long rides through sun-sparkled air.

But now he was old, and could not get up
When he tried to lay down and rest,
And my mind knew well what we had to do,
Though my heart rebelled at the test.

I patted his neck in the quiet stall,
He busily munched at his grain.
Then he turned to nuzzle me one last time,
And I ran out into the rain.

We owned him with pride and we loved him well,
And that time cannot take away.
But our world is less than it was before,
For our old friend died today.

Doby died November 4, 1970, with my daughter and the vet at his side. Doby was 30 and a bit more.

174

Norway Victorious
1989

They used to hide away their flags,
And hide their hearts as well;
But what is hidden still exists,
As anyone can tell.

Who once were Freedom's oldest friends
Invaders now had bound;
But friendship never really dies,
And courage stays around.

By treachery their land was gained,
And they must bend the knee;
But though the yoke was on their necks
Their spirits still soared free.

They showed the world what bravery was,
Their captors knew it too;
Unless you killed them to a man
They kept on shining through.

The little motto "We Will Win"
Sprang up just everywhere;
You might erase it every night -
Next morning it was there.

No threat of harm, no awful deed
Changed anything at all;
Free they had been, would be again.
Though silent, they stood tall.

Resistance was the watchword then,
To Country they'd be true;
And captors wondered, late at night,
If they weren't captives too.

...It was a lovely springtime day
When Peace came home again;
They met their Prince with shining eyes,
And souls without a stain.

I wrote this one about Norway's spirit during WWII.

Ern Pedler (1914-1989)
1989

Out of the shadows a lone man rode;
'Twas a Morgan Horse that the man bestrode,
Chestnut coat and a gleaming hide,
A prancing step and a look of pride.

A stallion he was, with spirit strong,
To carry a man where the miles were long,
To cross the gullies of rolling stone,
And to suit a man who would ride alone.

Then out of the dim a brightness grew,
Over endless vistas and mountains blue,
And the trail led up to a distant height
Where mustangs grazed in a meadow bright.

And the man turned his horse through the chaparral
Into piñon trees, past an old corral,
Breathing air as sweet as man ever knew,
Over grass that sparkled with morning dew.

While up ahead the mustangs twirled,
And ran away, leaving dust that whirled.
Then the man snaked his rope and laughed with glee -
"This is the Heaven for one like me!"

And late that night to a tall pine stand
By a campfire bright came an angel band,
To hear the tale of a lonely horse,
And of mustangers who had run their course.

While the stars winked down and coyotes cried,
'Til the night grew pale and the fire died.
Then the man saddled up his chestnut friend,
To ride the trails that would never end.

You may be familiar with Ern Pedler, the author of *The Big Lonely Horse, And Other Stories*. Ern was a family man, yet he still loved to go off into the back-country of Utah, with only his Morgan stallion for company, and track mustangs - not to harm or capture, but mostly for the sheer exhilaration of the chase. His stories were first published in *The Morgan Horse* magazine, and were much admired. In 1989, already ill, scant months before he died, a group got together for a last cattle drive, in which Ern participated, and during which time he read from his wonderful stories, as the video cameras rolled. The rare footage that was shot back in '89 still sits 'in the can', but there is hope yet of raising the funds to produce the film at last. I wrote this poem the night I learned that Ern Pedler had passed away.

The Beauty of Words
1989

I love the sound of words,
like heather,
pomander and
spice.
I love the singing sound
of words,
Like hyacinth and
Paradise.

I love the scented sound of
words,
like juniper and
Shalimar.
I love the trav'ling sound
of words,
like Mandalay and
Zanzibar.

Oh, words may seem like
simple things - all
mundane and
prosaic,
But some have lovely
picture-sounds
To form a speech mosaic!

Grown Old
2002

The saddle gathers dust these days,
The bridle's on the wall,
The barn has lost the scent of hay,
There's no horse in the stall.

My boots have truly lost their shine,
My chaps have gotten stiff,
And so have I, if truth be told,
And all hangs on "What If?" --

What If some decades fell away,
And I was young again,
To ride the mountains and the hills
And never feel a pain?

What If the Herefords grazed again
On long-remembered land,
And when the time for round-up came
I still could make a hand?

What If again those days of old
Became my present time,
When I could do once more those things
That I did in my prime?

What If that backward turn of time
Could truly come to be,
Would I relinquish my today
To be a former me?

What If I'd rather stow the thought
With boots and chaps and youth,
And with perspective keep the dream
As memory, not as truth?

I've kept my store of younger times
Bright-shining in my mind;
I may not ride a trail again,
But dreams are there to find.

From the time I was old enough to hang on to a carousel pony with the help of my Daddy, I've loved horses and riding. Even when I closed down my horse ranch and sold the last Morgans a few years back, I kept my chaps, my boots, my favorite braided reins and other essential tack, in case I decided to get myself another horse one day. Then I developed a health condition that turned me from a very active person, independent as the proverbial hog on ice, into one who moved slowly and carefully, and was next thing to housebound, and needed to be waited upon.

One night last January I got to remembering my long love affair with horses, thinking especially about the wonderful summers at Cold Creek Ranch – owned by Uncle Ed and Aunt Margit Titus, the ones who homesteaded in North Dakota years ago. There, I helped with haying (we still used Belgian teams, as it was during WW II), gathered and moved cattle, fished, swam, and rode for endless hours on my lovely, little sure-footed mare. Somehow, all that turned into the poem I called "Grown Old."

The Best Laid Plans
2003

I never intended to be an old cowpoke.
I planned to be richer than Midas by far.
I meant to start out with a few head of cattle.
I truly believed I could lasso a star!

But all of my plans seemed to soon come a-cropper.
I can't figure out why it had to be so.
No matter what venue I tried to succeed with,
I watched them all come, and I watched them all go.

I cobbled together a small herd of Herefords,
And set them to graze on Dakota's spring green.
I built a good barn and a little sod shanty,
And planted some willows to spruce up the scene.

But wouldn't you know, we had drought for three seasons,
And next came a winter of blizzards and freeze.
What stock I had left I just sold for a pittance.
Then all I had left was the land and dead trees.

My place went for taxes, and I left Dakota
With only my horse, tack and bedroll to show
For three years of work and a fistful of wishes,
And knowing that now I had no place to go.

I headed south-west, taking jobs when I found them,
Until I reached Texas and talk of "black gold."
"Ah ha!" said the dream that still lurked in my memory;
An oil strike might bring me those riches untold!

I found a good partner, and we went wild-catting,
But hit only dust on ten tries that we made.
Then Number Eleven came in like a winner,
And we thought we sure had it made in the shade!

I bought a fine Stetson, new boots and a Chevy.
My partner and I kept on drilling in vain,
Which ate up the cash from the well still producing,
As we slogged and drilled on through mud and through rain.

A man could grow old and worn out on that venture,
So we divvied up, and then went on our way.
He headed for Kansas, I thought I'd go westward.
I'd heard California was sunny all day.

The Chevy blew up when I hit Arizona,
And left me there, stranded and down on my luck,
Smack-dab in a desert without any shade -- I'd
Have sold the whole state for a smoke and a buck.

A man in a big car soon pulled up beside me.
He said he was headed out west to "L.A."
He eyeballed my Stetson and boots, and then told me
He made western movies out Hollywood way.

Said he'd need a stunt man for difficult film scenes,
When stars couldn't cut it, but someone must try.
My looks weren't half bad, he said; if I knew horses,
And had any interest I'd be the right guy.

With nothing to lose, and still dreaming of stardom,
I shook the chap's hand and thus settled my fate.
With too little thought of what surely must follow,
I took on a job I would soon come to hate.

Back then, too few cared if a horse took a tumble,
Or how a man hurt if he wasn't the star.
I banked lots of checks in ten years of B movies,
And dreamed of a ranch I'd call "Triangle Bar".

But luck never lasted, just smiled and then left me.
I sure did remember that quirk one sad day.
The scene called for racing between train and stagecoach.
The stage was to win -- it was timed out that way.

We lost; and I broke lots of bones when I landed,
All tangled with wreckage and floundering team.
The medical bills that I garnered that season
Stamped out the last wisp of my poor, fading dream.

I hobbled around Tinsel Town through that winter,
But no one could use a poor stove-up stunt man,
Until a Badlander who'd heard of my troubles,
Said he could use my help - "Come home if you can."

I caught the first train heading back to Dakota,
A shade of the man I had been in my prime.
I ride an old nag, checking fences for hours,
Draw minimum wages, and put in my time.

And that's how I came to just be an old cowpoke,
As far from a Midas as any can get.
I wonder what Fate still has plans to throw at me --
I know it's a corker, on that you can bet.

LaVonne parodied "The Best Laid Plans" with this:

I never intended to be an old lady.
I meant to be young to the end of my days.
I planned to go dancing on my hundredth birthday,
And ride in the mountains, if just for a ways.

But something called 'osteo' brought me a-cropper,
Afraid I'd break something if I merely sneezed;
So that was the end of my dancing and riding,
And doing whatever I doggone well pleased.

I had to adapt, then, to less of a lifestyle
Than that I had followed so nimbly before.
And that isn't easy when you're used to 'doing',
But there's one still open for every closed door.

The thing I've been able to keep right on working
Does make up a bit for the loss of the rest ---
I still can coin phrases, and keep up a rhythm,
And making up stories is what I like best!

The Fifth of July
2004

The fireworks are over,
Flags furled and put away.
The picnic spots are empty,
It's just another day.

The bows are out of horse tails,
Show saddles on the rack,
Good Stetsons boxed 'til Sunday,
We're back on normal track.

The Veterans' march has ended,
The floats are stowed once more;
No marching bands to cheer us -
Life goes on as before,

But, Oh, we should remember -
The pride that stirred the heart
So strong, and truly, in us
Must not so soon depart!

Let's not be "summer soldiers",
Flag-wavers for a day.
God bless our precious Country
All year, in every way!

The Down-and-Outer
2004

My Dad was full of platitudes.
He flung them out like jewels.
It took me years to realize
They were his teaching tools.

"The watched pot never boils", he'd say
When I just couldn't wait.
"Slow and steady wins the race"
Was one I came to hate!

"Birds in the bush" were gambles;
But "one in hand" was sure.
To "save the nine" that "stitch in time"
Was certainly the cure.

I never listened as I should,
But chased those bush-perched birds,
And squandered time on luke-warm pots
Despite all Daddy's words!

Those "pennies" I forgot to save
Could help no rainy day,
And "good turns" that I didn't do
No one could then repay.

I tilted windmills left and right,
And then felt like a dope
As in my mind I heard Dad say:
"You just can't push a rope."

It took me long to understand
The truth I wouldn't see.
The thing about it all is this:
The "rope" Dad meant was me.

The Christmas Miracle
2004

Only child on lonely outpost,
Not a soul to share his play.
Every night he kissed his parents,
Went off to his room to pray.

"Little prairie dogs, dear Father,
Play together, all the day,
Prong-horns too all have each other,
Could You send a child my way?"

Sighing deeply, little Robert,
"Fishes splash and have such fun!
Even eagles soar together -
Must I be an only one?"

"Mama says it soon is Christmas,
And I've been a real good boy!
If You just could send a brother,
I'd not ask for any toy."

"I have prayed a long time, Father,
And I hope You hear me still -
Send me soon someone to play with,
Father, if it be Thy will."

While he slept, a winter blizzard
Filled the world with whirling white,
Hid from view a silent struggle
Taking place that storm-tossed night.

Lost among the billowed snowdrifts,
Dark Wing clutched her child and cried;
Far away, the reservation,
Where her warrior brave had died.

Dark Wing held her bundle closely,
Weary, shaking from the cold,
Knew that she must keep on moving,
Struggling while the night grew old.

Far off, then, she saw a flicker,
Glowing dimly through the night.
Dark Wing whispered to her small one,
Staggered on toward the light.

From his warm cocoon of blankets,
Tuk-Wat-Se gazed at the star;
Wondered why they'd left the fire,
Why they had to go so far?

Round black eyes stared at the window,
While his mother stumbled on,
Little knowing that the candle,
Like her life, would soon be gone.

With a final desperation,
Dark Wing reached the cabin door,
Fell against it with a clatter,
Then lay dying on the floor.

Christmas Eve held three unlikely
Miracles before the dawn:
Dark Wing free, now and forever,
Going where her love had gone.

Tuk-Wat-Se gained home and parents,
Far from reservation's care,
And, as Christmas dawn awakened,
Robert got an answered prayer.

Tuk-Wat-Se = Buffalo Calf in Shoshone.

Cowpoke Philosophy
2005

Well, I read the evening paper,
And it scared me near in two,
With its columns-long palaver
About the world to-do.

Seems there's little wars all over,
And crimes and violence -
And you know, I got to thinkin'
That it surely don't make sense.

Why should neighbor shoot at neighbor,
And countries rattle swords?
I'm right sure they've all forgotten
That this whole big world's the Lord's.

Why, He made the sun to warm us,
And the evenings, just for rest;
And mountains filled with grandeur,
And mankind filled with zest.

And he made a horse to ride on,
And hills to ride him through;
A star-filled night to dream on,
And a wealth of things to do!

Well, I'd like to tell the gen'rals,
And presidents and such
If they'd just cut out the hagglin',
And get back into touch

With the things that God intended --
Like the beauty of the day,
Or the murmur of a forest,
Or the smell of new-mown hay,

If they'd just look at the wonder
Of nature all around,
Then perhaps they'd stop their feudin',
And we'd all have peaceful ground.

The Wanderer
2005

The prairie stretched before him, just
As endless as the sea.
The waving grass was stirrup-high,
No hint of shrub or tree.
A quest it was, that sent him West,
To lands not seen before.
But somewhere, he knew one for him
Held promises in store.

He'd traveled many lonesome miles,
And forded many streams,
But nowhere he had seen so far
Came knee-high to his dreams.
Perhaps he sought a Shangri-La,
Forever out of sight,
But somewhere in the West, he felt,
His place still shimmered bright.

His pack horse and his Pinto stud
Stepped deep through shifting sand,
And wild sage scented every breeze
That swept the barren land.
Strange rock formations speared the sky,
And then were seen no more,
While purple hills and silvered peaks
Loomed high not far before.

The climb was hard, and harder still.
Dismounted, he climbed too,
To save his horses, best he could,
For they seemed nearly through.
A valley high and mountain lake
Gave respite for the three.
A prayer of thanks flew Heaven-ward,
And sleep came easily.

Two days from then, they traveled on,
Through crags and drifted snow,
But still no glimpse of change ahead -
Just mountains more to go.
He found a pass, by luck it seemed,
A trail snaked down ahead,
And breaks between the peaks appeared,
As daylight went to bed.

Next morning, he tacked up and left.
The trail looked mighty steep.
A glitter showed up far ahead.
His heart began to leap.
A glimpse of green appeared below;
When they stopped on a hill.
It spread before him, far and wide
And held him, rapt and still.

Between the shining mountains and
The sparkling river's flow
A silent valley sweetly lay,
And set his heart aglow.
The long and lonely miles behind,
The dream that made him roam,
Were truly worth the time, for they
Had led the wanderer home.

Last Word
2007

T'was a night to be forgotten,
But few there were who could.
For sometimes nothing turns out
The way you think it should.

Now, I know you won't believe me,
'Though what I say is truth.
It happened many moons ago,
When I was in my youth.

Just a local, country bull ride,
To welcome in the Fall,
One round, and one round only,
With winner taking all.

All the bulls were rank and ready,
The men were set to ride -
Each hoping for the buckle
And cash to set aside.

I am glad I was too young then,
To risk my bones that night.
I never saw such critters,
So eager for a fight!

Each rider clamped his hat tight,
Gripped hard and with a nod
Rode in upon a whirlwind,
And then plowed up the sod.

There are long tales, also short ones,
And mostly there's a hero,
But seldom do they end so sad
As: "Bulls fourteen - Cowboys - zero."

I was watching the Rodeo Finals on TV one night, climaxed by the final round of the bull riding. Now, of course, this was not 'one round and one round only.' But it had the most unique ending that I could remember for such an important final event - it was "Bulls Thirteen, Cowboys One." That just cracked me up, and I kept trying to think of someway to dress it up a bit for a poem. This is how it turned out.

Warm Thoughts of Cold Creek
2007

I was young back in the 'forty's,
Just a kid, if truth were told,
So it only stands to reason
That by now I'm growing old.

But I haven't lost a memory
Of the many I built then
On the ranch I loved so dearly
In those days of "way back when."

Yes, I still remember clearly
How I loved that countryside,
With its Herefords out a-grazing
And my little mare to ride.

We would start out very early,
In the dawn's first pearly glow,
And go gather up the milk cows,
Though they didn't want to go.

We'd let them get far out ahead,
My horse just walking easy,
The grass all sparkling-wet with dew,
The air so sweet and breezy.

My horse would prance and toss her head,
Impatiently she waited,
And when I gave the cue to go
She never hesitated.

She'd take off at a full-out run,
So swift and freely striding,
While my heart fairly burst with glee
Because I was out riding.

If you had laid that ranch out flat
It would have made a county,
But it had hills and valleys too,
All rich with nature's bounty.

The creek was full of rainbow trout,
To catch if you weren't hasty;
Wild apple trees and choke cherries
And wild plums, oh so tasty.

Sometimes I'd take a bucket out,
And hang it from my saddle,
And gather up an old lasso,
And then I'd just skedaddle.

I'd ride up to an old fruit tree,
Rope high as I was able,
And dally to the saddle horn-
Fresh fruit would grace our table.

I loved to ride up through the hills,
And hear my saddle creaking,
When everything was peaceful-still
And not a soul was speaking.

I liked the silence in the woods,
The beauty spread below me,
Of meadow, trees, and grazing cows,
And my horse walking slowly.

Sometimes we'd startle up a deer,
Or spy an old coyote,
Or quail would whir up from the brush,
Or eagles high would note me.

The day the *Western Livestock* came
I'd head quickly for the lawn,
To read the latest, wondrous poem
By the great Bruce Kiskaddon.

He knew the West as it was lived,
By cowboys, harsh or gaily,
He spoke of simple, honest things
That happened to them daily.

I could relate to rain-wet boots,
Trail dust, or days all stormy;
His poems brought chuckles, or a tear,
And none could ever bore me.

Yes, I remember Cold Creek well,
Though it is gone now truly,
Gone as my childhood too has gone,
So quick, and so unduly.

In my mind still I roam those hills;
On Minnie I'm still riding.
I'm hooking pants on chaparral,
'Cause from Aunt Marg I'm hiding.

She'd rather have me doing chores,
Like dusting off the glassware,
But I'm off riding by the creek-
She'll call, but I won't be there.

In country flat I live my age,
This place I'm not forsaking;
But in my heart I roam the hills-
That dream's still mine for taking!

PROSE

A Heritage in Prose

LaVonne (age 5) and Cousin Don Landes
on Major, the Belgian gelding
at her uncle's ranch, 1930.
Photo courtesy of LaVonne Houlton.

Roots...in the Morgan World
1979

Some years ago my daughters and I went to visit one of my uncles and his wife. We took along several photos of our Morgans to show them. Uncle John looked at a couple of pictures of Blossom's Lass (013320 - Golden West National Junior Champion Mare of 1965), and said, "Yes, she's Morgan all right. She looks just like the team Dad used to have." Well! I really perked up at that, because it was the first I'd ever heard of Morgans in our family before mine.

My grandparents came from Norway in 1880, and first settled in Dakota Territory. Later, they farmed, and raised purebred Jersey cattle in Minnesota's lush Red River Valley. The farm was along the Thief River, a few miles from the village of St. Hilaire. The nearest town of any size was Thief River Falls, some eight miles north of St. Hilaire.

My mother was the youngest of ten children, so by the time I was born my grandparents were already 76 years old. Luckily, they lived 'til I was eleven, long enough for me to know and remember them well. Grandpa was very dignified and soft-spoken, and he walked straight as an arrow, even in his 80's. His hair and moustache were snow-white, his eyes were ice-blue. Though he always seemed so gentle and kindly, he loved to tease, and there was always a spark of mischief hiding in

Blossom's Lass, the mare that Grandpa's team was said to look like. Photo courtesy L.H.

those clear, blue eyes. It must have been really sparking the day he set out to get the Morgan team.

Going to town in those days consisted of hitching one of the work teams to the spring wagon and setting off down the dirt road. Grandpa's teams were O.K. in the fields, but on the road they had one speed -- plod. Everyone else's horses seemed to go faster, and finally Grandpa got left in the dust once too often. The next day he took off for parts unknown, and when he returned he was driving a beautiful pair of Morgans - one brown, one black. As Uncle John told me, "Nobody EVER passed Dad on the road after that!"

The Morgans weren't just a Sunday-Go-To-Meeting team, either. They did their stint in the fields along with the big teams, and Uncle John said they came in in the evenings in much better shape than the big horses did. The Morgans

My grandparents in Modesto, California, in their later years, about 1932, I think. When I was little, Grandpa and I would take walks down the long farm lane, holding hands, me chattering away in English, while he answered me in Norwegian (my grandparents would never speak English to me, which was a wonderful thing, really). Anyway, I was such a chatterbox that Grandpa called me his "little woodpecker" (in Norwegian of course). Photo courtesy L.H.

would be ready to go again after supper, driving the family to choir practice, or on errands, etc. My uncle couldn't remember where they had come from, or what their names had been.

When we got home, I wrote to my Aunt Mary, who was next-oldest of the children. She was then past 90, but she, too, remembered the Morgan team. She had good reason to remember, because the first night they were at the farm she took them out to the water trough, and as she was used to doing, dropped the lead ropes while they drank. The Morgans promptly raised their heads high, and headed for their old home, miles away. Grandpa was not pleased with Aunt Mary, and the next day he had the trip to make all over again.

Aunt Mary said the Morgans were beautiful horses, and very gentle. Grandpa was very fond of them. I had hoped she would remember just where they had come from, and that they might have had distinctive names that could give a clue to their breeding. What Aunt Mary wrote though was "We called them Brownie and Blacky." So much for pedigree-seeking.

They are all gone now, those old relatives of mine, and I will never know more about Brownie and Blacky than I learned from one conversation, one letter. But I like to think about Grandpa Brevik on the day he first drove his fine Morgan pair to town. I can just see him, sitting straight as an arrow, a small smile hiding beneath his moustache, and a big glint of mischief in his ice-blue eyes, as he left all the other farmers -- at last -- in the dust.

The Brevik family and their 10 children, taken just a few years after the Morgans came to the farm. Aunt Mary is the first lady on the left, back row; Uncle John is the 1st boy from the left, middle row, and my mother's the little girl standing between her parents, T. M. and Magnilda Brevik. Margit, the lady on the right, back row married E. R. (Ed) Titus, of whom I've spoken several times. This picture was taken in St. Hilaire, Minnesota. Photo courtesy of LaVonne Houlton.

I Remember
1995

Cold Creek Ranch was owned from 1939-1944 by Elbert ("Ed") and Margit Titus. The ranch was 10 miles from Ager on Beswick Road. It was a 1,280-acre property that spanned both sides of the road. On one side, the land was irrigated by a system of spring-fed ditches. It had small tree-shaded pastures, huge meadows that provided hay in summer and rough country beyond. The old, white two-story house, large barns, sheds, smokehouse, corrals and a big garden were on this side, as were willow and apple trees, wild plums and chokecherry trees. Cold Creek ran through this section – great trout fishing, even the ditches had trout in them.

On the other side of the road it was all dry land, with trees, lots of brush to snag the britches, grain fields, and grazing land for cattle. This section ran right up to the fire lookout.

When Mr. and Mrs. Titus came to Cold Creek Ranch from Modesto, California, they brought with them their best milk cows, two teams of Belgian horses and a fine Hereford bull, Prince Domino 14, that Titus had purchased from Canada some years before. Originally, the couple had homesteaded in North Dakota, and had many years' experience in the cattle business. At Cold Creek, they established a herd of Polled Herefords, which I think were the first in the area. They also kept a small dairy herd, sending the milk and cream to Montague via Major Spencer, who also delivered the mail.

Mr. and Mrs. Titus were childless. I was their niece, then in my early 'teens. I spent every summer at the ranch, which to me was the most wonderful place in the world to be. During those summers of World War II I helped with haying, herding and outdoor chores, as well as assisting Aunt Margit in the house. I also "sneaked off" whenever I could, with my horse. The McKenzie-Cheesbrough Ranch was below us and Ruth McKenzie and I became lifelong friends. We spent many happy hours together on our horses, "Pinky" and "Minnie." Fourth of July picnics at the McKenzie-Cheesbrough place were fun events those years.

Joe Silva lived some distance up the road from us. Once Ruth and I rode our bicycles to their place, forgetting that it was downhill all the way. After struggling up the grade awhile, we coasted back to Silva's and I called home to have someone come get us with the pickup. Joe had a pretty chestnut mare, "Balkitty," whose sire and dam were a part of the first band of registered Morgans brought to California from Texas, by Reginald Parsons in 1920. Balkitty was foaled at Parsons' Mountcrest Ranch, Hilt, California, in 1923. Joe purchased her as a three-year-old, and raised several foals from her. Byron White owned the only two of her colts that were registered – "Copco Joe" and "Copco Silva." Some distance beyond Silva's, Carl and Maude Crawshaw, from Ahwahnee, California, had purchased a small place, just before Pearl Harbor. Their son, Keith, was killed during the war. After Carl died (1947), Maude continued to live there alone for quite a few years.

Help was hard to find during the war, so Uncle Ed would recruit his hay crews from the "Hobo Jungle" at Montague. He had rigged a buck rake to the front of an old Jewett Coupe, and the Belgians pulled the mower and hay wagons.

One unusual thing was the finding of a tiny orphaned fawn. We raised it on a bottle, and it became a wonderful pet. "Laddie" had the run of the house, and never made a mess inside. He did become adept at filching pancakes from the plate while my back was turned, and he'd also snitch a cake layer set out to cool. When he got antlers, he sported red ribbons and a sheep bell during the hunting season.

One summer a saddle horse, bridle and rifle were stolen and we had a posse at the house, as they set out to track the thief. I remember that Louie and Byron White were part of the search. The mare went lame, and was found several miles away in the rough area we called "the lava." Uncle Ed leased 500 acres for grazing up there. The other stolen items were never recovered.

I think it was summer, 1943, that we held a cattle drive, taking a herd of Herefords from the ranch down to the railroad at Ager. From there, Uncle Ed and the hired man accompanied the cattle to the Los Angeles market, leaving my aunt and me alone at the ranch. A large group of young Herefords had just been vaccinated, and Uncle Ed cautioned me to get them under cover if it began to look like rain – they were not to get wet. Sure enough, one day thunderheads began forming over the high ridge to the south. Aunt Margit didn't ride anymore, so it was up to me to gather the cattle in from the huge back meadow. It was a pretty wild ride on a good cow horse, and the first raindrops began to fall just as Aunt Margit slammed the barn doors shut behind the last of the cattle. She told Uncle Ed of my success when he called home that night. When he returned, my uncle gifted me with a pretty scrapbook, a floral brooch and a beautiful gold cross necklace with my name engraved on the back. It was my proudest hour!

Age and failing health prompted the sale of Cold Creek Ranch around August 1944. Mr. and Mrs. Titus moved to a smaller property on the Klamath, at Horse Creek, where they raised Polled Angus cattle. Ed passed away in 1946 and Margit in 1956.

Cold Creek Ranch as I knew it no longer exists. The historic old house burned down years ago. The land was sold, and sold again. Only in my memory can I still hear the coyotes call in the night, or ride all day and never see the same spot twice. It was a beautiful, self-sufficient ranch, with white-faced cattle dotting the hills, and work that was hard but satisfying, a most wonderful place to be.

Cousin Don Landes
2003

You may have heard Oakdale, California called "the Cowboy Capital of the World," and Don Landes was a pretty well-known cowboy there back in the 40's and 50's, and he also was an unsung rider in many a Western filmed in the foothills around Jamestown, California. If you could ever get ahold of that wonderful old movie, "Smoky," and watch Fred MacMurray ride the bucking bronc, that's not Fred, that's my cousin Don. Looking at the Brevik family portrait, Don's mother, Helen, is second from the right in the middle row.

Don Landes
Photo courtesy L.H.

When I was five and Don was nine, the critter that we had to ride was Cecil, the clever burro. Don used to give the teacher a ride to the one-room little old red schoolhouse at Keystone in a cart behind Cecil. One time he and I were going to 'camp out' in the 'wilderness' on Keystone Ranch - we gathered up cans of beans (no can opener) some coffee (!) and I don't remember what else, except two old blankets for bedrolls. We went up in the hills, and thought a dry creekbed looked like a fine campsite. We unloaded everything from the sledge which Cecil had pulled for us. We were just getting our 'camp' nicely set up when a rattler rattled close by (the area was full of them) - Don grabbed my hand and ran; I fell down, and he continued to drag me across the stony creekbed, dumped me into the sledge, and off we raced, leaving all our gear behind. Boy, did I have skinned knees! We weren't very popular with our folks, either, because someone had to go back up there and retrieve all our stuff! Besides, it hadn't occurred to either of us to seek permission for such a camp-out!

That Keystone Ranch was also owned by our Uncle Ed Titus, who in turn owned the Triangle Bar Ranch in the Badlands, a dairy farm of the same name in Modesto, California, and later owned Cold Creek Ranch in Northern California.

Don passed away in Oakdale, in May 2001. He was 81 years old.

Don Landes, LaVonne (Hanson) Houlton, Summer, 1930, with Cecil and Ginger the dog at Keystone Ranch. (I had to laugh when I looked more closely at that picture. It must have been taken very soon after our excursion up into the hills - Mother always made me wear long stockings, even in summer, if I had skinned-up knees. Ever since that time I've always loved the smell of tarweed, though I sure hated having it stuck all over my legs and shoes if I walked out in it. I remember that we had a whole cigar box full of rattles, from snakes that had been killed at Keystone - sometimes Don and I would get a bunch of them out and see who could find the one with most rattles. Didn't take a lot to entertain us in those days, apparently!) Photo courtesy of LaVonne Houlton.

Don and Cecil (that old car, I think, is the Jewett - later at Cold Creek Ranch,
a buck rake was fastened to the front of it, and it was great at haying time!)
Photo courtesy of LaVonne Houlton.

World War II Memorial
May 29, 2004

Today I watched the World War II Memorial Dedication Ceremony in Washington, D. C. on television, through tears. My first thought, as the camera panned the audience was, "Oh, we have all gotten so old!" But then I remembered that we are called the Greatest Generation, and our spirits and faith were indomitable throughout the long, difficult years of the war. In our hearts, we are still young --- and we remember.

I was in grammar school when Hitler began invading the countries of Europe - including my beloved Norway. In high school, I bought war stamps for 25 cents each, rolled bandages, collected scrap metal and planted Victory Gardens. In Junior College, my major was Pre-Flight Aeronautics. I wanted to join the WASPS, but was still too young, so I was learning all the basics ahead of time. I also held a full-time job at Hammond General Hospital SCU1975, working in the Medical Detachment Office, during the summers. In April, 1945, I was a clerk-typist at the Army Supply Depot, in Lathrop, Ca. On a never-to-be forgotten morning our colonel came into our huge office crying, and announced that President Franklin Delano Roosevelt had died, at Warm Springs, Georgia. Everyone burst into tears, the flag was lowered, the office was closed, and we all went home.

On a more personal note, the war cost me my first love, my childhood sweetheart. The last time I saw him was the afternoon of December 7, 1941 - Pearl Harbor had just been attacked that morning. Not long afterward, he enlisted in the Navy, and served as a ship's gunner. His battery sustained a direct hit from the air just brief months later. I continued to correspond with his mother until she died, many years later, in a Gold Star Mothers Home in Southern California.

Eight of my American first cousins served in the Armed Forces, and miraculously, all came home safely at war's end. One was a Naval Air Corps pilot, decorated for his role in sinking a German U-Boat in the Atlantic. Three were in the Army - one in the Philippines (bothered forever after by bouts of malaria), one in the Italian theatre of operations, the third in Europe. One cousin was in the Marines, another in the Merchant Marine, one in the Navy, and another was a tail gunner on a B24 bomber over Germany.

In Norway, I had first, second and third cousins serving in the Resistance in whatever way they could. Most famous was Knut Haukelid, the "Hero of Telemark", but there were also Knut Rabbe of Røldal, three Bjaaen brothers in Setesdal and cousins in Ringerike who risked their lives just being links in the chain that saw messages passed along, hidden under certain rocks in the woods. One spent some time in the dungeon below Akershus Fortress in Oslo. I saw his stone cell years later - the low ceiling sloped so that one couldn't even stand erect.

Early in the war, there were rumors that the Japanese might be able to bomb the west coast. My Mother was hospitalized with cancer at that time, and one of my worries was how in the world could I help her if the bombers did come?? Meat, sugar, gasoline and many other commodities were rationed. We had black-out curtains on our windows at night, and frequently air-raid sirens sounded, to keep us on our toes, and watching the skies (we learned the difference in silhouettes between Japanese and American planes). We were sometimes afraid, often anxious. We looked forward to getting V-Mail letters from our friends and loved ones serving overseas. We loved our President - the only one many of us had known. He had seen us through the Depression, and we trusted him to see us safely through to Victory. We never gave up our belief that America would prevail. We celebrated D-Day, VE-Day and finally VJ-Day with great glee. Then, we couldn't wait for our loved ones to come back home, and for life to return to normal.

But we never forgot those chairs that remained vacant forever after. God Bless America!

Mr. Miley's Palomino
2005

One summer day during World War II, Mr. Miley came from Modesto to Cold Creek Ranch, pulling an empty horse trailer. His purpose was to buy a couple of Palominos, and Uncle Ed had told him there were several in our area that might suit his needs.

After all these years, I've forgotten Mr. Miley's first name. He was an old family friend from the days when he and my uncle had both farmed large properties out Old Oakdale Road from Modesto, in California's central valley.

Cold Creek's driveway. Photo courtesy of LaVonne Houlton.

The morning after he arrived, Mr. Miley and Uncle Ed drove several miles farther out the road we lived on to see the Spannaus brothers. The young men did have some Palominos, but for whatever reason they weren't what Mr. Miley was looking for. The two men then set out toward Yreka, to look at some other golden horses Uncle Ed knew about. Still, when the pair drove down our long driveway at the end of the day, the horse trailer was empty.

Next morning after breakfast the two intrepid horse-seekers set out once more, this time planning to drive over the Siskiyous into southern Oregon. Mr. Miley vowed stoutly that when they returned this time there would be two Palomino Horses in the trailer. We could count on it, he said.

It seemed like an especially long day, as we waited for the men to return. Because Mr. Miley had been such a critic of the horses they'd already seen, we just knew that whatever he bought was bound to be special.

We waited all that day, visions of gorgeous golden horses with flowing flaxen manes and tails running through our minds.

At last the truck and trailer came rumbling down the long drive, and we dashed out, eager to see what they had found. But, wait a minute - it didn't look like there were any horses in the trailer! When the rig quit rolling, Aunt Margit and I went to the back of the trailer. "Land sakes!" said my aunt, as I burst out laughing. One side of the trailer was empty.

Part of Cold Creek Ranch - Taken from the meadow - the land went clear up to the lookout on top of the mountain (see arrow) on the 'dry' side. Photo courtesy of LaVonne Houlton.

There, in the other side, contentedly munching hay, was a pretty little Jersey cow! "Well," said Mr. Miley, a bit sheepishly, "At least she's the right color!"

The Christmases of My Childhood (1930s)
Christmas 2005

I remember them as being so wonderful! Our Norwegian family seemed so big, and everyone was so happy to be together. Grandma and Grandpa lived with my Aunt Margit and Uncle Ed, so everyone congregated there for Christmas Day. The house was big, with large, high-ceilinged rooms. The star on top of the beautifully decorated, enormous tree just barely cleared the 12' ceiling. Presents were piled high beneath the tree. The house was redolent with the odors of roasting turkey and spicy pumpkin pies.

At home, early on Christmas morning, my little sister and I shared our own gifts, then sat down to a delicious Norwegian snack of lefse and fruit soup. Then we all set off for the big event!

First, I would run to meet Grandma and Grandpa -- "Glade Jul!" Grandpa, with his white hair and moustache and smiling blue eyes -- and Grandma, soft and cuddly as a feather pillow, her red hair faded to a look of apricots in whipped cream. Soon, family by family, everybody began to arrive -- until we numbered about 30 in all.

One Norwegian dish I could never learn to like was the lutefisk - hard-dried cod, that had gone through a series of water baths since Thanksgiving, to leach out the lye it contained. Now, here it was, all soft and white, with accompanying cups of melted butter. The dining room, large as it was, could only accommodate the grownups, so we children had our own table set up in the kitchen. It was like a 'rite of passage' in the family, to graduate to the 'big' table!

One of my father's crops on our ranch was Emperor grapes, a late table variety and so delicious that I've tried in vain to find them again ever since. Anyway, after the harvesters had left, Dad and I would glean the vineyard, getting quite a few lugs of various sized bunches. I would set up a little roadside stand and sell them, which gave me "lots" of money for Christmas presents. Everyone got a gift in those days - no drawing of names for us! On some special day before Christmas Mother and I would go to town, and she would deposit me in the wonderful Woolworth store. Here, I happily bought lace hankies, small jewelry, "Evening in Paris" perfume, things to embroider, men's handkerchiefs, socks and toys, all selected with a particular relative in mind. I have no memory of gifts I received on those long-ago Christmases, but I do still recall the thrill of making my own spending money, and buying and wrapping all those special little gifts for those I loved!

Uncle Ed Titus
2007

Ed was from an old New York Dutch family, and his wife Margit came to America from Norway, in 1879, as an infant. They first tried farming in Minnesota, but their land was too boggy, so they opted for a homestead in Dakota, and a sod house to begin with. The first couple of years Margit baked bread and rolls and sold them in Fryberg and Medora, and to neighboring bachelor ranchers, to help them get started.

The story of how they met is kind of interesting, too. E. R. (Ed) Titus left New York, heading for the Klondike and possible riches, working his way across the country as he went. He stopped near Stavanger Township, Trail County, North Dakota in1900 to work in the Grandin Farms grain fields for the summer.

Ed and Margit's 1901 wedding photo.
Photo courtesy of LaVonne Houlton.

Liking softball, he got together enough young fellow farm hands to form a couple of teams, to play on their day off. Their 'playing field' was right across the road from the ranch of Halvor A. Nash.

Recently widowed, Halvor had summoned his niece Margit Brevik from St. Hilaire, Minnesota, to help out with his children and cook for the hay crews. It didn't take Ed long to notice the pretty young lady across the road who seemed to work so hard. By September 1901 they were married, and the Klondike was a forgotten dream.

This is the couple in front
of their sod house.
Photo courtesy of LaVonne Houlton.

The photo above is my uncle Elbert R. ("Ed") Titus and one
of his Belgian stallions, "King," on the old Triangle Bar
Ranch in the Badlands of North Dakota, about1918.
The ranch was near Bullion Bluff and the "Little Mo" River,
and part now is in the Theodore Roosevelt National
Grasslands Park. I've been told that this barn could hold
up to 40 shod horses during the winter.
Photo courtesy of LaVonne Houlton.

Bibliography

Historic Horse Articles

"California Mare Families of the Twentieth Century." *Golden West Region 7 Morgan Horse Directory, Second Edition* 1977, pp. 10-16; reprinted in two parts as "California Mare Families of the Twentieth Century, Part I." *The Morgan Horse* March 2002, pp. 30 and 32, and "California Mare Families of the Twentieth Century, Part II." *The Morgan Horse* April 2002, pp. 34 and 36.

"California Morgans of Yesterday, 19th Century." *Northern California Morgan Horse Club, Inc. Pictorial Directory* 1966: p. 7.

"California's Morgan Sires." *Northern California Morgan Horse Club, Inc. Pictorial Directory* 1969: pp. 2-3.

"Dapper Dan – A Legend in his Own Time." *The Morgan Horse* January-February 1976, pp. 97-101.

"Early History of Morgan Mares in California." *Golden West Region 7 Morgan Horse Directory, Second Edition* 1977, pp. 5-9; reprinted in *The Morgan Horse* August 1980, pp. 58-61; second reprint in *The Morgan Horse* February 2001, pp. 26-28, 30.

"General Morgan and Black Bess." *The Western Horseman* February 1970: pp. 29, 66-67.

"Government Bloodlines…Their Influence on California Morgans." *The Morgan Horse* July 1975, pp. 56 – 61.

"LaVonne's Line: On the Road" (A 4-part series). *The Piggin String*, "On the Road August 1966," published October 1966: pp. 12 and 14; "On the Road September 1966," published November 1966: pp. 10-12; "October 1966 On the Road," published December 1966: pp. 14, 16, 18-19; "November 1966 On the Road," published January 1967: pp. 11-12.

"The Legacy of Linsley and His Sons." *The Morgan Horse* October 1995, pp. 76-83.

"Montpelier Men and Their Morgans." *The Morgan Horse* September 1968: pp. 38-39, 93-96.

"Morgan Breeding Stallions of the West." *Golden West Region 7 Morgan Horse Directory, First Edition* January 1975. Red Vermont, p. 4; Sonfield, p. 5; Redman, p. 7; Montabell, p. 8; Lippitt Morman, p. 9; Gay Mac, p. 10; Monte L., p. 11.

"Morgan Families Part II: The Working Western Family." *The Morgan Horse* August 1996 (Part II of a series on Morgan families), pp. 74-80.

"The Morgan Horse in California, 1849 – 1959." *Golden West Region 7 Morgan Horse Directory, First Edition* January 1975, pp. 12-16. Reprinted as "The Morgan Horse in the West." *The Morgan Horse* October 1980, pp. 57-60.

"Morgans in the West: The Development of a Type, Part I." *The Morgan Horse* August 1984, pp. 63-70; and "The Development of a Type, Part II." *The Morgan Horse* September 1984, pp. 79-86.

"Morgans of Yesterday in Nevada and Arizona." *Golden West Region 7 Morgan Horse Directory, Third Edition* 1981; reprinted in *1990-91 Arizona Morgan News Special Edition*, pp. 17-22.

"Morgan Stallions in California: El Don." *The Morgan Horse* July 1969: p. 35.

"The Morgan Story." Introduction to the promotional brochure, *Justin Morgan Had a Horse . . .and you too can enjoy a Morgan*, The Morgan Horse Club, Inc. 1969.

"The Mysterious Narragansett Pacer, Part I." *The Western Horseman* February 1971: pp. 66, 147-148; "Part II." *The Western Horseman* March 1971: pp. 26-27, 126; "Part III." *The Western Horseman* April 1971: pp. 7, 134-141.

"The National Stud Farm." *The Thoroughbred of California* March 1967: pp. 412-413, 504.

"The Redman/Blackman Story." *The Morgan Horse* July 1992, pp. 50-55.

"Richard Sellman's Morgans, Part I." *The Western Horseman* March 1967: pp. 12, 101-103; "Part II." *The Western Horseman* April 1967: pp. 68, 102-106; "Part III." *The Western Horseman* May 1967: pp. 80, 160-163.

"Roland Hill and his California Government Morgans." *The Morgan Horse* August 1975, pp. 13-18.

"The Spanish Jennet: Its Origin and Influence, Part I." *The Horseman's Courier* February 1968: pp. 8, 40-41; "Part II." *The Horseman's Courier* March 1968: pp. 14, 42-43.

"William Randolph Hearst and His Morgan Horses." *The Morgan Horse* July 2001, pp. 128-131 and 133.

Cowboy Poetry
Most of these poems have been posted on the Cowboy Poetry Website: www.cowboypoetry.com. LaVonne sent me these poems to include: "A Sheltie Will Do", "The Beauty of Words" and "Norway Victorious."

"A Brighter Day." (1969).

"A Journey into Yesterday." (February 23, 1962).

"A Sheltie Will Do." (1960s).

"Ace." (1968). *The Western Horseman* April 1968, pp. 76-77.

"The Beauty of Words." (1989).

"The Best Laid Plans." (March 26, 2003).

"The Christmas Miracle." (2004).

"Cold Creek Remembered." (1958). *The Morgan Horse* September 1984, p. 86; reprinted in *The Morgan Horse* July 2005, p. 74.

"Cowpoke Philosophy." (2005).

"Doby." (1970).

"The Down-and-Outer." (July 9, 2004).

"Ern Pedler (1914-1989)." (1989).

"The Fifth of July." (July 5, 2004).

"Grown Old." (2002).

"Joseph." (1959).

"Last Word." (2007).

"No Home on the Range." (1967).

"No Sale." (1960s).

"Norway Victorious." (February, 1989).

"Spring Love." (1963).

"Town and Country." (1965). *The Western Horseman* May 1966, p. 109; reprinted in *The Clover Collection of Verse*, Vol. VI, 1973.

"The Wanderer." (2005).

"Warm Thoughts of Cold Creek." (2007).

"What Grandma Told Me." (1964). *Piggin String Magazine* 1960s.

"The Wreck of Buckboard Number Nine." (1969).

A Heritage in Prose
Most of these prose pieces have been posted on the Cowboy Poetry Website: www.cowboypoetry.com. LaVonne sent me these prose pieces to include: "I Remember" and "World War II Memorial."

"The Christmases of My Childhood." *Cowboy Poetry Website*, http://www.cowboypoetry.com/, 2005.

"Cousin Don Landes." *Cowboy Poetry Website*, http://www.cowboypoetry.com/, 2003.

"I Remember." *The Siskiyou Pioneer and Yearbook*, Vol. 6 #8, of the Siskiyou County Historical Society, 1995, pp. 129-131.

"Mr. Miley's Palomino." *Cowboy Poetry Website*, http://www.cowboypoetry.com/, 2005.

"Roots...in the Morgan World." *Northern California Morgan Horse Club KORRAL* May 1979; also posted on the Cowboy Poetry Website, http://www.cowboypoetry.com/.

"Uncle Ed Titus." *Cowboy Poetry Website*, http://www.cowboypoetry.com/, May 21, 2007.

"World War II Memorial." Sent by email to family and friends, May 29, 2004.

Index

Photographs and Illustrations